The New York Times

Long Island

ARTS AND ENTERTAINMENT

From the Summer of '50, Luminous Drawings

In Multiple Layers of Charcoal and Pastel, Ary Stillman's Creations Revel in Intensity

By BENJAMIN GENOCCHIO

Ary Stillman, who died 40 years ago after a life spent traveling, painting and looking for a place to call home, was among the more talented of the many artists who immigrated from Eastern Europe to the United States during the early 1900s.

Born in 1891 in Slutsk, in what is now Belarus, he emigrated with his family to Iowa in 1907, living there for a decade before returning to Europe. Moving around would become a pattern.

Most of his early work was representational, including portraits, still lifes and landscapes in a Post-Impressionist style. World War II, however, had a powerful impact on the artist, who began making abstractions in 1945 and continued to do so for the rest of his life. As he explained at the time, "The world of surface realities is no longer paintable, for nothing is as it formerly seemed."

ART REVIEW

Mr. Stillman's abstractions were mostly oil paintings on canvas, along with some embossed drawings in charcoal and pastel on paper. The show at the Pollock-Krasner House concentrates on the drawings, in particular a group of them produced in Sayville in the summer of 1950. We don't know for sure why he was out there; art historians speculate that he was visiting friends, though he may also have been lecturing at an artists' club.

In the embossing process, the surface of a material is indented with a design. Mr. Stillman embossed his drawings by hand, scribbling the designs onto a sheet of paper with a nonwriting stylus, then rubbing over the paper with a flat-sided stick of charcoal or pastel to reveal the white outline of

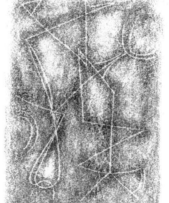

THREE-DIMENSIONAL QUALITY
Both by Ary Stillman: left, "Sayville No. 23" (1950, embossing charcoal and pastel on paper) and right, "Sayville No. 11".

the drawn design; the pigment covers the surface but does not enter the embossed grooves. He then enhanced the shading to give his work a three-dimensional quality.

Mr. Stillman's Sayville drawings are striking in their immediacy and intensity. That is partly a reflection of the spontaneous, improvisational quality of the creative process, the artist allowing his subconscious to direct the movement of his hand. Sometimes the designs take on a totemic quality; at other times they resemble doo-

dling. More often than not they are dense, biomorphic abstractions.

The best of them have a luminous, atmospheric quality that owes itself to the artist's fluid, free-flowing line and the delicate contrast of light and shadow deriving from the subtle application of multiple layers of charcoal and pastel. Among my favorites are "Sayville No. 23" (1950) and "Sayville No. 26" (1950), both of which are larger than the other works here.

Sometimes the drawings suggest the influence of Cubism, specifically that of Picasso or Paul Klee. Perhaps Mr. Stillman had met these artists, for he spent most of the 1920s as an expatriate painter in Paris. He did not seem to show an interest in the emerging movement of Modern art, however; there is nothing very avant-garde about his early work, which can often remind you of the paintings of Pierre Bonnard.

In 1933, fearing Hitler's rising power, Mr. Stillman moved from Paris to New York. Arriving with an established reputation, he slipped easily into the local art scene, showing with prominent galleries and participating in meetings at the Artists' Club on East Eighth Street. He even shared a podium with Mark Rothko to talk about abstraction at a 1947 forum for painters and sculptors in New York.

Everything seemed to be going right for the artist until the early 1950s, when declining vision in one eye, coupled with the loss of the lease on his studio, brought on a bout of depression. He then made a fatal career mistake: with abstract art at the height of its popularity, he left New York for Paris. He moved about, eventually settling in Cuernavaca, Mexico, where he continued painting in relative obscurity until his death in 1967.

To learn more about Ary Stillman, visit www.stillmanlack.org

Praise for *Dispensing Beauty in New York and Beyond*

"Annette Blaugrund fuses fan's enthusiasm, a scholar's resourcefulness and a storyteller's craft in this engaging, enlightening biography. Praised for her 'gentle manners and sympathy for the suffering and hardships of others,' Harriet Hubbard Ayer emerges from Dr. Blaugrund's portrait as an innovative entrepreneur, crack reporter, and pioneer of the American feminist movement."
—Sidney Offit, author, teacher, curator emeritus, recipient of the George Polk Journalism Award and former president of the Author's Guild

"Just when we thought there were no more original American characters, along comes Annette Blaugrund's fine biography of the little-known feminist pioneer Harriet Hubbard Ayer—her harrowing struggles, her inspiring achievements, her unexpected triumphs. What a marvelous tale written in a riveting manner!"
—William A. Johnson, professor emeritus of philosophy, Brandeis University

"An excellently researched mixture of history and biography about a maverick Victorian woman who made beauty her business and thereby changed the way women perceived themselves. Harriet Hubbard Ayer prevailed in a man's world, but what a high price she paid!"
—Barbara Goldsmith, author of *Other Powers: The Age of Suffrage, Spiritualism and the Scandalous Victoria Woodhull* and *Obsessive Genius: The Inner World of Marie Curie*

Dispensing

Beauty *in*

NEW YORK
& BEYOND

The Triumphs and Tragedies
of Harriet Hubbard Ayer

To Kathy,
With great appreciation for
your help, Annette Blaugrund

ANNETTE BLAUGRUND

Charleston H London

THE
History
PRESS

Published by The History Press
Charleston, SC 29403
www.historypress.net

Front cover: William Merritt Chase (1849–1916), *Portrait of a Lady* (Harriet Hubbard Ayer), 1880 [detail]. Oil on canvas, 27 1/4 by 22 1/4 inches. *California Palace of the Legion of Honor, Fine Arts Museums of San Francisco. Gift of Henry K.S. Williams.*

Back cover: Harriet Hubbard Ayer (1849–1903) photograph, circa 1872, in Margaret Hubbard Ayer and Isabella Taves, *The Three Lives of Harriet Hubbard Ayer*; Advertisement, Scribner's Magazine, June 1890; Advertisement, fall 1886.

First published 2011
Manufactured in the United States
ISBN 978.1.60949.279.3

Blaugrund, Annette.
Dispensing beauty in New York and beyond : the triumphs and tragedies of Harriet
Hubbard Ayer (1849/1903) / Annette Blaugrund.
p. cm.
Includes bibliographical references.
ISBN 978-1-60949-279-3
1. Ayer, Harriet Hubbard, 1849-1903. 2. Cosmetics industry--United States--History. 3.
Businesswomen--United States--Biography. I. Title.
HD9970.5C672A933 2011
338.7'66855092--dc22
[B]
2011008136

Contents

CONTENTS

Preface

Memory is a complicated thing, a relative of truth, but not its twin.
—*Barbara Kingsolver,* Animal Dreams *(1990)*

As an art historian, I came upon Harriet Hubbard Ayer through a portrait. She was painted three times by two well-known American artists. I then read *The Three Lives of Harriet Hubbard Ayer*, an undocumented biography written in 1957 by her daughter Margaret Hubbard Ayer (Cobb), with the help of Isabella Taves, a professional writer. Margaret's aim, late in her life, was to nullify misinformation about her mother (namely that she was insane), to make sure that her mother would be remembered and perhaps to assuage her own guilt for having denounced her publicly in the past. While Harriet's daughter had access to letters that are no longer extant, I have discovered newspaper articles, court records and other data that tell a more complete story and contradict many of the dates and facts in Margaret's imaginative reordering of the material. Margaret's son, Hubbard Cobb, in notes for an unpublished book of his own, wrote: "Mother told me lots about her early life but I was never sure of what was fact and what was fiction. She had, after all, been on the stage and like most theatre people enjoyed telling a good story even if it was not always accurate. Anyway there is no body around now that can say it wasn't."

Although the 1957 book preserved much of what is known about Harriet and has served as the basis for many biographical dictionary entries and articles, I decided her life deserved a more comprehensive biography. By the time the 1957 book was written, Harriet's life had been obscured, with no vestige of her earlier accomplishments evident. In fact, for all her success with a registered business, as a single woman she was never included in a U.S. census. All that remained was her name, bought by people who used it for new and different cosmetic companies through the 1950s. While Elizabeth Arden, Hazel Bishop, Estée Lauder and Helena Rubinstein are held in high regard as early women entrepreneurs in the cosmetic field, it was Harriet Hubbard Ayer who made beauty her business before any of them. First with her creams and balms and then with her words and ideas, between 1886 and 1903 Harriet Hubbard Ayer influenced and encouraged several generations of women to look and feel good about themselves.

Acknowledgements

Acknowledgements frequently end by thanking family members, but at the outset I wish to recognize the love and encouragement of my husband, Stanley Blaugrund, who has willingly (and sometimes unwillingly), listened to and read many versions of this book. My children—Andrea Nevins and her husband, David, and Jonathan and Jeb Blaugrund and their spouses—have also provided suggestions. I want to single out Dr. Alicia Longwell, chief curator at the Parrish Art Museum, for introducing me to the portrait of Harriet Hubbard Ayer that initially aroused my interest. During my research, I was privileged to meet Professors Melanie S. Gustafson of the University of Vermont and Susan M. Yohn of Hofstra University, both of whom shared with me their work on Blanche Howard and her relationship to Ayer. Susan S. Wallach and Professor Emeritus William A. Johnson read my manuscript in full and offered sage advice. Editors Kathleen Luhrs, Jaime Muehl and Joan Sanger were very helpful, as were my friends the authors Sidney Offit and Peter Blauner. Franklin Feldman Esq. facilitated my understanding of the legal documents, while Dr. William A. Frosch assisted in interpreting the psychological subtext; I am grateful to them both. My Chicago connection, Betty Blum, contributed to my research in myriad ways, and I greatly appreciate her participation. Bronxville Village historian Eloise L. Morgan generously shared the information she had gathered for her article about Ayer's institutionalization. I am indebted to Joseph Ditta, Eric Robinson and Mariam Touba at the New York Historical Society Library; Lesley Martin at the Chicago Historical Museum; the staffs at the New York

Public Library and the Newberry Library; the R.G. Dun & Co. Collection at Baker Library, Harvard Business School; the George J. Mitchell Department of Special Collections & Archives at Bowdoin College Library; the Abplanalp Library, University of New England; and other libraries across the United States and in France, for their wholehearted assistance. New York Historical Society curator Marilyn Kuschner graciously gave me access to the Bella C. Landauer collection of Business and Advertising Ephemera. Diane E. Richardson, special collections librarian at the Psychiatry Department's Oskar Diethelm Library at Weil Cornell Medical College provided the backgrounds of the alienists. Local historian Wayne Wood, OD, generously sent me information about Ayer's unfinished house in Jacksonville, Florida. Literary agent Andrew Blauner offered guidance about agents, lawyers and publishers and led me to Lisa K. Digernes, who gave me sensible legal advice. Diane P. Fischer, Jessica Gumora and Joanna Sternberg, researchers I hired, provided invaluable aid. Thanks go to the many people who assisted me in obtaining the images in this book, including the curatorial staff, particularly Sarah Cash, at the Corcoran Gallery of Art; Timothy A. Burgard at the Fine Arts Museums of San Francisco; and Chris McNamara at the Parrish Art Museum, as well as the helpful people (Ila Furman, Sue Grinols, Glenn Castellano and Sam Bridger Carroll) who facilitated rights and reproduction permissions. Special thanks go to the Graham Wiliford Foundation for American Art for the image of Harriet's feet. Most heartening was the enthusiasm and attention of Whitney Tarella, commissioning editor at The History Press, which preempted other publishers. Last but not least, I wish to thank Margaret Garguilio, Deke Simon and Ben Berry, descendants of Harriet Ayer, for their interest and support. Because of them, I feel as if I have a physical connection to my subject.

Introduction

G reat women are the products of their inner strengths, social environment
and economic circumstances. From a shy, unattractive, sheltered girl
born into a rich, socially prominent Chicago family, Harriet Hubbard Ayer
metamorphosed into a beautiful, sophisticated, intelligent woman whose
life evolved from extreme wealth to reduced circumstances and back again
several times. Each period in her life revolved around a disappointing
relationship with a man. First, her father, Henry G. Hubbard, died when
she was barely four years old, leaving her mother, Juliet, a despondent,
disinterested parent; second, her husband, Herbert Ayer, turned out to be
a philanderer and alcoholic; third, the man she loved, General E. Burd
Grubb, forsook her for a younger woman; and finally, James M. Seymour,
the man who befriended her by funding her business, proved to be a swindler
and a rake. Despite these unfortunate relationships, Harriet's innate powers
of regeneration turned each obstacle into a life-altering opportunity. While
she never directly participated in the women's rights movement, her actions
defied the prudery and restrictions of the era into which she was born.

What gave this Victorian woman the strength to withstand her adversaries?
How did she develop the know-how to start a business when it went against
all societal conventions? Herein is the romantic saga of her triumphs and
tragedies. By examining her upbringing in Chicago, her values, attitudes,
strengths and weaknesses can be better appreciated.

PART I
Chicago's Founding Families

1

The Hubbards

In the mid-nineteenth century, Chicago was the fastest-growing city in the West. Until the completion of the Erie Canal in 1825, it was an isolated trading post at the edge of American settlement. The Erie Canal was responsible for a commercial outburst that led migration to the west because it opened up the water highway between New York and Chicago. In 1848, another canal connecting the Chicago and Illinois Rivers was completed and linked to the Michigan Canal; ultimately, the canals connected the Great Lakes with the tributaries of the Mississippi, and via the Mississippi to the Gulf of Mexico, forming one giant circulatory system. Soon, however, transportation by steamer was surpassed by the railway system, with Chicago as its hub by the 1850s.

Henry George Hubbard, a descendant of the Hubbards of New England, came to Chicago around 1830. His parents, Ahira and Serena Hubbard, eventually left Middleboro, Massachusetts, to join their son in Chicago.[1] Henry was lured to Chicago by his cousin Gurdon Saltonstall Hubbard, a founding father of Chicago, who had arrived as early as 1818.[2] Chicago became an incorporated town with a population of about 350 people after a final treaty by which the Potawatomi, Ottawa and Chippewa Indians ceded their land in 1833. Because of the commercial opportunities, the population soon soared to 4,000, and on March 4, 1837, the city of Chicago was established. Strategically located at the mouth of the Chicago River and the southwest corner of Lake Michigan, this swampland became the center of transportation for lumber, grain and livestock in the nineteenth century.

Henry Hubbard, Harriet's father, entered into a partnership with Gurdon and Elijah K. Hubbard (1812–1839), another cousin who came from Middletown, Connecticut. Although short-lived, Elijah became a major real estate investor and developer in Chicago during the 1830s. In 1835, Henry, Gurdon and Elijah were also partners in Gurdon's warehouse, a forwarding and commission business; thus, the three cousins became wealthy by investing in real estate in and around Chicago and from their other businesses.[3] By 1843, however, Henry had become a clerk of the circuit court of Cook County and was listed in the city directory at the clerk's office, with a home on Lasalle Street, between Washington and Madison Streets, in Chicago.[4]

"Henry was full of fun and prone to indulge in pranks…He was fond of hunting and kept a number of trained dogs and horses for that purpose." Others said that he was generous and lovable.[5] Hank, as he was called, was engaged in several businesses, one of which compelled him to move to the country where he developed congestive fever, a malaria-like illness that forced his return to Chicago. His last employment was with Cyrus McCormick's Reaper Works.[6] In 1847, McCormick built a reaper factory in Chicago, which was so successful that he cornered the national market.

Harriet Hubbard was born into this pioneering, rapidly developing city on June 27, 1849, just twelve years after it was formally incorporated. Her parents, Henry George Hubbard and Juliet Elvira Smith, were married in 1837, and as Henry became more and more financially stable, he built a large brick house not far from Lake Michigan, on the corner of Michigan Avenue and Hubbard Court, in about 1845.[7] According to Henry Hamilton, Henry Hubbard's cousin, this house was considered one of the most attractive in the city. Set on a piece of property that extended to Wabash Avenue on the north side of the block, it was surrounded by gardens that contained many varieties of flowers, shrubs and vegetables and enough strawberries to send to market. Yet this little paradise was surrounded by construction on all but its lakeside.

It was while working for the McCormick Company that Henry went to Sandusky, Ohio, in 1852, where he contracted cholera, a fatal disease of rapid dehydration and diarrhea transmitted by ingesting contaminated water or food. He died that year at the age of forty-three, leaving his wife, Juliet, with four young children.[8] Shortly after her husband's death, at the urging of her sisters, Louise and Sarah, Juliet left her children with them and went alone to Paris to recuperate from the depression caused by her loss. Her sisters were married to important Chicago city fathers: Louise to Dr. Levi Boone, a doctor who became the seventeenth mayor of Chicago (1855–56) and, incidentally, was a great-nephew of Daniel Boone; and Sarah to Stephen Francis Gale, who founded the first bookstore in Chicago, was chief engineer of the fire department from 1844 to 1847 and invested in real estate, among many other things.[9] Clearly, the backgrounds of the extended Hubbard and Smith families were interwoven with the history of Chicago.

Juliet Smith's father, and Harriet's grandfather, Theophilus W. Smith, was an Illinois Supreme Court judge. Born in New York, Smith studied law and was admitted to the New York bar in 1805. In 1814, he moved to southwestern Illinois and settled in the town of Edwardsville, where in 1825 he was elected associate justice. He was impeached for corruption and oppressive conduct, but the impeachment proceedings against him failed. In 1836, Judge Smith moved to Chicago, where he was assigned to the Seventh Judicial Circuit in Cook County, and he practiced law there until 1842. Judge Smith was married to Clarissa Harlowe Rathbone, with whom he had several children, including Juliet and her sisters, Louise and Sarah. As was common then for circuit court judges, Smith traveled miles on horseback to hold court in small towns, often taking Juliet with him.[10] In Chicago, he became acquainted with Gurdon Hubbard and very likely Henry, since both the judge and Henry worked in the same circuit court.[11] Thus the match between Juliet Smith and Henry Hubbard was realized. Henry and Juliet Hubbard had seven children, but as was typical of the time, only four of their children survived.[12] When Henry Hubbard died, Jule, the eldest surviving child, born on November 10, 1845, was just seven years old. Henry, the second child and only boy, born in 1847, was five. Harriet, the third child and second daughter, had just turned four, and May, the youngest, born in 1851, was only eleven months old.

Juliet returned from Paris as Madame Hubbard, an affectation she retained for the rest of her life.[13] Paris gave her the opportunity to recover from her husband's death and to visit with American friends abroad. She never bothered to learn French, nor was she interested in the culture of the country. The beautiful and vivacious Juliet, after surviving multiple pregnancies and tragic deaths, took to her bed in her mid-thirties and became a semi-invalid who left the children's upbringing to the servants. This depressed woman was unable to cope with the responsibilities of single motherhood and spent much of her time in her room reading, lost in the world of books and bonbons. Juliet probably suffered from neurasthenia, a term coined in 1861 by Dr. George Mitchell Beard (1839–1883) of New York to describe exhaustion of the nervous system.[14] The diagnosis encompassed many symptoms, including headaches, fatigue, depression and the desire to escape from responsibility. Dr. Beard's famous cure was rest and removal from all sources of stress.[15] The treatment consisted of isolation, confinement to bed, diet and massage for his women patients, while his male patients were shipped off to the West to find peace and virility.[16]

Whether Juliet's isolation from her children was prescribed by a doctor or was a self-imposed cure, she sequestered herself in her bedroom for long periods of time, her illness providing a solution for not dealing with life's problems. Fortunately, she had the resources to retain servants, who took over her daily responsibilities. For the most part, this fragile Victorian woman, living in a beautiful brick house on Michigan Avenue, supported herself and her children by periodically selling the valuable property her husband had left her. Thus, Harriet's mother set an example of invalidism that had an impact on her daughter's future behavior. Juliet, however, did instill in her children two important traits: cleanliness and proper etiquette. Absent her mother and father, Harriet still grew up in a world of wealth, governed by carefully delineated rules and rituals that proscribed and restricted her behavior.

Of the four surviving Hubbard children, the least is known about Henry Jr. As a boy, he was mischievous and not inclined to study. In 1866, the Chicago city directory listed him as a commercial merchant living at 381 Wabash Avenue. He lost money and property in the Great Chicago Fire of 1871 and disappeared after that, leaving behind a wife and three daughters. Later, it is said, he moved to Montana, where he became a forest ranger.[17] The imperious and self-centered Jule, allegedly an exceptional beauty, boasted twenty-nine marriage proposals.[18] She was known to make fun of Harriet, who was shy, fearful and lacking in confidence. May, the baby of the family, fared better, with the love of her brother and Harriet.

As a middle child, Harriet was picked on. Her nose was deemed too large for her freckled face, and her blonde hair, lashes and brows did not properly set off her dark blue eyes. "Freckles," Harriet wrote many years later, "are not pretty."[19] In addition to being physically unattractive, Harriet was sickly, and Jule teased her mercilessly about her dread of the dark. Harriet panicked in dark places, a fear she sustained for the remainder of her life. Her plainness and reputed lack of academic achievement were a disappointment to her mother. These childhood interactions, as with most children, played a role in determining Harriet's future personality.

With her father dead and her mother inattentive and undemonstrative, the young Harriet was an unhappy child and surely felt unloved. It was probably the household servants and tutors who provided any attention she received (an Irish maid called Nora is mentioned). She considered herself physically and intellectually inadequate, feelings that can often lead to either defeat or defiance. In Harriet's case, however, they provided the fuel that drove her to great aspirations and future successes. But that growth and inner confidence took several years to develop. Her family, especially her mother and older sister, never anticipated the brilliance, resilience, perseverance and, most remarkable of all, physical beauty that would surface as she matured.

Harriet is said to have been able to read by the age of four or five and could quote from Shakespeare at a young age. She was initially tutored at home because "she was extremely delicate."[20] Perhaps she was even given dancing lessons as part of her social education. It was not until 1861, when she was twelve years old, that she was finally sent to the Academy of the Sacred Heart for her education. The academy, founded in Chicago in 1858, had recently bought twelve acres on the west side of Chicago and opened its new school building to 350 students in August 1860.[21] The curriculum at the school, in addition to religious instruction, may have been based on the writings of Catharine Beecher, who recommended that "much less time should be given to school and much more to domestic employments, especially in the wealthier classes."[22] Beecher, whose books were widely read, recommended needlework, drawing and music, alternated with domestic skills, plus enough general information that would assist women in social situations. Harriet proved to be highly intelligent, and later articles asserted that she was the best in her class.[23]

2

Hubbard and Ayer Families Unite

One sultry day in July 1865, fifteen-year-old Harriet was lolling about when her mother ordered her to go out and exercise. Harriet, at a loss for what to do, took her hoop and rolled it down to Lake Michigan, not far from the Hubbard home. Skipping rope and rolling hoops were the proscribed play for girls at that time. Dressed in the fashion of the day, the hem of her wide skirt, consisting of yards of fabric and petticoats held up and out by a wire hoop, caught on the construction materials around the lakeshore. The young city of Chicago was being built up at the time, and wood walkways protected people from the mud and debris below. Two young men, John Lockwood and Herbert Ayer, both reeking of whiskey, came to Harriet's aid as she tumbled to the ground and tried to pull her skirt free. Herbert, the short one with a moustache, elegantly dressed in a fashionable suit and a panama hat, tried to help Harriet and insisted on escorting the embarrassed young girl home.[24]

Madame Hubbard, curious about the unfamiliar visitors, left her bed to come downstairs and greet the young men. Once she established their social credentials, she decided that Herbert would make a fitting suitor for Jule, since the eldest daughter was supposed to be married first. Consequently, Madame Hubbard pressed Herbert to focus his attention on Jule. The more she insisted, however, the more he fancied Harriet. Even John V. Ayer, Herbert's father, was surprised that his son, who was fourteen years Harriet's senior, would select the plain younger sister over the beautiful older one, and he vigorously objected to the marriage.

Nevertheless, Herbert was attracted to the simple, unaffected young girl he had recently rescued.

The man who had rescued Harriet had a complicated early history that the newspapers embellished almost every time they wrote about the Ayer iron company. Herbert Copeland Ayer was a relative newcomer to Chicago in comparison to the Hubbard family.[25] He was born in New Orleans in 1835 to John Varnum Ayer and a southern belle named Sarah Lynch.[26] John Ayer came from a poor family that had settled in Wisconsin, but he was well educated.[27] John persuaded his friend Samuel Hale, who had some money, to buy cheap land in Ohio in order to establish an iron mill. Then he left for New Orleans in the 1830s to earn money by teaching in order to invest in the iron business with Hale.

He fell madly in love with Sarah Lynch, a wealthy girl from Charleston, South Carolina. Despite the objections to the marriage by both sets of parents, the lovers eloped. After their marriage, John went back to teaching, and Sarah was forced to live in John's small boardinghouse rooms, which were hardly up to the standards of this spoiled southern girl. Although John worked hard to support his wife, they argued about money and expenditures; he ultimately went to Chicago looking for other business. He planned to send for Sarah, but she returned to her family, who convinced her to divorce John. Several versions of what happened after exist. Some say that both John and Sarah developed yellow fever. Each was led to believe that the other had died. Sarah's father actually put an announcement in the New Orleans newspaper the *Bee* on June 17, 1833, listing Sarah, "consort of John V. Ayer, aged 20 years, a native of New Jersey," as dead on June 12, along with a son named Montravill B., who died on the fifteenth at the age of seven weeks and six days.[28] Given that a yellow fever epidemic occurred almost every other year in New Orleans during the 1830s, John believed that Sarah was dead. "Broken down by grief, he was unable to return to the South" and devoted himself to work in order to earn enough money to join Sam Hale in Ohio and invest in the iron business.[29] Eventually, Sarah married another man, a Mr. Copeland. John, too, married again in the late 1830s, this time to an older woman from Wisconsin named Elida Manney, with whom he had three sons.[30]

Another version of this story said that John knew his wife was pregnant, but her parents broke up the marriage anyway. Brokenhearted, he allegedly left his shoe business in New Orleans and went to Washington, D.C., where he prospered in the lumber business. He then received a letter from his lawyer notifying him that his wife had died in childbirth; it even described her grave and epitaph. This story corroborates the false death announcements in the *Bee*. Furthermore, the story claimed that in 1861 John Ayer visited New Orleans, where he recognized his former wife. She had married a rich plantation owner in Rapides Parish who was impoverished by the war and had died. When he found that his son was still alive, he procured letters to release his newfound son from the Confederate army. In addition, he gave Sarah $150,000 so that she could survive comfortably in New Orleans and brought his son, Herbert, back to Chicago, where he "lavished upon him all the money he could spend."[31]

Herbert was about thirty years old when John allegedly bought his release from the army.[32] Rich men did not have to serve in the army, since for $300 or more they could purchase a substitute. In the South, toward the end of the war, men between the ages of eighteen and fifty were conscripted, and the cost of buying a substitute rose to thousands of dollars. A later article claimed that John paid $8,000 for Herbert's release.[33] Since no records for Herbert Copeland serving in the Confederate army could be found, it is entirely possible that he never served.[34] The Union army had captured New Orleans by the spring of 1862, so perhaps Herbert was just unable to leave New Orleans and his father had only to release him from the city in the grip of Union forces.

Harriet's daughter Margaret claimed that about 1863, during the Civil War, John Ayer traveled to White Sulpher Springs, West Virginia, where, since the eighteenth century, wealthy Americans vacationed.[35] While enjoying the hot spring baths and social life, he chanced upon his first wife, Sarah, dining with a young Confederate soldier. Sarah by now had gray hair and had changed physically, but he recognized her.[36] Her husband's plantation was in ruins, and she had suffered the hardships of war in the South. The boy, who bore Sarah's second husband's surname, Copeland, turned out to be John's son.[37] A slightly different version of John Ayer's discovery of Herbert Copeland recounted that during a business trip to New Orleans in 1864, while dining at the Planters' Hotel, John spotted "a woman who bore such a remarkable resemblance to the first Mrs. Ayer that he made inquiries about her and was astonished to learn that the latter was living, that she was the woman he had seen and that the young man with her was his son, of whose existence he had never even heard."[38] The important point of these various versions is that father and son were reunited, most likely late in 1864. Herbert was suddenly propelled into a new way of life, turning from a New Orleans southerner into a Chicago northerner; from the genteel poverty of his stepfather to the wealth of his actual father, who by this time was very successful; and from a mother who seemingly adored him to a stepmother with three sons of her own.

John Ayer had rejoined Sam Hale before the Civil War began. The Hale & Ayer Iron Company was established in 1859. In 1862, they bought an interest in Brown and Bonnell Iron Company in Youngstown, Ohio. That company consisted of four of the largest iron rolling mills in the country, three blast furnaces, a large iron mill and, nearby, a large coalfield, coking ovens and a limestone quarry. The mills produced bar iron, railroad spikes, sheet and tank iron, nails, links, coupling pins and other light railroad iron products. Business soared during the Civil War. The company had unlimited credit and reaped immense fortunes from John's "shrewd and successful management." With the advent of the Civil War and the growth of the railroad system in Chicago, John V. Ayer became a very rich man. Industrial growth, from agriculture to manufacturing, was enormous, and after the Civil War some thirty thousand miles of railroad tracks were laid across the United States. Hale & Ayer supplied some of the materials. Hale disagreed with John about further expansion and changes in the company and eventually left around 1870, which served John well since he planned to take his sons into the business.[39] Herbert, who was working for the Stock-Yards National Bank, then began to work for his father along with his stepbrothers. Eventually, John became a member of the elite Chicago Club, founded in 1869 by and for the wealthiest and most influential men in the city.

Obsessed with his newfound heir, his love child, John Ayer laid his hopes and ambitions on Herbert's shoulders, tutoring him in the business he would ultimately inherit. Herbert was first listed in the 1866 Chicago directory as living at home with his father and three stepbrothers at One Park Place, on a street of elegant attached townhouses.[40] In 1862, John's sons Philip and George were salesmen for the Hale and Ayer Company, while the youngest, John M., was a law student.[41] The sudden appearance of an older stepbrother must have caused some friction, jealousy and resentment among the Ayer boys.[42]

When Herbert met Harriet in 1865, he and his stepbrother John were listed in the directory as students at Bryant and Stratton Business College, on Clark Street and the corner of Washington. A spoiled, cocky young man, Herbert was already bored with school and his job and frequented bars with his friends. Nevertheless, his heart belonged to the delicate and unassuming young girl who was unlike his flirtatious mother and Harriet's sister Jule and her friends.[43] He did not mention the subject of marriage to his father or to Harriet right away but waited until the Civil War was almost over. His father had hoped that he would wait and marry after he took over the family business, but John Ayer was impressed with the Hubbards and eventually consented to the marriage.

According to contemporary etiquette, Elida Ayer called on Madame Hubbard to talk about the marriage arrangements, but Juliet assumed that Herbert wanted Jule's hand. The retiring Mrs. Ayer was made to feel ridiculous by Juliet's imperious but mistaken reaction.[44] Herbert had to insist that it was indeed Harriet he wanted and that he was willing to wait until she was seventeen to marry. While most biographies persist in writing that Harriet was married at the age of sixteen, even some that were written while she was alive, they are inaccurate.[45]

Madame Hubbard finally consented to have her younger daughter marry first because she truly believed that her ugly duckling might not have any other marriage prospects. Harriet acquiesced, probably thinking, as many girls did then, that marriage was her only escape from the boredom and unhappiness she experienced at home. That someone thought her attractive gave her confidence, and she basked in the attention and affection Herbert showered on her. That her own mother tried to persuade her suitor to consider her sister instead could only have increased her feelings of being unloved. Such disregard by her family surely provided the motivation for her future emphasis on the importance of appearance.

Although Herbert's education had been neglected and he was known to be a gambler and a heavy drinker, he was a good-natured fellow who apparently demonstrated some aptitude for business. John clearly favored Herbert and placed him over his other sons in the firm, perhaps to assuage his guilt for having abandoned Herbert, although unintentionally, during the young man's formative years.

Spring 1865 brought both good and bad news to Chicago. The Civil War, fought by over three million Americans, was finally over. In the end, the South was left poor and the North rich. Chicago profited, and John V. Ayer prospered. However, on April 14, Good Friday, President Abraham Lincoln was assassinated. He was killed by a bullet to his head while he attended Ford's Theatre in Washington, D.C., and died the next day. Headlines in Chicago papers proclaimed, "The Death of President Lincoln." The lines below told more: "J. Wilkes Booth the Murderer, Andrew Johnson Sworn into Office."[46] On May 1, Lincoln's coffin was paraded up Michigan Avenue, a main thoroughfare in Chicago. Nearly forty thousand people attended the funeral and procession. His flower-coated coffin lay in state at the courthouse for several hours before it was moved to another city.[47] Harriet was hardly impacted by the war because no men from her immediate family had been involved. Her father was dead, and her brother was too young to join the Union army. Nevertheless, she could not have avoided seeing the caskets and funerals of Chicago's dead in addition to the walking wounded. On this occasion, Harriet went with John Ayer to view the body at midnight, and the two of them began to bond. Herbert, a southerner and former Confederate soldier, did not go.

By 1866, the marriage had been agreed upon by both families. Preparations for the wedding took place, with Harriet in charge of the decorations in the house, especially the flowers. The white satin wedding dress and bridesmaids' dresses were made in New York. Nora, one of the Hubbards' Irish servants, sewed Juliet's Venetian lace onto Harriet's gown. Jule was totally upstaged, jealous and outraged and therefore more obnoxious than usual. Madame Hubbard remained in her room to avoid Jule's tantrums.[48] Not to be outdone, a week before the wedding, Jule secretly eloped with Herbert's friend John Lockwood and fled to New Jersey, where they resided for the rest of their lives.

During the usual pre-wedding tensions, John Ayer became better acquainted with his future daughter-in-law and began to appreciate her refreshingly open and unaffected personality. Although unfashionably dressed and physically unattractive, he found her blonde hair and dark blue eyes appealing. On October 2, 1866, seventeen-year-old Harriet Hubbard became Mrs. Herbert C. Ayer in a ceremony at the family church followed by a reception for the family and a few friends held in the beautiful Hubbard home. Madame Hubbard presented her daughter with a Bible soon after the wedding. A short announcement appeared the next day in the *Chicago Tribune*.[49]

The newlyweds spent their honeymoon in White Sulpher Springs, West Virginia, at a hotel affectionately known as "Old White's." Harriet realized how poorly dressed she was in comparison to those around her. While Herbert played cards at the hotel, she went for fittings of the latest Parisian dresses. Herbert and his father provided her with a bank account, and for the first time in her life, she had some financial independence. She enjoyed shopping for clothes and dressing well and even began to wear a corset to improve her figure and to show off her new wardrobe.[50] Most women wore laced corsets to reduce their waist size, although in later years Harriet advocated garments that did not require corsets, or else the use of corsets without bones.

When Harriet and Herbert returned to Chicago, they lived with John and Elida for a while, until John rented a small white frame house for them at 309 Huron Street.[51] With his new responsibilities, Herbert devoted himself to business, starting at the lowest level in his father's firm, while Harriet concentrated on becoming a proper wife and homemaker. Appearances were important, therefore Herbert's wife had to be fashionably dressed and keep a well-appointed home. She was to cook, sew, embroider, wash and iron clothes—or at least know how to supervise the servants in those activities. A wife's main role was to give pleasure and comfort, to produce children—preferably boys—and to obey her husband.

Herbert and Harriet became part of Chicago's young married set and went to parties where they both enjoyed dancing. Little by little, Harriet adjusted to married life and sought to fit in with her peers. Her mother had not taught her to keep house, and she depended on one servant named Lizzie to help her. She made mistakes that amused Herbert but worked hard at developing her household and culinary skills. John Ayer, having only sons, was enthralled with his new daughter-in-law and visited almost daily. He enjoyed Harriet's quick mind and taught her Latin and other subjects that reminded him of his days as a teacher in New Orleans. His attention to her enraged his son, who reacted to Harriet's newly acquired knowledge by becoming inebriated, presaging future problems.[52]

Harriet soon became pregnant and was sick with blinding headaches that were bad enough to necessitate hospitalization. The cause was probably preeclampsia, a condition of some pregnant women marked by high blood pressure, severe headaches, dizziness, nausea, vomiting and swelling of the feet, among other symptoms. It occurs frequently in teenage pregnancies, and Harriet, who was just eighteen at the time, could have died. Hospitalization was unusual among the wealthy, so Harriet's symptoms must have been severe. Taking her own food, sheets and nightgowns from home, she was admitted to either the Chicago Hospital for Women and Children or, more likely, St. Luke's, an Episcopalian hospital that had accommodations for those who could pay, as well as for the poor.

While in the hospital, she began to read the novels of Charles Dickens, her mother's favorite author. Dickens's writings awoke in her sympathy for Chicago's poor. She empathized and tried her best to help those within her immediate surroundings, even supplying food and clothing to some of the families of hospitalized women. Although isolated from the poor most of her life, she became aware of the needs of the people around her and befriended and aided several indigent patients. She was kind and thoughtful, and her help was greatly valued. One family would demonstrate their appreciation four years later during the great Chicago conflagration.

As was customary, Harriet returned home to have her baby. Her daughter was born on a hot August day in 1867. Herbert was pleased and insisted that the baby be named Harriet; the name was shortened to Hattie, which was Madame Hubbard's nickname for Harriet. Hattie was given the middle name Taylor. Although John would have preferred a boy to carry on the family name, he came to adore the pretty little girl. Now he stopped by to see both Harriets, and he showered the little one with gifts. Within a couple of years, Harriet was pregnant a second time and once again was bedridden. Most likely, the preeclampsia recurred, and bed rest was all that could be done during those years. This time, she insisted on staying at home to care for little Hattie rather than going to the hospital. With a household dominated by an ailing wife and a lively little girl, Herbert sought his entertainment outside the home. Excessive drinking was considered normal socializing among men, and he often came home late and intoxicated.

The second baby, Gertrude Griswold, born on October 10, 1870, was a disappointment not only because she was not a boy but also because she was sickly. Harriet, a loving and devoted mother, insisted on caring for the baby herself instead of allowing Nora, the Irish servant her mother had sent, to care for the child. It was then that Madame Hubbard advised her to pay more attention to her husband or else he might be tempted to stray. For the first time, she noticed that her daughter had matured into an exceptionally beautiful young woman. (See Figure 1.) She also recommended that Harriet purchase new clothes and begin entertaining again. John and Herbert also noticed the change in Harriet's physical and intellectual development. Herbert worried that she would turn into a vacuous woman like those he had known in New Orleans—or worse, that she would become too intellectual. Both alternatives were threatening to him because of his own inadequacies.[53] Perhaps, too, there was an unspoken competition between father and son.

3

The Great Chicago Fire

Life went on as it did for other well-to-do families in Chicago. Harriet furnished their home, took care of the children and organized entertaining dinners with the help of her servants. That lifestyle disappeared in a single day. On Sunday, October 8, 1871, fires broke out in various parts of the city. The weather had been hot, and the city had been without rain for so long that a conflagration was almost inevitable. It was not, as legend has it, Mrs. O'Leary's cow kicking over a lantern alone that started the fire. Current thinking suggests that the cause was multiple fires bolstered by the heat and spread by wind. The city was vigilant about fires because of its huge stores of coal, lumber, grain elevators, mills, warehouses, wooden churches and wooden houses. However, it lacked sufficient firefighting equipment and water to combat this conflagration.

The blaze spread quickly and consumed hundreds of commercial and industrial buildings, except for the famous stone water tower and pumping station. Designed in a castellated Gothic style by W.W. Boyington on North Michigan at Chicago Avenue in 1868–69, the waterworks, as the two structures were called, was inadequate, yet the rusticated stone tower, which hid a 138-foot standpipe, and the pump house across the street withstood the flames. The fire, one of the worst disasters of the nineteenth century, burned a three-and-a-quarter-square-mile path of destruction. It left 90,000 people homeless, including Harriet and Herbert Ayer, and about 300 dead out of a population of 300,000 inhabitants. Despite the destruction of the physical city, Chicago retained its importance as a commercial and industrial hub because of its geographic position as a center for railroad, canal, river and lake transportation.

Harriet was home alone with the children and Nora when the fire began. As it spread closer to her frame house, she decided to retrieve her horse and carriage from the stable several blocks away and bring it back to the house. She told Nora to bundle the children in blankets and ready them for the ride to her in-laws' house on the south side of the city. People were frantic, leaving their homes in droves and crowding into the streets. From the chatter outside, she learned that the lumberyards were in flames and the opera house, among other structures, had burned to the ground.[54] She had almost reached the stable when she saw Herbert, who told her that their carriage house had been destroyed and their carriage stolen. Together, they fought their way back to the house, trying to beg a ride from people in vehicles, but to no avail. When they arrived at the house, they spotted a lone wagon parked there. The wagon driver was the husband of one of the women Harriet had helped when she was in the hospital. In gratitude, that woman had sent her husband to rescue Harriet and her children. The man hardly recognized Harriet, who was covered with soot from the encroaching fire and smoke. He refused to help her, saying:

> *I am going to save the kindest lady on the north side—the lady who took care of my wife and children, who cooked their food with her own hands after buying it for them. I ain't a man what forgets a kindness like that. I'll save that good lady or die in the attempt.*[55]

The much-repeated story relates how Harriet left her jewels and clothes behind in order to save some neighborhood children. The horses, frightened by the embers, smoke and commotion in the street, became unmanageable, and the driver declared that he could not control them. Some men came along and blindfolded the horses, yet the terrified driver could not continue, so Harriet took the reins and drove the children to safety. This dramatic version fails to mention Herbert. With the children and Nora on board, Harriet made her way to the senior Ayer's house and found it filled with strangers seeking refuge from the fire. John Ayer put mattresses in the basement for people to rest and sleep, and Elida and her servants made sandwiches and coffee to offer to passersby. Elida was greatly relieved when her daughter-in-law and grandchildren arrived, but baby Gertrude, who had asthma, ultimately did not survive the smoke she had inhaled on the way to her grandparents' house.[56]

Gertrude's breathing was labored, and Herbert, after great effort, was finally able to persuade a doctor to come see the child. There was not much the exhausted physician could do, but he did give Harriet, who was beside herself with worry about her baby, a shot of morphine to relieve her anxiety. A common treatment then, this may have been the beginning of Harriet's dependence on the drug. Gertrude suffered for two months before succumbing on December 7, 1871.[57] Harriet, who had nursed the child during that period, was grief-stricken. While Gertrude's death was due to her frail condition, in general, mortality rates for children before the age of five ranged from 18 to 20 percent during the second half of the nineteenth century. Chicago had a 50 percent survival rate for that age group in the 1870s.[58]

Although the fire was finally extinguished, the smoldering embers remained for days. Harriet's frame house, as those of other property owners, was destroyed. In a stupor of heartbreak and sadness over Gertrude's death, Harriet worked with the other women in her family to give aid to the poor and helpless victims of the fire. Everyone became a pioneer under these circumstances, united in a common effort to clean up their city and rebuild their lives. Most of the city's birth, death and marriage records were lost. Madame Hubbard was in New York with Harriet's younger sister May at the time of the fire.[59] Depositing May with her friends the Wetherills in Philadelphia, Madame Hubbard returned to Chicago to find that although her brick house survived the fire, vandals had looted it. She decided to sell it and return to New York.

Devastated by the loss of her child and her home, Harriet was encouraged by her mother and her father-in-law to travel to Paris to recuperate, just as Juliet had done after the death of her husband. Herbert was disturbed by his wife's departure but more so by her taking away his precious little Hattie, to whom he was quite attached. In mid-December 1871, Harriet sailed on the steamer *George Washington* for the long ocean voyage to France.[60] While marriage and motherhood were distinctive milestones in Harriet's life, her trip to Paris to recover from the death of her daughter changed her definitively.

PARIS

Dressed in black mourning clothes, Harriet arrived in Paris just one year after France lost the Franco-Prussian War. On September 19, 1870, the German armies besieged Paris for four months during a winter so severe that food supplies ran out. Paris, therefore, was still somewhat in shambles when Harriet, along with her mother and daughter, arrived. Reminiscent of the city they had just left, people had lost loved ones, and destruction was visible everywhere. Harriet rented an apartment on the Champs-Élysées that came with two French-speaking servants. Neither Harriet nor her mother knew the language, but little Hattie picked it up rapidly. Soon, Harriet set herself to the task of learning French while her mother made herself understood in English by raising her voice.[61] Harriet found a young Frenchwoman, Mademoiselle Frochard, who gave her two-hour lessons every morning, and then Harriet spent afternoons practicing verbs and writing. She and her teacher, who had lost family in the war, united in their grief and became lifelong friends.

As Harriet recovered, she again began to show interest in her appearance and laid aside her mourning clothes. Paris offered the advantages of the latest fashion, art, food and entertainment. Although the House of Worth had closed during the Franco Prussian War, it reopened in 1871, just as Harriet was reenergizing. Charles Frederick Worth (1826–1895) had moved to Paris from England in 1845, and within three years he established his own atelier, transforming couture into high art and big business. Each outfit was custom fitted and fabricated from luxurious textiles. Like Harriet, many Americans favored his gowns, and his business flourished. (See Figure 2.)

Worth designed several original gowns expressly for Harriet. Her fluency in French apparently impressed him, and he took her under his wing, advising her on her hairstyle, her jewels and her general appearance. With a hairdresser, he created a soft bang of curls to cover her forehead, and the rest of her golden hair was drawn into loose curls at the back of her head, different from the typical American style of tight chignons.[62] Her avant-garde coiffure, which she retained for many years, was more appreciated by her Parisian friends than the Americans living in Paris in the early 1870s.[63] The American community was fairly insular and preferred living in the newer buildings on the Boulevard Malesherbes or around the Champs-Élysées. Harriet knew people like Sir Henry Drummond Wolff (1830–

1908), a well-known English diplomat and politician, who came to her aid on a later visit to Rome.[64]

Harriet also used her time during the winter of 1872 to wander through the antique shops and bookstalls along the Seine. She bought books on a variety of subjects to improve her mind and read voraciously. She also scoured the antique shops for furniture and bric-a-brac for her new home. During her meanderings, she found a chemist's shop on the Boulevard Malesherbes. The shop specialized in making perfumes and creams. The proprietor, Monsieur Mirault, talked to Harriet at length and was duly impressed with the seriousness of her interest and the intelligence of her questions. He invited her into his laboratory, where he formulated the scent of Parma violet that Harriet used for years.[65] Monsieur Mirault also told her about a cream that his family made for Jeanne Françoise Julie Adélaïde Bernard Récamier (December 4, 1777–May 11, 1849), a famous French woman who was a leader of the literary and political circles of the early nineteenth century. This cream was responsible for keeping Madame Récamier looking young. He offered to show it to Harriet when she next visited the shop, an enticement that became the basis of her future endeavor.

Another preoccupation of Harriet's was the theater. She attended frequently in an effort to improve her French, and toward the end of her visit to Paris, she settled on shows presented at the Odeon Theater. The Odeon, located on the Left Bank near the Luxembourg Gardens, was one of France's five national theaters. Harriet attended the same show every night because of the quality of the acting and the precise diction of the actors. She sat in the same box each time in order to observe their faces and then transcribed the dialogue for Mademoiselle Frochard and recited passages. She went so often that friends refused to continue going with her. Thwarting contemporary conventions, she went alone, even though the theater was some distance from her apartment, which led people to gossip and suspect that she was flirting with the male star. Actually, she left Paris without ever meeting him. On board the French ocean liner she took home, she impressed the captain with her fluent, flawless French.[66]

Harriet arrived home in love with France and all things French. Her education abroad made Chicago social life seem provincial. Travel changed her perspective on history, art, food, décor and culture. Just as her mother appropriated the salutation "Madame" after her trip to Paris in 1852, Harriet took on the persona of a cosmopolite. She proceeded to take Chicago by storm, much to the discontent of her husband and the jealousy of her peers. Like the protagonist Edna Pontellier in Kate Chopin's book *The Awakening*, published in 1899, Harriet reassessed her personal priorities and began pursuing her own interests. Her awakening, however, was in conflict with Herbert's patriarchy and instigated the demise of their relationship.[67]

4

Grown Up in Chicago

Harriet's newly acquired cosmopolitan manners, dress and cultural pursuits made Herbert uncomfortable. Her sophistication also signified her increasing social emancipation. As time went on, their differences—not only age but also upbringing and education—became more evident. Pretty, vivacious and hungry for life, Harriet was ready to entertain and perform, while Herbert preferred a social life of a different sort. Fourteen years older than his bride, Herbert had little patience for or understanding of the changes he observed. Harriet had become increasingly beautiful, but he preferred her as the innocent girl he first met and could control. Herbert was more pleased to see Hattie than his wife because his daughter did not threaten him or make him feel inadequate.

Herbert met Harriet and Hattie in New York, but they did not linger; both were eager to return to Chicago, albeit for different reasons. Harriet wanted to see the new house John Ayer was building for them and to observe the reconstruction of the city in her absence. Herbert, ill at ease in New York, wanted to return to his work and his drinking cronies at home.[68] Madame Hubbard, not wanting to return to her looted house, remained in New York and did something very tender: she replaced the Bible she had given Harriet on her wedding day. The unemotional inscription reads, "To my daughter Hattie replacing her wedding gift of October 2nd 1866 destroyed during the great fire of October 9, 1871."[69]

Upon her arrival in Chicago, John Ayer, and most especially Elida Ayer, who was ill, greeted Harriet warmly. Because Elida hardly ever ventured an opinion on any subject of importance, her husband and children ignored her. But she empathized with her daughter-in-law and realized that Harriet's return to Chicago would renew heartbreaking memories of Gertrude's death. Harriet spent time with Elida while she and Herbert boarded with the senior Ayers until their own house was ready. The household also included Herbert's stepbrothers, Philip, George and John M. Ayer. From 1872 through 1874, they were listed in the city directory as living at One Park Row, off Michigan Avenue near Twelfth Street, a block-long street near the lake. Among the city's most fashionable addresses, it consisted mainly of elegant attached town houses.

The new house Harriet's father-in-law built for them was simple, located in the so-called Gold Coast because so many millionaires moved there. The 1875 directory lists the Herbert Ayers at 467 Dearborn Street, a street of elegant town houses on standard-sized lots of about twenty-five square feet. Harriet spent her days shopping not only in Chicago but also at the exclusive furniture house of Sypher & Co. in New York. Late in October 1874, the young couple moved into their new home.

Harriet's first dinner party in her new house was on Christmas 1874. She decorated the table with red roses floating in crystal bowls and used red and gold French-made china in which she served French food. She wore her beautiful white satin Worth gown to offset the ruby and diamond necklace and bracelet Herbert and John had given her.[70] The young Ayers were happy in their new home. Like other wealthy, socially prominent residents of the city who entertained lavishly at home, Harriet spent a good deal of time decorating her table and selecting interesting menus and wines.

One would hardly have known there was a depression in 1873 by the way Harriet spent money on luxuries and did nothing to curtail her expenditures. Although the Panic of 1873 began on September 18 in Philadelphia when a major financier involved with promoting railroad construction declared bankruptcy, the Ayers were able to withstand the crisis. Thousands of businesses fell into bankruptcy. Banks failed, the New York Stock Exchange closed for ten days and the country found itself in a major depression. It was so catastrophic that it was known as the "Great Depression" until it was superseded by the even greater disaster from 1929 to 1933. John Ayer, however, had taken precautions, and his company continued to thrive, as iron goods were needed for many industries.

Sometime later, Herbert reported that Harriet's purchases were excessive. "The last year I lived with Mrs. Ayer it cost me $96,000 to pay for her extravagances."[71] While he objected to her reckless spending, he was secretly proud of showing off their home décor and his ability to afford it. Their wealth was also publicized by such charitable donations as an Italian marble font placed near the main entrance of the recently rebuilt St. James Episcopal Church, completed in 1874.[72] The baptismal font, deeply carved in Carrara marble by the American sculptor Augusta Freeman, depicted three angels holding up the basin. It is dedicated to the memory of Gertrude Griswold Ayer and is inscribed with her birth and death dates, as well as biblical quotations. St. James was the church to which the family belonged; Herbert invested in a pew, number 158, for the family for $750.

After her return, Harriet had had a series of miscarriages that left her weak and depressed. The 1876 Centennial Exposition in Philadelphia provided an excuse for Harriet to get away and visit with Jule and May. May was staying in Philadelphia with her in-laws, the Wetherills, and Jule was living in New Jersey with her husband, John Lockwood, and their son, Herbert. Little was known about postpartum depression then, although most doctors connected all women's diseases and moods to their uteruses. The fair provided a stimulating diversion from her problems.

The Centennial Exposition marking the 100th anniversary of the signing of the Declaration of Independence was the first official international world's fair in the United States.[73] It was held from May through November 1876 in Fairmont Park along the Schuylkill River. Ten million visitors came from all over the world to see the national and international scientific, industrial, cultural and artistic displays that promulgated each nation's industrial, commercial and cultural accomplishments. This fair emphasized American history, exhibiting Colonial-style rooms that initiated the vogue for historic American objects. At the opening ceremonies on May 10, 1876, Harriet spied a tall, handsome, dark-haired man on horseback who was to become her great romantic interest and, eventually, one of the several disappointing men in her life.

Harriet had not seen her sister May since 1872, when she attended her wedding to Alexander Wetherill in New York, and most likely, she had no contact with Jule since her older sister eloped with John Lockwood in 1866. May led an interesting life, traveling with her husband, Second Lieutenant Alexander Macomb Wetherill, a career soldier in the Sixth United States Infantry who was raised to the rank of captain in 1890. She had recently returned from his various posts in the Dakota Territory.[74] Boarding with the Wetherills (her mother's old Quaker friends), Harriet met May's little girl, also named May, for the first time. Jule did not attend the Centennial Exposition, nor did she attend May's wedding in New York, because her husband was "unwell." Harriet and May were determined to visit Jule since she had become completely estranged from their family.[75] The Lockwoods moved several times to various addresses in New Jersey during the 1870s and '80s. Although Harriet would have liked to have brought nine-year-old Hattie with her to meet her aunts and cousins, she left her at home to placate Herbert.

Harriet and May ventured by train from Philadelphia to Elizabeth, New Jersey.[76] The formerly vivacious Jule was waiting for them at the station. Her two younger sisters were surprised by the change in their once beautiful but spiteful sister. Jule, dressed in drab, matronly attire, drove them to her home, a simply furnished place with cheap oak furniture and no curtains or draperies. Draperies, while providing privacy and protection from drafts, were also a symbol of affluence. Referring to her husband by his last name, she said that Mr. Lockwood, who was in the water business in Manhattan, did not allow curtains because of the dust. He did, however, appreciate flowers and vegetables, which were abundant in the garden.[77] Like his old friend Herbert Ayer, he was very fond of whiskey and grew churlish when drunk (the state Jule referred to as "unwell"). That Jule called her husband "Mr." was a sign of their hierarchical relationship, one that put the formerly arrogant Jule in a position of being the property of her spouse, as many women were in those days. Once married, women, regardless of class, surrendered rights to property and person and had no legal recourse. After a short visit, May and Harriet, with sighs of relief, departed for Philadelphia, despondent about the life of their sister.

As a guest of the Wetherills, Harriet was formally introduced to the man she had admired from afar, General Edward Burd Grubb (1841–1913). It was he who led the honor guard for celebrities visiting the Centennial Exposition in Philadelphia. He came from an old American family, just as Harriet did. Born in New Jersey to Edward B. Grubb, an owner of an ore mine, and his wife, he was educated at Burlington College. Soon after graduating in 1860 at age nineteen, he enlisted in the Third New Jersey Volunteer Infantry. As a Union army officer during the Civil War, he served in three regiments, commanded two of them and ultimately was made a brevet brigadier general for his gallant services. He was also a notable businessman and subsequently a politician and diplomat. Married to Elizabeth Wadsworth Van Rensselaer in 1868, Grubb was obviously unhappy, for he was smitten with the voluptuous, sparkling young Harriet when they first met. Grubb later ran for governor of New Jersey in 1889 but lost; he was appointed ambassador to Spain from 1890 to 1892.

At a dance hosted by the Wetherills, the two spent time together. While Harriet had refused to dance with others, she could not resist a dance with this man whom she found so attractive. The feeling was mutual, and he asked if he could call on her the next day. He brought her violets from his greenhouse, declaring that no one could wear them as well as she. Every afternoon thereafter he called on her and sent fresh violets. Harriet mentioned to May that she thought Grubb was attractive. The proper Mrs. Wetherill and her daughter-in-law, knowing both were married, tried to discourage their meetings and were relieved when Harriet finally left Philadelphia. As she departed, the general told Harriet that she could call on him for anything.[78] This subliminal romantic interlude presaged Harriet's disregard for period conventions when it served her and also underscored her discontent with her marriage. By dancing with Grubb and accepting his flowers, she signaled her openness to receiving his advances.

When Harriet returned to Chicago, she found Herbert more churlish and rude than ever before after visits with his mother, Sarah Lynch Ayer Copeland in Youngstown, Ohio. He was drinking excessively. Harriet tried to confide in her father-in-law about her marital problems, but as was typical of the period, his response was to encourage her to make the marriage work. He had noticed their increasing estrangement and convinced Harriet to settle with Herbert. Thinking that perhaps she had not made a strong enough effort toward reconciliation, she moved back into their bedroom, which she had left because of his drinking. She endeavored to be congenial and patient, and Herbert even stopped drinking for a while.[79]

Mrs. Herbert Ayer, listed in the 1876 *Chicago Social Directory*, performed in amateur theatricals and entertained friends and Herbert's business acquaintances, along with such celebrated actors as Sarah Bernhardt, Clara Louise Kellogg, Edwin Booth, Richard Mansfield, Ellen Terry and Henry Irving. While she never asked her guests to perform, there were nights when some of them did. On other occasions, she actually hired musicians and then sat them at the table with her guests, highly irregular in Chicago. At a banquet for the actor John McCullough that the Ayers could not attend, "a handsome floral offering was the gift of Herbert C. Ayer."[80] Herbert was also listed as a patron of a concert given at Lincoln Park by Mr. Hand's orchestra.[81] At least in name, Herbert took part as a patron of the arts.

In 1878, Harriet lent "an old carved chest, dated about 1650, a very rare and valuable specimen," to an exhibition that included European paintings, Dresden porcelain and Oriental embroideries, corroborating her taste for antique furniture.[82] She continued to buy and collect antique furniture, but her interests were wide ranging, encompassing politics, theater, economics and literature. Her library was filled with books she had purchased in Paris and after. She read Henry Wadsworth Longfellow, Ralph Waldo Emerson and the newest American author, Mark Twain, whose *Adventures of Tom Sawyer* had just been published in 1876. She even read the work of the English philosopher Herbert Spencer. Her subscriptions to the *Nation* and the *Atlantic Monthly* upset Herbert, who accused her of being a bluestocking—or even worse, a suffragette—because she read so much.[83]

Although Harriet may have been sympathetic to their objectives, she was not a member of any women's organizations. She did, however, accomplish much of what they were advocating within the next fifteen years. No longer the shy, innocent young girl he once adored, Herbert no longer loved the cosmopolite she had become. Try as she may to make a success of her marriage, the differences between them became increasingly magnified. Harriet continued to read and learn, while Herbert continued to drink excessively, cavorting with his cohorts and other women.

During a short cessation of hostility between them, Harriet became pregnant, but once again she was ill throughout the pregnancy. There was a fundamental lack of understanding between most men and women then. When she came close to term, Harriet sent Hattie to spend time with her grandmother Hubbard, who was staying at Chicago's newly built Palmer House during the spring of 1877. Margaret Rathbone Ayer was born in 1877, a disappointment to her father and grandfather because she was not a boy. With the birth of a new child, Harriet sublimated her feelings for General Grubb. Fortunately, unlike Gertrude, Margaret was healthy. Harriet took pains to keep Hattie from becoming jealous of the new baby and spent extra time with her. She wanted to counter the experience she had as a child when her mother made her feel inferior to her older sister. There was a ten-year difference between the two sisters, but because of

Harriet's reputed psychological awareness, the girls remained close to each other.[84] Harriet knew her interest in giving her daughters a better education than either she or Herbert had enjoyed made him feel inferior. Nevertheless, she persisted in giving the girls all kinds of lessons. She hired a German governess for Hattie and encouraged her musical talent by giving her piano lessons.

Between 1873 and 1882, Harriet Ayer was a leading socialite in Chicago. Even as her marriage was failing, she continued to live lavishly and spend excessive amounts of money on luxuries. John Ayer died of pneumonia at age sixty-five on April 30, 1877, and his death was followed a month later by that of Elida, at age seventy-two, on May 30, 1877.[85] Harriet, who felt affection for her in-laws, helped to take care of John and Elida during their final illnesses. John left the family house on Park Row to Elida, his wife of almost forty years. He left Herbert a thriving iron business. Herbert was as inclined to spend money as Harriet, and in September 1880, he purchased a 200- by 133-foot plot of land on Dearborn Street from the Roman Catholic bishop for $20,000.[86] This may account for the address change in the directory soon after, from 467 Dearborn to 362 Dearborn, the property on which the Ayers built their limestone mansion and for which they ordered three portraits.

THE PORTRAITS

While their marriage was falling apart, the Ayers kept up social pretenses and commissioned three portraits of Harriet. Divorce was not an option most people considered during the Victorian era. Herbert contacted William Merritt Chase to paint the first portrait of Harriet. The commissioning signaled Herbert's status as an independent, wealthy man two years after the death of his father. Herbert and Chase were similar in that they were both seeking greater recognition. Chase was aspiring to be a famous, financially successful artist, while Herbert's goal was to be a captain of industry. With his father's estate settled, Herbert assumed leadership and ultimately full ownership of the iron company in 1877, and it came to be known as John V. Ayer Sons. The Gilded Age was associated with fortunes such as the Ayers enjoyed, built through industry and commerce. The intense amassing of goods and art to fill grandiose homes was part of the optimism and anxiety of keeping up with rich neighbors. These accumulations of objects defined the wealth of nouveau riche families, for wealth was synonymous with culture. A work of art, therefore, was an expression of a family's claim to high society, to which Herbert was aspiring and part of which Harriet had always been.

In 1879, Chase was an exuberant and talented emerging artist, having recently returned from Munich, where he had studied from 1872 until 1877. He set up shop in New York's most prestigious artists' building, the Tenth Street Studios, where he rented the building's largest studio, the former exhibition gallery. He decorated it with the fabulous antique and exotic objects that he had collected in Europe so that the studio became symbolic of his sophistication. His furnishings would have appealed to Harriet, since she had recently decorated her own house with antiques and bric-a-brac acquired abroad. Chase spent more than he earned on his accessories and needed portrait commissions to finance his purchases. Harriet, too, even when things in her life were amiss, continued to spend extravagantly on furnishings and clothing.

Because of approbation in the press before he returned, Chase was already acknowledged as a leading American artist. He had sent paintings to the 1876 Centennial Exposition in Philadelphia and the National Academy of Design Annual Exhibitions in New York, where it is possible that Harriet had seen them.[87] In keeping with Harriet's sophistication and appreciation of the arts, she and Herbert chose a daring, yet probably still affordable, portraitist. She could have selected other, more celebrated artists like John Singer Sargent or some of the European portraitists plying the American market at that time, but Chase was distinguished enough for her and Herbert. The first portrait, painted in 1879, was of Harriet in a black lace Worth gown, one of several she had purchased in Paris. The painting portrayed her as a beautiful young socialite with style and charm, confident yet modest, heir to her family's status and Herbert's family's wealth. (See Figure 3.) Chase charged about $2,000 for full-length portraits.

Chase painted an additional portrait the following year. Perhaps it was because Harriet wanted a smaller, less formal painting of herself, or perhaps it was because she liked the experience of sitting for Chase. It was probably Chase who instigated this second painting in the hope that it would attract clients from Chicago. In the second picture, Harriet wore a directoire gown and bonnet, likely from Chase's collection of antique clothing. The depiction was less formal—a woman who looked like one of Chase's student-models. I have proposed elsewhere that Harriet may even have posed as the anonymous model in Chase's 1881 portrait of his studio, as he enjoyed using well-known socialites to promote himself and his artistic accomplishments.[88] A woodcut by Frederick Juengling was made of the second painting of Harriet and published in an article about Chase by the art critic Mariana Van Rensselaer in January 1881. (See Figure 4.) Van Rennselaer raved, "His blues and yellows and pinks are paler, softer tints…an almost evanescent purity of effect, are the results. Success had justified its audacity."[89] Chase exhibited the painting under the title *Portrait of a Lady* at the Society of American Artists in 1880 where it was favorably reviewed and subsequently at the Interstate Industrial Exposition in Chicago in 1881.[90] (See Figure 5.)

Herbert was not at all pleased when he previewed the second painting, nor was he happy with its publicity. In a fit of anger, jealousy and suspicion (because the painting took so long), he informed Chase that the only things right about the painting were her feet. Annoyed at this response, Chase cut off the lower portion of the painting and sent it to Herbert with his "compliments."[91] (See Figure 6.) Perhaps what Herbert disliked was that Harriet allowed herself to be painted in a costume that flaunted both her beauty and her lack of proper comportment. It is this playful image, however, that provides a clue to the woman she would become, one who broke with society's conventions and became a successful entrepreneur.

Only one year later, Harriet and Herbert ordered a third portrait, this one by Eastman Johnson (1824–1906), another highly respected and recognized American painter. Perhaps Johnson was selected to teach Chase a lesson and to assuage Herbert's dissatisfaction with Chase's second portrait. Since Harriet frequently traveled to New York to shop, posing in Chase's New York studio would have been both convenient and pleasurable. For Johnson's portrait, however, she had to travel all the way to Nantucket in 1881, where Johnson had a summer home. Johnson had studied in Germany and Holland, and by the mid-1870s, he was exploring the subtle aspects of Nantucket home interiors; later, he focused on genre paintings of cranberry pickers in Nantucket, but from 1880 on, he concentrated on portraits. Different from Chase, he depended on a full oil sketch before attacking the finished canvas.[92] Johnson's paintings were more traditional than Chase's in the sense that he included a fully detailed interior that might have been his parlor in Nantucket. Harriet was portrayed as a proper Victorian woman. (See Figure 7.) These paintings were meaningful to Harriet, and while she was forced to sell her possessions several times, she held on to the paintings and left them to her daughters.

That the paintings were commissioned during the Ayers' disintegrating relations is astonishing. Yet Harriet continued to attend functions in Chicago and to entertain. Her sophistication drew admiration from her peers, although some thought she put on airs, some thought she rejected social rules and some were just plain jealous. As the young couple grew apart, Herbert found his entertainment elsewhere on overnight trips. In 1880, the Ayers built a larger house at 362 North Dearborn Street, near Maple Street.[93] Herbert was now forty-five and Harriet was thirty-one when they moved into their third house together, a four-story limestone building in the English Renaissance style designed primarily for entertaining. While both houses were on the Gold Coast, the second house was more elaborate and had a dining room with walnut paneling taken from an English house that seated forty people. It also had an Empire drawing room, a library, a kitchen, quarters for fifteen servants and a huge stable.[94] Although fifteen servants could be accommodated, the 1880 census revealed that there were only four servants and a coachman. Given Herbert's personality and Harriet's interest in interior design, this house was more a symbol of Herbert's ascending role as the new owner of the Ayer ironworks than of his father's aspirations for him.

Harriet had brought back from Europe Oriental rugs, Dutch and French antiques and Venetian glass that had decorated both of her houses. She continued to shop at Sypher's in New York, taking short trips and perhaps staying with her mother. While many households were eschewing ornate Victorian furniture and dense draperies for the lighter aesthetic movement pieces, Harriet loved that heavy ornamental style and bought richly carved pieces that she highlighted with her collection of Venetian glass, mirrors and bric-a-brac. Her taste paralleled that of many tycoons of industry who were also amassing antique furniture in Europe to decorate their newly built mansions in Chicago and New York.

The well-known aesthete Oscar Wilde declared the Ayers' home to be the most beautifully decorated in the West.[95] While Chicago newspapers listing the families with whom Wilde had dined made no mention of the Ayers' abode, later newspapers recalled, "During Oscar Wilde's visit to Chicago he was a caller at her home, and went into ecstacies [*sic*] over the aesthetic furnishings of her parlors. He said he had seen no more beautiful decorations in America." Wilde's aesthetic dedication to art and beauty was underscored in the lecture he gave at Chicago's Central Music Hall on February 13, 1882, and another in March of that year.

In this setting, Harriet gave large, elegant dinner parties, as well as Sunday breakfasts, at which she served classic French food accompanied by French wines and black coffee. To these events she invited such celebrities as the actors Edwin Booth, Lawrence Barrett and John McCullough. While other socialites would not consider inviting actors to their dinner tables, Harriet identified with these professionals, and her dinner parties became a cause célèbre in Chicago's social world. One newspaper later noted:

> *Mrs. Ayer was a woman of imposing figure and striking personality—a type of pure blonde, with a complexion that became famous as probably the most perfect in the country. Her entertainments were celebrated for their sumptuousness and perfect taste.*[96]

The Ayer dinners became known for their fascinating and amusing conversations. Invitations were sought after, and people began to save their favorite anecdotes to tell there. While Herbert was much admired as an important businessman, he did not cherish the role of social leader and usually drank too much wine before excusing himself from the table.[97]

Herbert was persuaded to attend Harriet's amateur theater performances.[98] According to the writer Caroline Kirkland:

> *Mrs. Herbert Ayer was atypical of the strait-laced, conventional community in which she lived. She became a devotee of amateur theatricals and in a north-side club, the Anonymous Club, which flourished in the seventies, and was a prime mover in many dramatic entertainments in which the club delighted. Some of these were given in private houses and some in the parlors of Unity Church.*[99]

On February 1, 1880, the Anonymous Club of the North Side advertised a theatrical entertainment, *School for Scandal*, to be held at Brand's Hall.[100] This was a satire by Richard Brinsley Sheridan, written in 1777, perhaps with Harriet playing Lady Teazle. Victorian parlors were transformed into an artistic, theatrical environment. People often forgot their lines, and in one performance Harriet was supposed to faint or play dead but fell so close to the edge of the stage that she had to draw in her feet to avoid the descending curtain and certain catastrophe. Herbert thought it hysterically funny. On the other hand, Harriet's popularity with her acting friends and other admirers made him jealous, resentful and moody. Kirkland continued:

> She loved all things gay and pretty, clothing, furnishings, food and wine, most especially everything French including books and plays. She read and spoke French fluently as well as some German and Italian. Her French was good enough for her to translate some French plays into English.[101]

While pursuing an amateur acting career, Harriet kept up with her French by translating and adapting the French play *The Widow* (1877), a comedy in three acts by Henry Meilhac (1831–1897) and Ludovic Halevy (1834–1908), who often supplied librettos for the composer of operettas Jacques Offenbach.[102] As Harriet matured, she surpassed Herbert and outclassed him in family background, education and, most certainly, social behavior.

After vacationing on Block Island, New York, with the children, Harriet returned to Chicago at the end of the summer of 1882. Hattie, whom Harriet left in the care of her sister Jule, was enrolled at St. Mary's School at 8 East Forty-sixth Street. Although Harriet was an Episcopalian, she had gone to a Roman Catholic school and was now sending her own daughter to one. That summer, Harriet had bought some land in Riverside, a suburb of Jacksonville, Florida, for $4,000. She began building a southern-style mansion and took out a mortgage for $3,000, but alas, the house was never completed. Her extravagance and Gilded Age excess were revealed in the design, which included porches all around, a cupola on top, a large dining hall, a private theater and at least ten rooms upstairs (one article claimed twenty-five bedrooms).[103] The lot, shaded by beautiful trees, had two hundred feet of river frontage, with a wharf to accommodate yachts and steamers. This winter retreat probably served as a place for her to hide her money if and when she left Herbert. With the failure of Herbert's business, she never finished nor used the mansion, but she had already spent $38,000 of the $50,000 it would take to complete it. In 1891, the house was on the market for $15,000.[104] Ultimately, it was sold under duress for a pittance, to pay for expenses incurred when she was committed to an insane asylum in 1893.

Grown Up in Chicago

The story of Harriet Hubbard Ayer's independence began at the end of 1882, when this Chicago socialite left her husband after sixteen years of tolerating his drinking and infidelities. With her two daughters, Hattie and Margaret, she joined her mother, Madame Juliet Hubbard, in New York, where she established her family in a town house. Her mother's presence did not necessarily mean financial or psychological support. In fact, Juliet was embarrassed by her daughter's bold actions. Contrary to her mother's withdrawal from her children in response to adversity, Harriet threw her energy into the education and upbringing of her children.[105]

5

A Wrecked Society Queen

By Christmas, Harriet, believing that financial support would be forthcoming, had decided that she would never return to Herbert, a very bold move for a woman at that time. She was a thirty-four-year-old mother of two when, in December 1882, she moved to New York City, removing herself from an untenable marriage to an alcoholic adulterer. Herbert had become increasingly abusive in his treatment of her during their sixteen years of marriage.

According to one newspaper article:

> *Twenty years ago she was confessedly the leader of Chicago society. She had education, taste, talent, wealth. Her eminence was naturally and legitimately won. If such a thing as social leadership belongs to anyone by birth or succession, she would have been placed among those entitled to that rank. A devoted mother, a reproachless wife, a faithful friend, there seemed to be everything in her life to round it completely. To Chicagoans it would be a needless opening of old wounds to recall the ruin that a man's fault brought on a home.*

The article went on to praise Harriet's literary abilities, her charm and her friendships, while implying that Herbert was at fault for both the loss of his iron business and his family; it marked Harriet as "a wrecked society queen."[106]

The limited choices for most women in the United States to obtain respectability were to be someone's wife, daughter, sister, mother or servant. Cultural traditions dictated that marriage and motherhood were women's destiny. Women had few legal civil rights, a subject that dominated conversations during the second half of the nineteenth century. It was not until August 26, 1920, that the Nineteenth Amendment to the Constitution giving women the right to vote was actually passed. Even the medical establishment warned against changing women's domestic status. Overexertion, they claimed, could drain an individual's nervous system, which would lead to a breakdown.[107] Of course, they specifically meant women. In case of a divorce, custody of children automatically went to the husband. Therefore, it was both daring and risky for Harriet even to contemplate divorcing her husband. Harriet's move to New York removed her from the embarrassment of newspaper headlines, as well as the daily censure of neighbors and relatives in Chicago.

Rebelliously, Harriet secured a town house to accommodate her children and servants. The house, at 120 West Thirteenth Street, bordering Chelsea and Greenwich Village, was not too far from Sypher's Antique Furniture shop, where she would eventually obtain work.[108] She was listed at that address in the New York City directory from 1883–4 through 1889–90. "Mrs. Ayer was worth $150,000" when Herbert left her, because "he cleared up the titles on all of her property and left it free from debt."[109] According to Herbert, part of the money he gave her came from the sale of the bric-a-brac in the mansion.[110] Harriet was not totally destitute, just not nearly as rich as she had been.

Built in brick trimmed with reddish brown sandstone, her house extended the full width and length of the small lot and was bracketed on either side by similar units. Usually, the parlor and dining room were on the main floor; the kitchen and service area were located on the lower level in line with the small backyard; the family's bedrooms were on the second floor; and the servants' quarters or guest rooms were on the third or top floor. Harriet's little town house seemed meager when contrasted with the large limestone mansion she had vacated in Chicago. Yet this quiet, tree-lined street in the West Village featured the best Greek Revival building in the city: the Thirteenth Street Presbyterian Church at 143 West Thirteenth Street.[111] Between 1860 and 1910, retail stores such as Tiffany and Company, Lord and Taylor and others opened, making Broadway and Sixth Avenue, from Ninth Street to Twenty-third Street, into a shopping mecca. Known as "Ladies' Mile," this fashionable shopping district gave

New York its reputation for sophistication. The earliest stores above Fourteenth Street were on Broadway, as was Sypher & Company at 860 Broadway, the firm Harriet heavily patronized when furnishing her homes. Harriet had moved into a neighborhood that sparkled with entertainment, culture and commerce.

Because she was accustomed to having servants, Harriet immediately hired Lena Raymond, to cook and clean, as well as a German governess for five-year-old Margaret. Of mixed black and white parentage, Lena was self-educated and very bright. Her voice was cultured, her penmanship excellent and her standards of cleanliness outstanding.[112] Domestic work was one of the few options open to her; she could cook, sew, wash, iron and keep house very well. Her education probably derived from an African church that offered classes as well as services. When Lena requested a salary comparable to that of the Hubbards' Irish maid Nora, Harriet was taken aback but granted her request. Racial prejudice was widespread in the nineteenth century and was reinforced by southern-born Herbert, who refused even to hire or pay blacks. Lena proved to be not only a valuable servant but also a loyal companion.

Once settled, Harriet wrote to the man she had met in Philadelphia in 1876. Although she had not seen him in six years, she remembered their mutual attraction and boldly invited General Grubb to visit her when next he came to New York. Her first Christmas in New York began sadly, for Harriet was all alone. She was putting the finishing touches on the tree late in the evening when she heard a knock on the door. Lena, who ordinarily would have answered, had gone to bed, as had the children. With some trepidation, Harriet opened the door, and much to her surprise and delight, there stood General Grubb, covered with snow with presents in his arms.[113] It seems odd that he would come calling late in the evening. One can only conjecture that this unconventional visit, after so many years apart, was most likely due to his impatience to see her again. Without telephones, he had no way of letting her know he was in town. Both he and Madame Hubbard visited the next day and played with five-year-old Margaret and fifteen-year-old Hattie, bringing about a happy Christmas for all. Margaret, who could not pronounce the word general, called him "Ginger," a nickname that endured. When Grubb had a moment alone with Harriet, the first time since 1876, he told her that he was seeking a divorce from his wife and that he wished to court her. Harriet was ecstatic about being sought after by this man she had admired from afar for so long. It would require great patience to wait for him to obtain his divorce and for her to acquire her own, but he promised to write to her and to send violets from his greenhouses every day.[114]

After the holidays, Hattie returned to St. Mary's School in New York. The German governess, who was off for the holidays, returned to care for Margaret, and Lena took care of the house and cooking. Harriet explored the bustling and growing city, visiting museums and art galleries. The Brooklyn Bridge, connecting Manhattan and the then separate city of Brooklyn, long in construction, finally opened in May 1883. With the advent of passenger elevators, the first skyscrapers were appearing in lower Manhattan in the 1880s. New York was becoming a vertical city. By 1882, there were electric lights on Broadway from Fourteenth to Twenty-third Streets. The influx of immigrants gave the city ethnic diversity and excitement that had not previously existed. The Metropolitan Museum, founded in 1870, opened its doors in 1872, and the New-York Historical Society, founded in 1804 and at the time housed on East Eleventh Street and Second Avenue, remained the city's attic. When furniture went out of style or family portraits were no longer cherished, they were given to the historical society, thereby creating a historical collection for the delectation of future generations. Portraits of Harriet met a similar end several generations later. There was much for Harriet to do and see.

Harriet's Chicago friend, Mrs. Lyon, the wife of stockbroker John B. Lyon, wrote and told her that Herbert's business had gone bankrupt and that he desperately needed money. With the news of the demise of John V. Ayer Company, Harriet's world suddenly collapsed. She placed little Margaret with the nuns at St. Mary's School, let the German governess go and left for Chicago to see for herself. Lena offered to stay on without wages. For the first time, Harriet became fully aware of her husband's dire financial straits and wrote to him, once again requesting a divorce in stronger terms. Herbert's answer was to inform her that he had sold their house and most of its furnishings for $50,000. She boarded a train to Chicago as soon as she could, taking with her the jewels the Ayers had given her for him to sell. When confronted, Herbert brusquely explained that he owed about $100,000 to the banks and needed immediate cash.[115] Actually, he was in debt for much more.

FAILURE OF JOHN V. AYER SONS

When John Ayer died on May 30, 1877, his obituary noted that he was a "respected citizen and a successful merchant" and that he was looked upon "as a man of worth and strength, and one whose departure from the world is to be generally lamented. He was noted for his integrity and his attention in his dealings, and his devotion to his business interests resulted in his amassing a fortune."[116] Herbert took over the iron business, which was then located at 78 Michigan Avenue. He managed to alienate the other company directors, including his stepbrothers, with his rude and cocky behavior. Only Henry I. Higgins, whom his father appointed in 1875, when Herbert's stepbrother Philip died, remained—at least until a year before the company's labor force went on strike in 1882.

Left to his own devices after his father's death, Herbert bought out the partners of Brown and Bonell in 1879 and became sole owner. There were some legal entanglements about the sale that were aired in the *Chicago Daily Tribune* in January and June 1879.[117] Herbert made a number of major improvements at the Youngstown mills at a time when the market for iron products was waning. The mills employed about four thousand men, who were unhappy with their wages and struck for higher salaries. Between 1881 and 1905, there were more than thirty-seven thousand strikes in the United States, many of them bitter, violent struggles pitting labor against management.[118] Herbert, apparently aware of the unrest among his laborers, was unsympathetic to their demands so did nothing to appease them. A strike occurred in the summer of 1882, forcing the mills to close for four months. Although he spent much time at his Youngstown mills and nearby coal fields, it was only when he was in Chicago that he asked the militia for protection because he feared violence. Herbert refused to give the men a raise as some other mills had done, yet the workers eventually went back to the mill. It was, however, a Pyrrhic victory because the financial loss after being closed for four months was substantial. Herbert attributed his losses to causes other than his stubborn refusal to negotiate. He blamed it on depression in the industry and the inability of Congress to act on a tariff bill and reductions he had hoped for in tariff duties. Although there was a short recovery period from 1878 until 1882 following the severe depression of 1873, Herbert had not foreseen a depression in the iron industry (as his father might have), and was not properly prepared for the recession that lasted from 1882 until 1886.

A Wrecked Society Queen

By February 1883, the *Chicago Times*, in a lengthy article, described the history of the company and its current problems. The article stated that the company was formed in 1859 as Hale, Ayer & Co., dealers in merchant iron, and that it was as "well-known throughout the country as any firm or corporation in that line of business, and at the same time one of the oldest in the west."[119] It is true that a series of outside events, such as the reduced market for iron products, the downfall of the steel tariff and the suspension of the Union Iron and Steel Company with over $3 million in liabilities, exacerbated the situation. But the immediate precipitating cause for Herbert was "the refusal of the Union National Bank to cash a piece of paper for $15,000 maturing" on February 17, 1883. This seems like a small sum for a multimillion-dollar company, but other such loans amounting to $100,000 and more were coming due in rapid succession, and that bank was the primary lender. Given the losses Ayer incurred during the four-month strike, the company could not redeem the loans. Clearly, Herbert had overextended his financial capacities and had not calculated for the extreme losses incurred during the strike.

The news spread everywhere: New York, Chicago, Cleveland, Youngstown, Boston and beyond—a large blow to Herbert's already fragile ego. He was forced to sell everything to pay his debts, including the beautiful house he had recently built, with all the expensive furnishings Harriet had so lovingly bought and arranged. He only received $50,000 for the house, nowhere near its value and certainly not enough to pay his debts. He left Chicago to escape the shame and the creditors, deserting Harriet and the children. Although he had promised to give Harriet $500 a month to take care of her and the girls, he was unable to do so. He left for Europe and was joined there by a well-known "Chicago adventuress."[120] Some say he had planned his escape with this woman long before. Although Harriet had already made up her mind to leave Herbert, his desertion left her, for the first time in her life, without regular financial or familial support.

Herbert had gambled and lost the company his father founded. It was not only because he overexpanded the Ayer iron business but also because he mismanaged it. He had eliminated his stepbrothers George and John from the company, as well as the advisors his father had put in place. Herbert was a mess; he stopped shaving, and his clothes were soiled. Most of his old cronies deserted him, although it is said that a few lent him some money.

Harriet's mother, who had spent most of the fortune she had inherited from her deceased husband Henry, could help her daughter only a little.

Nevertheless, Harriet had already decided that although she had very little left in the bank, she would not take money from anyone, including General Grubb. Nor did she want to live in genteel poverty or move to Europe, where many people in difficult financial straits expatriated because it was less expensive to live there. She convinced Herbert to give her a divorce, and he agreed on the condition that she pay for the lawyers.[121]

On her return to New York, Harriet fully appreciated her predicament. Her acquaintances Reverend Dr. Clinton Locke, the rector of Chicago's Grace Episcopal Church; his wife, Adele; and their daughter, Fanny, drove her to the train station. Fanny, who was just a little older than Hattie, spoke of her forthcoming studies in Stuttgart, Germany, with the popular American novelist Blanche Willis Howard.[122] Fanny asked if Hattie could join her, a request that previously would have received a positive answer but was now no longer affordable.[123] This was the critical moment when Harriet realized the consequences of her reduced finances. In her determination to give her daughters all the advantages they would have had before Herbert's bankruptcy, she became a woman who would forge a life and a living on her own. Although not destitute, since she could still afford household help, a house and private schools, given her past income and extravagance, she felt poor. From this time forward, she particularly focused on being able to send Hattie to study abroad with Blanche Howard and to provide herself and her daughters with a standard of living similar to the one they had enjoyed previously. She wrote a diplomatic letter to Herbert asking for her freedom, trying not bruise his ego further.

6

From Queen to Clerk

Touted "both as a petted daughter of luxury and fashion, and since her adversity as the brave, self-reliant breadwinner for her children," Harriet not only set herself up in her own house in New York but also found a job.[124] For a Chicago socialite to enter the workforce was uncommon, and her mother's friends surely gossiped about her. In fact, her mother, who was also living in Manhattan, was at first ashamed to tell her friends that Harriet had moved there. The children had adapted fairly easily to life in Manhattan, especially young Margaret. Hattie, who was in school, had a more difficult time adjusting to the loss of the father who adored her. Nevertheless, she excelled in her music classes at St. Mary's, and the nuns encouraged her to continue studying music.

In October 1883, the *Chicago Daily Tribune* announced in an article about New York, "A former Chicago Lady of Fashion Clerking in Sypher & Co.'s Store."[125] It was just as Sypher's furniture and bric-a-brac store had expanded that Harriet began to work for the company. She said that she did not actually seek employment but merely consulted Obadiah Sypher for advice about several other job offers. Knowing what a connoisseur of antique furniture she was, he offered her a position in his firm with many perks. She was to travel to Europe in search of antiques and eventually work from home. Sypher remarked, "She was once one of our largest customers, having purchased at different times no less than $40,000 worth of curios and antiques." In another version of the story told by Harriet (for she seemed to change various aspects of her life history for different reporters), she said:

Fancy me then. I was utterly without money, though used to spending it like water. I had my two children to support and nothing to commence on. I walked the floor of my room thinking what I could do. Finally I asked Sypher & Co., of whom I had bought thousands of dollars worth of goods, if they would not give me a position. They did, and also offered me a commission on all my sales. I remained with them until I found that I could do better alone. I then established a purchasing agency, and my profits ran into the thousands.[126]

Obadiah Sypher understood that Harriet's social background and good taste would be advantageous to his business and that some of her friends might become clients. However, she had never worked before and only knew how to spend money frivolously. Still, she proved to be hardworking and able to persuade customers to buy the merchandise at Sypher's. In fact, she was so adept at her work and sold so many expensive pieces that within one hour she had sold more than $1,000 worth of goods. She earned a year's salary during her first week and gained her co-workers' respect.[127] Her personal warmth, charm and charisma, of course, played a role. In addition, she was able to apply the Europeanized taste she had acquired during her many trips abroad to help newly wealthy patrons achieve the rudiments of the décor that fit the social status they desired.

Sypher's was a pioneering company in bric-a-brac, tracing its origins to 1840. Obadiah Lum Sypher, who was later joined by his younger brother, Asa Mahan Sypher, owned the business. The store sold antique and reproduction furniture, silver and porcelain, some of which was imported from Europe and the Orient. It also specialized in fine tapestries and textiles. After the 1876 Centennial Exposition, it produced faithful colonial reproductions, fulfilling the demand for American furniture. In the basement gallery of the newly built 860 Broadway store (1884), Sypher's displayed interior settings to show how such colonial reproductions and other antiques could be incorporated into a room.[128]

In 1883, Harriet rented her house on West Thirteenth Street to British actress Lillie Langtry, who thought it the most elegant house in America. In the meantime, Harriet stayed at the Colonnade, in one of the town houses fronted by a two-story row of Corinthian columns, located on Lafayette Street, one of Manhattan's most elegant areas.[129] Therefore, she was acquainted with the actress before using her as an endorser for her future cosmetic business. It is possible that she made some money by renting her house before she was fully established at Sypher's.

Almost immediately after Harriet had secured a position as a saleswoman, she wrote to Herbert's friend, a Mr. Cobb, and informed him that she planned to take a job in a furniture store. As if seeking Herbert's permission to work, she asked Mr. Cobb to convince Herbert of her urgent needs. She felt that while she was young and healthy, there was nothing to stop her from working until Herbert was able to support her and the girls again. She went so far as to say that she would drown herself if she did not have something to occupy herself during this sorrowful period of her life.[130] Her reaction, while dramatic, may have held some truth, but it more likely revealed her determination to make the best of a difficult situation.

Herbert may have been embarrassed to have his wife work as a sales clerk, but there was not much he could do about it. He had to accept and appreciate the fact that she was willing to take care of herself. On the other hand, he may not have cared in the least since he was off to Europe to live with another woman. He resided in Paris with his lady friend for about three years in order to avoid his creditors. Harriet wrote to him again in response to his letter of July 29, 1883, giving reasons for the divorce and her handling of the children.[131] Their divorce, while agreed upon, was not finalized until almost four years later because Harriet had to earn enough money to pay lawyer and court fees. A sympathetic journalist wrote, "Mrs. Harriet Hubbard Ayer is a remarkable instance of what pluck and talent can do for a woman who found herself, while still young, hampered with poverty and beauty."[132]

Friends tried to persuade Harriet "to take a position as a governess or companion, or some other such position as is usually sought by women who have to support themselves."[133] No one realized the seriousness of her commitment when she accepted the job at Sypher's, except Mr. Sypher, who advertised that Mrs. Ayer had been added to the staff and would welcome customers. People she knew came to check on her, and some of them even purchased a few items. Acquaintances and curiosity seekers come to pry, and other nasty gossips came to gloat at her reduced circumstances and addressed her as if she were a servant, which hurt her feelings.[134]

Although it was unusual for a woman of Harriet's social standing to work, there were other women who worked because they wanted to. Often, they could do so because they came from wealth or married into it. Candace Wheeler (1827–1923) and Rosina Emmett Sherwood (1854–1948) were women who lived at approximately the same time as Harriet. Wheeler founded the Society of Decorative Art in 1877 for the training of economically deprived gentlewomen. She offered instruction to women in the design field and gave them marketing advice to make them financially independent. Two years later, in 1879, she established Associated American Artists, her own textile manufacturing business, in partnership with such distinguished artists as Louis Comfort Tiffany. Like Harriet, she had married at the age of seventeen, but she did not begin her career until she was fifty. By the 1890s, she was the leading woman decorator in the United States. Harriet was thirty-four years old when she started to work as a decorator and clerk at Sypher's, which, coincidently, sold Associated American Artists textiles. It is, therefore, likely that Harriet actually knew Candace Wheeler.[135] The same is true for the painter Rosina Emmett Sherwood, who studied with William Merritt Chase in the mid-1880s and may have met Harriet in his studio. So, while there were numerous women challenging feminine stereotypes during the last quarter of the nineteenth century, they usually were women of strong character.

The *New York Times* later said that when Harriet came to the city she was

> *practically penniless…Her training and tastes led her into a pursuit which not alone provided her with support, but enabled her to spend a great deal of time in Europe and to live in the best style. She became a buyer of works of art, antiques and fine furnishings for wealthy people who desired to enrich their homes…She was apparently born with a genius for business, and for several years it was estimated that she was making from $10,000 to $15,000 per annum* [during the time she worked for Sypher's].[136]

Sypher frequently sent Harriet abroad to find antiques, and he ultimately allowed her to work at home on commission, advertising her home as "Artistic Furnishings and Shopping." Some wealthy women did not care to shop publicly, so Sypher's accommodated them at Harriet's town house. She went to Chicago in 1884 to expand the firm's customer base by renting sales rooms in the Palmer House, at 163 Wabash Avenue.[137] Sypher listed the company in the directory three times—under Harriet's name, under furniture and alphabetically. This flexible arrangement permitted her live comfortably in New York, support herself and her daughters adequately and even afford servants. She traveled to London for business late in the summer of 1884, returning on the ship *Oregon* from Liverpool on September 29, 1884.

While Harriet made a decent living with commissions, she still she had to maintain a tight budget at home. Lena introduced Harriet to such money-saving practices as buying cheaper cuts of meat and removing ruffles from her petticoats to save on laundering. Managing household budgets and accounts provided invaluable business training for nineteenth-century women. While Harriet was willing to sacrifice luxuries, Hattie, the apple of her father's eye, who was brought up in great comfort, was resistant. News of her father's difficulties and the pending divorce naturally upset her. For Harriet, sacrifice meant that she could achieve her goal of sending her talented daughter abroad to study music. She never forgot about Blanche Howard's finishing school.[138]

Although patronized and pitied by women of her class, Harriet remained vivacious and charming to her clients, which meant increased sales and commissions. She began to understand and sympathize with people who had to work or who were poor. She also began to recognize her own strengths and, by contrast, the weaknesses of her husband. She worked long hours, neglecting Margaret, who was still at home, yet she knew Margaret was well cared for by Lena, whom the young girl adored. Madame Hubbard advised her not to work so hard, but Harriet admitted that she really loved her work.[139]

One day, probably late in the summer of 1884, Harriet answered her door to find a tall, handsome, well-dressed man in his late forties standing before her. He introduced himself as James Seymour and told her that a well-known railroad magnate had recommended her to him.[140] Many events shaped the life of Harriet Ayer: her marriage at the age of seventeen in 1866, the death of her baby daughter Gertrude after the great Chicago Fire in 1871, her subsequent visit to France in 1872 and her separation from her husband at the end of 1882. Still, the encounter with this man irrevocably changed her life and ultimately caused her more heartache and suffering than she could have possibly imagined.

7

The Villain: James M. Seymour

The man who appeared at Harriet's door in 1884 was at once courteous, solicitous and charming, yet he was ruthless. His passport of 1877 described him as five feet, ten inches tall, with dark brown hair, a prominent nose and a large mouth set in a long, oval-shaped head.[141] A later description characterized him as "a small, slim, aristocratic-looking man."[142] Harriet may even have heard of him when he was a commodities broker in Chicago from 1875 to 1879, a period when she was considered one of the most beautiful and cultured women in Chicago. The reason for Seymour's visit was that he had just purchased the steam yacht *Radha* on August 6, 1884, from Pierre Lorillard IV (1833–1901).[143] Lorillard was a tobacco manufacturer and thoroughbred racehorse owner who helped to establish Rhode Island as a yachting center. For Seymour, a former grocer, to upgrade to a yacht owned by this fabulously wealthy, old-family yachtsman was an achievement. Who was this man who would affect Harriet's life so negatively?

James M. Seymour was born on September 13, 1847, in Galveston, Texas, where he was in the grocery business. Before coming to Chicago, he was involved with the Vulture Mine in Arizona in 1874. The following year, in 1875, when he was in his late thirties, he moved to Chicago, bringing with him his wife and two sons, Allen Lewis and James M. Jr. (both born in Galveston, Texas, on October 5, 1867, and 1877, respectively).[144] In Chicago, Seymour became a member of the board of trade that promoted and monitored commerce, in particular agricultural products. The board monitored brokers like Seymour, who gambled in futures.

The Villain: James M. Seymour

Seymour, a partner in Seymour and Hunt & Company, had some disputes with the board. In 1879, he moved to New York without Joseph A. Hunt, who had supposedly retired, possibly because he and Seymour filed a bill in the circuit court against the board of trade and its officers to restrain them from expelling the company.[145] Apparently, the company had come under investigation for selling wheat illegally, and that may have been one of the reasons for Seymour's relocation. Yet Seymour persisted in business with Hunt until about 1884 from his offices on Lexington Avenue and Forty-seventh Street in New York, where he sold "all kinds of country produce on commission." In 1881, an agent for R.G. Dun & Company, the nineteenth-century credit-reporting agency (forerunner of Dun & Bradstreet), wrote that Seymour's "credit is favorably spoken of...out of town...responsibility uncertain." R.G. Dun & Company sent agents into the field twice a year to evaluate the credit rating of various businesses, especially those that borrowed or lent money. By 1885, Seymour's commission business no longer existed. (Harriet's business was never rated.)[146]

Subsequently, Seymour started a new firm in New York, Seymour, Baker & Company, a stock and grain business with offices at 30 Broad Street. Baker replaced Joseph Hunt, and the company was listed at various addresses in the financial district until 1892–93. By 1885, Dun & Co. reported Seymour's worth at $1.5 million but added that "it is very difficult to obtain a definite confirmation of a broker's statement."[147] Seymour started his commercial activity with a gold mine called Central Arizona, and he advertised for small investors in New York and Chicago to purchase shares. He manipulated the stock so that he earned over $1 million while everyone else lost money. This fiasco forced him to hire bodyguards when he traveled between the home he built in Orange, New Jersey, and his office in the financial district. He repeated this process with another mine called South Pacific and earned over $1.5 million while his investors were ruined. His largest coup was with a bank that lost $2 million while he cleared that same amount.

Phoenix was Seymour's fourth mine adventure, although he denied that he owned the mine,[148] yet according to the *Boston Globe*:

> *everybody has heard of the Phoenix mine...it appears it was originally owned by James M. Seymour, one of the most reckless gamblers on the street. Seymour came here from Chicago with a high reputation as an operator in grain. He also made a specialty of mines. Some of them turned*

out well. Some of them ill…Seymour at one time held a majority of the Phoenix stock, and under his manipulation it rose point by point, till starting at 6 it touched 14. That was good enough for the first trip, and somewhere in the neighborhood of 12, Seymour unloaded his stock and quietly stole away. Down fell the Phoenix barometer, not quite so quickly as it had risen, but still quite quickly enough to bring discomfort to the speculators who had purchased Brother Seymour's shares. When it reached its original point strange portents were visible in the journalistic firmament. Hostile paragraphs were published against the property. Questions of title were raised, and an old and forgotten lawsuit was raked up. Obscure persons were found to claim that they once owned the mine and thought they owned it still. The air, in short, was filled with dark hints and mysterious innuendos. There was dismay among the holders of stock, for the mine had become a popular craze and the shares were widely held by people of all classes. Rumors were started that the whole thing was a bubble. Fears of its collapse were everywhere entertained. The stock, which had fallen to 6 stayed there obstinately and spasmodic attempts were made to [save] it. All were intellectual. It leaks out today that the fall of the stock, like its rise, was engineered by Mr. Seymour.[149]

Ostensibly, Seymour's trick was to sell when the stock was high and buy it back when it had fallen to half price, a practice by which he "made a fortune…these are the tactics of Wall Street…verily we live in a wicked world." It was the greatest mining fiasco of recent times. The press denounced it, in unmeasured terms, as the cruelest swindle ever known. The governing committee of the stock exchange made an examination, withdrew the stock of the mine from its list and "made things so unpleasant for Seymour that, last November, he retired from business."[150] Some investors in the Phoenix Mining Company on Cave Creek in Maricopa County, Arizona, brought suit against Seymour, claiming some of his profit.[151]

In October, there was yet another article that reported that Mr. Seymour was willing to sell his Phoenix Mine shares for one dollar: "While he thinks that the stock may be cheap enough at a dollar a share on its merits, yet if Mr. Seymour sells out there will be no one left to manipulate any appreciative movement in the stock, and holders would have to depend entirely upon the merits of the mine." The advice put forward was for shareholders to get out at a dollar a share.[152]

The Villain: James M. Seymour

Yet another judgment against Seymour appeared in June 1887, and by November 1888, his firm had been dissolved.[153] George Treadwell began a new suit against Seymour to recover $400,000, about one-third of the value of the Phoenix Mine. Treadwell was a mining engineer who worked at the mine with the proviso that he would be paid one-third interest in the mine. The 500,000 shares of stock were sold at $1 a share and were listed on the stock exchange. When the stock rose to $14, Seymour sold his shares at an average of $6 a share, as mentioned above, but he refused to give Treadwell his share of the interest. Seymour, it seems, was in constant litigation for his breach of contracts.[154]

R.J. Dun recorded in 1883 that Seymour and his son, Allen Lewis Seymour, were worth about half a million dollars and were deemed "a safe house with which to do business," and by 1886 they had three bank accounts and did not have to borrow money.[155] Seymour had enough to invest in Harriet's new enterprise in 1886, with the hope that he could share in the profits and perhaps find a role for his son. However, the following year, in 1887, there were judgments found against them, and their firm was dissolved in 1888 with no succession and no office listed in 1889.[156] Another suit against Seymour was brought in 1889 by John C. Eno, the fraudulent president of the Second National Bank, but because a juror disappeared, the case was thrown out. It did not come to trial again until 1890, and the case lingered until it was decided that Seymour's actions were not fraudulent.[157]

Even Seymour's negotiation with Lorillard for the purchase of the *Radha* was devious. The asking price for the boat was $65,000, a great reduction over the original cost of $138,000. Seymour tried to obtain an even lower price, but Lorillard refused. Seymour came late to the designated sale meeting and offered $50,000. Lorillard refused to bargain and considered the sale off. Only then did Seymour produce a certified check for the asking price, which he had with him all along.[158] It was soon after that purchase that Seymour hired Harriet, despite the fact that she had no experience with yachts. If Harriet was aware of how Seymour made his millions and still wanted to work with him, it reveals how desperate she was to earn money—or how naïve she was. After she accepted the assignment to decorate his yacht, they became good friends, each respecting the other's drive and motivation. He needed her expertise and social standing, while she needed his money. And so, on her trips abroad for Sypher's, Harriet also worked on Seymour's yacht. Price was no object, so she planned to duplicate the interior décor of the Prince of Wales's yacht.

Harriet may have understood from the way Seymour treated her that he had in mind more than a business relationship because she was careful never to mention his name in her letters to General Grubb, who was off on a safari to Africa at the time. Harriet was so preoccupied with her work that, to some extent, she begrudged the time she did spend with Grubb when he came to New York to take her to dinner and the theater.[159] Her business ambitions began to interfere with her personal life, and she clearly preferred her independence and the challenges of work. Before she left on another shopping trip to England, Seymour, aware of her ardent desire to support herself, explained that there were opportunities for anyone to become rich, even a woman with half an idea. He explained that nobody ever got rich on commissions and advised her to find something she could make and sell, a business with volume. He implied that men dealt with things like mines and railroads, while women should provide products for wives, something that every woman wanted or needed. If she came up with a good idea, he offered to finance it.[160]

In the late summer of 1884, Harriet went abroad to order what she needed for Seymour's yacht, as well as to buy objects for Sypher's, where she still worked. She was well received by the Parisians, who thought she was dazzling, even though she could no longer afford Worth gowns. Her beautiful face framed by blonde curls, her pleasingly round figure and her vivacious personality combined to make her very attractive and perhaps a bit of a flirt and tease. While she was busy combing antique shops for her clients during the day, at night she attended lively French balls and dinners. She remained faithful to General Grubb, the man to whom she had given her heart, and he continued to send violets to her daily from a florist in Paris. Her freedom and joie de vivre, her unusual beauty and her pride in her new life turned older members of the American community in France against her for what some called her "loose ways." The French, however, found her charming and engaging.[161]

The dealers Harriet had previously patronized were surprised by her change in attitude about cost. Formerly, she never questioned their prices, even when she knew that she was being overcharged. Now she haggled adroitly for her clients. Because of her excellent command of French, she was able to buy beautiful objects and resell them for a profit. She bought, among other things, antique paneling from a French château and ancestor portraits for ambitious clients who had none. Harriet's trip ended in England, where she ordered custom-made fabric and other costly items for Seymour's yacht. He never complained about price; after all, he was perhaps comparing himself with Lorillard. While she was in Europe, Seymour curried favor with her by ingratiating himself with her daughters.

In Paris, Harriet visited with her former French teacher and friend, Mademoiselle Frochard, who had become Madame Duval, now a mother of three. She returned to Monsieur Mirault's chemist shop to buy some more of the Parma violet perfume he had created for her and chatted with him about the change in her life. He thought she could no longer afford the perfume he made for her, but she said she needed it more than ever to keep up her morale. Harriet then remembered the skin salve his grandfather had made for Madame Récamier and asked him to make several jars for her to sell to her rich clients. He advised her to charge a sufficient amount so her clients would appreciate its exclusivity.[162] This was a time when most upper-class woman used little makeup, perfume or face cream, but Harriet remembered Seymour's advice about finding something special that women in America would want, something that could make her a fortune. That idea, which Seymour had implanted in her mind, resurfaced. Harriet boarded the ship *Oregon* in Liverpool and hurried back to New York on September 29, 1884.

After yet another trip abroad in June 1885, Harriet again rushed back, this time for her daughter Hattie's graduation from St. Mary's. Hattie had won many prizes and played the piano at the ceremony. Little Margaret was thrilled by her eighteen-year-old sister's honors. Much to Harriet's surprise, James Seymour appeared at the graduation, claiming that the nuns had invited him. He acknowledged that he came not only for the girls but also to see their mother; clearly, he wanted Harriet as his mistress. The two adults talked about business, and Seymour announced that the *Radha* would soon be ready. He told Harriet that he did not make promises lightly; he was fair with friends but never forgot a slight.[163]

The inauguration of the *Radha* was the end of Harriet's involvement with the yacht but not with Seymour himself. As early as September 1885, however, Seymour sued Pierre Lorillard for the $65,000 he had paid for the boat and an additional $50,000 to repair the leaking hull. The fee probably included the amount he spent decorating the yacht. The self-possessed Lorillard appeared in court on December 17, 1886, and claimed that the boat was in perfect seaworthy shape when he sold it to Seymour. He told how Seymour tried to reduce the asking price, even though that amount was half of what the boat was worth. Between December 3 and 22, 1886, the story made the headlines, and by December 23, Seymour had won $40,000. Lorillard paid the judgment rather than appeal.[164]

Twenty-year-old Lewis Seymour paled in the shadow of his father, causing Harriet to feel sorry for him. He was immediately attracted to Hattie when he met her on one of the *Radha*'s maiden voyages. Harriet's reaction to him was similar to her mother's when Herbert Ayer had courted her. Hattie spoke German and French and was well educated in music and literature, while Lewis had been taken out of school at the age of ten and put to work as an office boy on Wall Street. His father believed he could learn more on the job than at school.[165] Hattie was only eighteen years old, and Harriet did not want her daughter to make the same mistake she had made by marrying someone intellectually beneath her. She immediately arranged to send Hattie to Stuttgart. Nevertheless, she urged Hattie to be nice to Lewis so that her business relationship with his father would not be jeopardized. She believed that their infatuation with each other would end when Hattie left the country. She was wrong about this, and about her future dealings with this boy's ruthless father, whom she was compelled to take to court in 1889.

The Famous Authoress Blanche Howard

B y 1885, Harriet was earning enough money on commissions both at Sypher's and from her own "purchasing agency" to be able to afford to send Hattie to Stuttgart. She wrote to Mrs. Clinton Locke, whose daughter Fanny had first mentioned Blanche Howard's finishing school to her in 1883, to ask about the cost. The answer soon came that it was $150 monthly for room, board and music conservatory fees, plus about $100 for Blanche's chaperoning fee. The steamship fares and clothing allowance were additional. Harriet then wrote to Blanche Howard, who happened to be in Bangor, Maine, visiting relatives in 1885, and received a speedy answer informing her of Hattie's acceptance.[166] Harriet quickly prepared Hattie for the journey to Europe. Blanche added that she admired Harriet's courage in supporting and raising the girls on her own, but her laudatory words rang false.

Blanche was a complex person. While not beautiful, her charm and accomplishments made her attractive; in a word, she was a woman who made the most of what she had.[167] She was born in Maine in 1847, and after graduating from high school in Bangor, she spent a year at a boarding school in New York and another year with her married sister in Chicago. Her first novel, *One Summer* (1875), sold fifty-four thousand copies, and the book was reprinted as late as 1912. She went abroad in the fall of 1875 with a commission to write weekly articles for the *Boston Evening Transcript* about Americans living in Europe. Her book *One Year Abroad* (1877) resulted from those articles. Her books introduced American audiences to life and customs in Europe. Blanche chose to live abroad because of the cultural stimulation. She settled in the beautiful town of Stuttgart to study philosophy, sociology, science and particularly music, for she was an accomplished pianist. Stuttgart contained many noteworthy art collections and a music conservatory.[168]

In order to support herself; her widowed sister, Marion Smith; her two nieces, Marion and Christine; and two nephews, Howard and Harold, Blanche started to take in American girls for the study of music, art and languages. Like Harriet, Blanche had to work for a living but apparently did not join any of the women's rights movements. "It is hardly reasonable to suppose that in view of the fact that I have worked since I was eighteen years old, I should lack sympathy with the welfare or progress of women."[169] She continued to write a new novel almost every other year through the 1880s. In 1890, she married Dr. Julius von Teuffel, the court physician to the king of Wurttemberg, but by 1892 he had become insane. Perhaps signs of his dementia were already apparent when he allowed Blanche to misuse the drug he prescribed for Harriet. Baroness Blanche Willis Howard von Teuffel, who died in Munich in 1896 at the age of fifty-one, was to become another of Harriet's adversaries, one who interfaced with James Seymour during the 1880s. Blanche, who was approximately the same age as Harriet, had no children of her own and experienced child rearing vicariously by caring for the children of others. She charged a goodly sum for chaperoning the girls and lived more comfortably in Europe than she could have in the United States. Nevertheless, money worries were always a concern.

Under the supervision of Blanche, in October 1885, Hattie Ayer left for Stuttgart aboard a steamer. She shared a room with her Chicago friend Fanny Locke, who had already been with Blanche for two years. Transatlantic travel aboard luxurious ocean liners began in the 1880s. Such ships had grand ballrooms, libraries and facilities for the privileged, who dressed in formal attire for dinner. It must have been very exciting for eighteen-year-old Hattie to go on this voyage with girls her own age yet a little frightening to leave the security of her home. Although Harriet often traveled to Europe on business and was able to visit with Hattie on many occasions, she still missed her eldest child. In 1885, she sailed back from Le Havre on the *Normandie*, a two-year-old luxury liner that crossed the ocean in just eight days. Once on board this grand ship, she began to suffer from insomnia and blinding headaches, the kind she endured during her pregnancies. She took the pills that her physician, Dr. George F. Schrady, had prescribed, but they put her into a morbid state of mind.

Harriet wrote to General Grubb about Hattie's departure but more importantly told him that she was going to consult a lawyer about a divorce, if she could afford it, whether or not he was free to marry her. To this letter, the general replied that before his return from Africa, his wife had become ill, and he was advised that she was too sick for him to consider a divorce at the moment. This may have been an excuse because of Harriet's unconventional lifestyle.[170] Time, distance and circumstances also may have diminished his feelings for her. Or perhaps he was having an affair with another woman, something he could do without repercussion. While Harriet was tempted to wait for him, she came to the conclusion that she enjoyed her independence and success in business. When she saw him again, she insisted that under the current circumstances (his not seeking a divorce and seeing other women), they had to stop seeing each other so that she could provide a proper role model for her daughters.

On October 20, 1885, Harriet wrote to Hattie, mentioning that James Seymour's son, Lewis, had asked for her several times. She added that she missed her daughter but that she was pleased Hattie was in the hands of such a wonderful prototype as Blanche Howard. Harriet also mentioned that Mr. Seymour visited on Sunday and had gone with her to see Margaret, who was attending St. Mary's School. She described how he bought Margaret a lot of "trash." She asked Hattie to describe everything in Stuttgart—her room, the people she met and her daily activities. Harriet promised to try to visit during the winter, if she could afford it, and cautioned Hattie to be good so that she would be deserving of "Miss H.," a really charming, generous woman whose sunny disposition was worth emulating. She went on to compliment Hattie for her generous, sympathetic traits but noted that persistency was her evil demon because she persisted right or wrong. In flowery prose, she reiterated her love for Hattie, blessed her and asked her to send her love to Miss Howard. "My own little love, I long to see you, and I am coming unless some accident—a financial one it will be—prevents. She ended the letter: "*Addio—t'amo tesoro mio, Sa Madre.*"[171]

Hattie and the other girls did not live with Blanche; rather, they stayed in nearby pensions. Since Blanche often worked on her books late at night, she did not have the girls visit until the afternoon. One of the several houses she rented was spacious and well run, with a staff of servants including a butler, a cook and a housemaid, but because of monetary problems, Blanche changed residences frequently. Some of the houses were less grand.

Luncheons were perfectly prepared and served so that the girls would learn proper etiquette and develop high standards from the elegant ambience and the delicious food. They learned how to look for the best rugs, draperies, furnishings and antiques. They studied German and French and were exposed to theater, opera and concerts. They were introduced to visiting artists to learn art history and drawing. The girls were required to go to the gymnasium (German high school) and conservatory for their basic training in literature, language, science, math, music and art. After church on Sundays, they visited art galleries, and at their next lunch they described and discussed what they had seen. Hattie, who had musical talent, attended the music conservatory.[172] Miss H.'s girls were dually introduced to culture and the refinements of life in which they were expected to excel. Their minds were stimulated in a variety of ways, including politics. Not all the girls benefited to the same degree, but Hattie and Fanny Locke (circa 1870–1939) did. Fanny went on to write plays for the Broadway theater with her second husband, Frederic C. Hatton, the drama editor for the *Chicago Post*.[173]

A frequent visitor to Blanche Howard's house, Dr. Julius von Teuffel provided medical care for the girls. The doctor was a widower with two sons, Ernst and Erwin. He was enamored of Blanche, who defended him when he became a scapegoat for medical mishaps in the royal family.[174] Blanche was manipulative and set her mind to attracting Baron von Teuffel, as well as earning Harriet's confidence and trust. She wanted Harriet to have faith in the good doctor and arranged for them to get to know each other. Blanche's guests were encouraged to relax and enjoy her nightly dinners, which included visiting diplomats, politicians, musicians, writers, painters and poets, all of whom contributed stimulating conversation. Harriet preferred the evenings that ended early enough for her to visit Hattie in her pension. There were times when Harriet could not fall asleep because of her chronic insomnia, and she would then help herself to some liquor and read until early morning in this relaxed atmosphere.

On her business trips to France and England, Harriet enjoyed visits with Blanche. She confessed to Blanche that she was taking morphine more frequently than prescribed by her doctor for sleep, although she was cautioned not to take the powder too frequently. Her physician, Dr. Schrady, had told her that half of his patients in New York were suffering from a similar malady because of the pace in that city and that all she needed was more rest and less worry. Nevertheless, the strain of making enough money from commissions to keep her daughter at boarding school and pay all her other expenses was enough to cause Harriet anxiety and insomnia. Her childhood fear of the dark probably exacerbated her sleeplessness. Blanche suggested that she consult the "brilliant" Dr. Teuffel, claiming that the Germans knew more than American doctors.

Blanche also questioned Harriet about little Margaret, who was now at the Convent of the Sacred Heart in Manhattan. When Blanche heard that Margaret was difficult to manage, was not yet reading and was inattentive and lacked focus, she suggested that Margaret come to Stuttgart, insinuating that Harriet was too busy to spend much time with this child, who seemed to have special educational needs. James Seymour had even nicknamed Margaret "Grasshopper" because of her short attention span.[175] Blanche may have been right when suggesting that Harriet was an inattentive mother. Like her own mother, but for different reasons, Harriet relegated the care of Margaret to Lena, the nuns and governesses.

Harriet protested that she could not afford to send both daughters to Stuttgart. Blanche suggested that Margaret live with her, thereby reducing the cost of room and board. She would provide private lessons and would only charge Harriet a fee for chaperoning.[176] Blanche said that Margaret would have her nephews and nieces for company since they were coming to stay with her in the spring. And so it was in 1886 that Harriet committed Margaret, who would turn nine in the spring, as well as Hattie, to Blanche Howard's care. Although she hated having both children gone, she thought it best for them to have an education abroad with this woman whom she still thought of as a perfect role model. It also freed her to concentrate on her new business endeavor.

At first, Margaret did not want to leave her mother and her beloved Lena to go to Stuttgart. In spite of her misgivings, however, when she arrived in Stuttgart, it took very little time before she was won over by Blanche. Blanche's house at the time was beautiful, located near the woods, where Margaret could walk and play. She had companions of her own age, in addition to her sister, whom she had missed during the past year. Since everyone seemed to adore Blanche, Margaret felt privileged to live with her. Blanche allegedly was thrilled to have a child younger than her usual students, one whom she could mold and wean away from Victorian conventions.[177] While Harriet, whom Blanche seemed to admire for her unconventional accomplishments, disregarded many traditions, she still retained a strong Victorian bias.

Harriet ruminated about the cost of keeping two girls in private school, even with a reduction in price. She then remembered James Seymour's advice about finding something every woman needed or wanted and then selling it to earn more than her current commissions. While Seymour had invested what little surplus money Harriet earned, the return was not enough for her to manage tuition for two children in 1886, even though by 1885, she had left Sypher's and was working for herself, importing objects from Europe for her own clients. While she earned an adequate living, she felt that she had to earn still more money to regain her earlier wealthy status.

9

Divorce

In September 1886, the same year Harriet launched her new business, Récamier Preparations, Inc., she filed for divorce. She was thirty-seven years old when she hired Cyrus Bentley Jr. of the Chicago solicitors Bentley and Bentley to represent her. The proceedings occurred two months later, in November 1886. Her irresponsible, alcoholic husband was served with a bill of chancery that accused him of deserting her in October 1883 until the present time. While he had promised to send $500 in child support on the first of every month, these monies never appeared. Although Harriet had written to him from time to time requesting his financial support, he had never "contributed one single cent directly or indirectly" between October 1883 and November 1886. The legal petition to dissolve the marriage and giving Harriet full control and custody of the children was introduced into the court and summoned Herbert, the defendant, in November 1886 to answer the charges.[178]

Harriet's testimony was recorded in the certificate of evidence and presented to the Honorary Gwynn Garnett, the presiding chancellor of the Superior Court. Although she was living in New York at this time, she testified that she was still a resident of Chicago and "from time to time sojourned" to New York "for business purposes entirely." Probably it was the opposite, for she lived in New York and from time to time sojourned to Chicago. She swore that she regarded Chicago as her permanent residence and intended to remain there permanently. An article in the *Boston Globe* claimed that Harriet, for a time after the separation, earned her income by writing gossipy letters about "the metropolis. Then she was given charge of Sypher & Co.'s Wabash Avenue branch of their Chicago establishment for artistic house furnishings, and elegant bric-a-brac."[179] Therefore, at least in 1883 and 1884, Harriet was splitting her time between New York City and Chicago.

During the divorce proceedings, Harriet stated that her daughter, Harriet Taylor Ayer, was nineteen years old and that Margaret Rathbone Ayer was ten. When asked where she was in the fall of 1883, she answered that she was in New York at the direction of her husband, who was departing for Europe. Herbert asked her to remain there until further instructions. The whole story of not receiving money—"not a farthing"—was repeated. Cyrus Bentley, her lawyer, then asked if Herbert had returned. She answered that she read in the papers that he had, but he had not contacted her. Bentley then pressed her about why she made no effort to reach him. Reluctantly, she answered that she could not because he was living with another woman in France and did not return for two or three years. He took up residence at the Manhattan Club in New York, where he was living when Harriet brought suit for divorce.[180]

Henry Kirtland, a butler who worked for the Ayers for about six months at the end of 1882 and into 1883, spoke on her behalf. Bentley asked about Herbert's behavior during that period:

Well, it was very brusk [sic] *to Mrs. Ayer and most of the time I considered that Mr. Ayer was under the influence of liquor during the whole time; he used to have poker parties there every other night, frequently lasting until 3 or 4 in the morning.*

When asked specifically about Herbert's treatment of Harriet, Kirtland responded, "He didn't seem to have any affection for her at all; he treated her more as a servant than he did his wife; he didn't seem to like her company much, or anything of that kind." As for Mrs. Ayer, he said, "I never knew Mrs. Ayer to do anything that was wrong or unbecoming a lady. I thought she was a perfect lady in every sense of the word." He added that he never saw Herbert strike Harriet or do anything violent, but they did quarrel at least once or twice a week in language that was unbecoming for a man to use with his wife. Herbert was often foul tempered because he started drinking early in the day. Kirtland remarked that the couple did not have breakfast together, and often, when Herbert came home drunk, he would fall asleep before dinner. As for the children, Herbert did not mistreat them.[181]

The *New York Times*, on September 21, 1886, citing an article from the Chicago papers of September 20, reported:

> *The bill of Mrs. Harriet Hubbard Ayer against her husband Herbert C. Ayer, the iron merchant, was filed in the Superior Court to-day. She says that she was married to him on Oct. 2, 1866, at Chicago, and lived with him until October 1883, when he said that he was going to Europe on business* [yet she was listed in the 1883–4 New York City directory] *but would give her $500 a month for the support of her and the children. She claimed that he had deserted her and has never returned, nor has he contributed anything since to her support or that of their two children, Harriet and Margaret.*[182]

Harriet told the judge that she had not heard from Herbert since his departure for Europe and that her investigations found that he was traveling and living with a woman in Europe. Upon his return to the United States, Herbert had never been to see her, nor had he sent any money. Divorce was only possible when one spouse had committed a marital offense, such as adultery, cruelty or desertion, or if the husband was not able to support his wife financially. Herbert, of course, was guilty of all these offenses. He was indeed no longer able to sustain his wife and children. Harriet, proper as she was, had severed her relationship with General Grubb before working toward her divorce, especially since reporters frequently monitored her activities. It took from 1883, when Herbert said he would grant her a divorce if she paid the lawyers, until 1887 for the divorce to transpire.

As she told her tale of woe to Judge Garnett, she burst into tears but controlled herself and continued. "The court asked Mrs. Ayer whether she had made any overtures looking toward healing the breach between herself and her husband to which she tearfully replied" that she had not under the circumstances. Mrs. Lutie Mason, Harriet's private secretary (since June 1884) testified that she opened all of Harriet's mail and had never seen any correspondence or money from Herbert, which of course corroborated Harriet's testimony. The judge thought the evidence insufficient to warrant a decree of divorce and continued the case, as he was familiar with the newspaper accounts of Mrs. Ayer's activities and of her articles and advertisements for her products.[183]

Although he had returned to the United States, Herbert never appeared in court, despite the subpoena. Ultimately, the court found that all Harriet's allegations were true and granted her the divorce, as well as "custody, control and education of the children, without any interference on the part of defendant, until further order of this Court." It was further ordered that she pay all of the court costs. "The Court reserves the consideration of alimony for a future order and decree herein."[184] The divorce decree was entered on February 28, 1887, but the possibility of Herbert being granted custody of the children at a future date was stipulated legally. Even with evidence that Herbert was a womanizing, alcoholic scoundrel, as a man he had the legal right to custody of the children, to which Harriet would never have agreed. In any event, Herbert did not contest the decision. Nevertheless, the possibility of his appealing the court's decision at any time in the future remained, and at a later date Herbert did exercise his rights.

Just as Harriet launched her own company in 1886 and finalized her divorce in 1887, General Grubb's wife died. In a letter to Hattie in 1888, Harriet spoke of her total exhaustion and admitted that her former liaison with "Ginger," Margaret's childhood name for Grubb, had ended. She indicated that the general had had an affair and that she could not forgive him. General Grubb ultimately found a much younger, less prominent and preoccupied companion than Harriet, whom he married in 1890. For him, Harriet's business association with James Seymour was likely a bone of contention, as was her unconventional behavior. In addition, the reputation of Blanche Howard, with whom Harriet's daughters were living, also came into question. The general refused to place his own daughter Effie in Blanche's finishing school, although Harriet suggested it, because Blanche allegedly attempted to seduce him, a fact Harriet was unaware of at the time. At this moment, Harriet was still pleased with the progress of her daughters. Hattie was charming and well educated; Margaret had learned to read and was doing well academically. Harriet had very high moral standards, but Grubb's were even more stringent, not only because of period double standards, but also because he was politically active in New Jersey.

Harriet's relationship with the general had deteriorated not only because she suspected that he was seeing other women, but also because she was so preoccupied with her business that she found it difficult to make time to see him. Frictions grew and the relationship soured. A draft of a rambling letter to Grubb was found among her papers after she died:

> *Yet I would not if I could forget the few moments in which I have clearly seen Life's wondrous possibilities…I have tried to think myself the blame, but that is absurd…From the first, it was overwhelming and I could do nothing but wonder and be glad, so though we never see each other again I insist that you must not regret it, for me. Life will not, cannot, be harder for me with the conception I now have of its possible pleasures.*[185]

It is impossible to know whether Harriet and the general ever consummated their love, although "conception I now have of its [life's] possible pleasures" might be interpreted as such. Clearly, it was a revelation to Harriet that there were human relationships better than the one she had with Herbert. By the time Grubb and Harriet both had their freedom, they each had other social, commercial and familial commitments. After waiting three years for her divorce, spurred on by the possibility of marriage to the upright, outstanding, wealthy general, Harriet's plans were thwarted by her own unconventional activities (albeit prompted by necessity), by her preoccupation with her business and by bad timing. Her courage in seeking a divorce, violating Victorian mores and actual legal constraints, ultimately undid her in the nineteenth-century world concerned with public opinion and proper behavior, especially when it came to women. Surely, her early years as a member of an important yet dysfunctional family provided the tenacity for her future endeavors in New York and beyond.

PART II
Founding the Cosmetic Company in New York City

10

Crafting Récamier Preparations

O n one of her frequent buying trips to Europe in search of objects for her clients, Harriet decided to revisit Monsieur Mirault, the chemist whose home and shop was on the wide residential Boulevard Malesherbes. It was he who had concocted the scent of violets she always wore since her extended stay in Paris in 1872. She importuned Monsieur Mirault to sell her the formula to the cream that his grandfather had created for Madame Récamier, the one that supposedly kept the Napoleonic beauty looking young for so many years. The chemist resisted her offer, telling her he would go into partnership with her; he would produce the product and she would sell it to rich Americans.[186] She persisted, and at last he gave in and sold her the formula for a reasonable, yet expensive (for her), price. There was a certain amount of risk associated with this purchase, since she did not know if she could even obtain the proper ingredients to reproduce the cream in the United States. However, motivated by the idea James Seymour had lodged in her mind, she believed she had a product that was widely needed and could earn her more money.

Employing the formula she had just bought, Harriet began to experiment in her kitchen late at night. Test tubes, pots and porcelain-lined teakettles were all the tools she had to work with to perfect the cream until it resembled the one Mirault had produced.[187] Training in business methods and pharmacy procedures was not readily available to women. Harriet taught herself and started a one-woman manufacturing operation in her kitchen with little financial capital. She tested the cream on herself and on acquaintances, selling it "in a small way until she accumulate[d] money enough…to advertise, and within a year from this small beginning she is today doing a large business."[188] Although her own skin was naturally radiant, despite her chronic insomnia, it showed improvement after using the cream. She asked her mother to try her newly formulated cream, and although Madame Hubbard, like other upper-class women of the period, initially resisted, claiming that she never used cosmetics or creams, she eventually obliged her daughter. Soon, she was back for more.[189] Harriet had found the key to her future success, giving women what many of them truly wanted and needed—a clear complexion and radiant skin.

So frowned upon was the use of makeup, especially during the 1870s, that Harriet insisted that her products were patent medicines. "In the nineteenth century the term patent referred to medicines and beauty preparations sold through specific techniques of national advertising and distribution."[190] Cosmetics, some with added color, were disguised as cures for sunburn, freckles and other blemishes. The idea that Harriet's choice of business was cosmetics astonished Madame Hubbard. Women were supposed to be delicate, pale and fragile; some even drank vinegar or ingested arsenic to achieve a white pallor. Makeup was for actresses, prostitutes and lower-class women; anything akin to it had to be camouflaged as a medical ointment or patent medicine. According to *Secret Nostrums and Systems of Medicine: A Book of Formulas*, compiled by Charles W. Oleson, MD, in 1889, Harriet's cream contained a homogenous mixture of glycerin, zinc oxide, grains of a corrosive substance and spirits of rose.[191] Zinc oxide is still used in cream form to prevent sunburn and for minor irritations.

The mixture was set in a delicate blue china jar similar to a covered sugar bowl, and the handles were tied with a ribbon to keep the cover attached. (See Figure 8.) She also placed the balm in a cut glass container finished off with a bow. The presentation of the cream—and soon after, the balm—was almost as important as the ingredients. When she considered her product ready, Harriet presented it to James Seymour, who had previously offered to sponsor her if she came up with a good business idea.[192] With her former romantic interest, General Grubb, now out of the picture, she no longer had to keep her business relationship with Seymour a secret. She was ready to accept his generous proposal to finance her venture. Intrigued, he opened the jar and smelled the cream, to which Harriet had added her special Parma violet perfume. Harriet had not thought about a price, but Seymour helped her determine her expenses and revenues while she explained the pedigree of the cream.

Crafting Récamier Preparations

Madame Récamier, she explained to Seymour, was a beauty of the Napoleonic era who had used this formula to keep her skin looking radiant. Even in old age, this accomplished, intelligent, beautiful Frenchwoman never lost her attraction, and her name was well known in America through various publications. Seymour recommended $1.50 per jar (when the ingredients cost no more than ten cents) as the selling price and gave her $50,000 (over $1 million in 2011 dollars) to launch the company. His other important contribution was to suggest that she incorporate her own name and family crest with that of Récamier's name, thereby exploiting her position in society.[193] It took great courage for Harriet to exploit her family name.

The Harriet Hubbard Ayer Company was founded in 1886, and the earliest advertisement appeared in May of that year, claiming "Never Before Manufactured for Sale." Harriet immediately changed the origins of the formula, "positively made from the recipe used by Mme. Récamier, obtained by Mrs. Ayer in Paris from a French Countess, relative of the famous beauty. One bottle of Récamier Cream Balm will be given to every purchaser of Récamier Cream for the next thirty days."[194] Just as she was introducing the cream, she was already touting an additional product. Ayer advertised Recamier Cream and Récamier Cream Balm, each at $1.50. Madame Récamier's picture was prominently displayed, taking at least one-quarter of the entire advertisement. (See Figure 9.) The ad ended with a list of endorsers that included her Chicago friends the Lockes, some church representatives, a politician, a retired opera singer and a society woman. She had all her bases covered.

The cosmetic industry was one of the few avenues open to the entrepreneurship of women during the second half of the nineteenth century. Harriet filed an application for registry of trademark, which included the words "Récamier Cream," her family crest and a facsimile of her signature. The following year, in 1887, she assigned the trademark, along with other property used in the business, to the Récamier Manufacturing Company, a New York corporation. This trademark was placed on all of her products. Advertisements stressed the fact that without her signature on the product, it was not genuine.[195] In the certificate of Incorporation, dated April 9, 1887, she listed Récamier Cream and Récamier Balm, together with other creams, balms, powders and compounds of medicinal nature. The amount of stock was valued at $50,000, and three trustees were appointed: Harriet, Albert Mason and Lutie Mason (not related).

After the loan and advice from James Seymour, Harriet issued one thousand shares of stock in her company. She insisted that Seymour take stock as collateral for the loan and that the stock should be returned after she reimbursed him. Naïvely, no binding legal contract was signed, even though she knew Seymour's reputation as a ruthless wheeler-dealer. His mining fiascos had been publicized in the newspapers many times, but Harriet was so determined to start her own business that she overlooked his unscrupulous business practices, as well as his obvious licentious desires. No one else had offered financial backing. Besides, she actually admired Seymour's business acumen and success and willingly overlooked his unsavory reputation. Desperation and determination drove her decision.

In promoting the consumption of beauty products, Harriet had to confront both the stigma cosmetics held for women of this period and that of divorce. The truth was that many women subtly enhanced their looks with powders and rouge, which they concocted themselves and then applied ever so lightly so as not to be noticeable, but in public they denied it.[196] The word "cosmetic" usually referred to creams and lotions that would correct skin problems, while "paints" referred to products that covered the skin. Harriet recalled that women often requested that her beauty products "be sent in a plain wrapper." Good and bad women from time immemorial, she countered, used cosmetics; however, no other woman before her in the United States had developed her own cosmetic business.

One might point to Lydia Pinkham (1819–1885), who established, manufactured, marketed and sold a vegetable compound that was said to cure or alleviate women's gynecological problems, or to Madame C.J. Walker (1867–1919), who developed hair products for African American women. While Pinkham's formula was mostly herbs and vegetables, it included alcohol, which she believed was therapeutic as well as useful as a preservative. Pinkham advocated mild exercise, healthy food and hygiene, specifically looser clothing and cleanliness. Different from Harriet, hers was a family business that involved her husband and children. And while Madame C.J. Walker's hair products for African American women were marketed aggressively, her business was established years after Harriet's Récamier Preparations. Many other women went on to establish cosmetic businesses thereafter: Elizabeth Arden (1884–1966), Helena Rubinstein (1870–1965) and Estée Lauder (1906–2004), but Harriet Hubbard Ayer was the first.

Crafting Récamier Preparations

Almost immediately, Harriet rented space at 27 Union Square West for the retail sale of patent medicines and cosmetics, with offices for herself, as president, at 30 Park Place. At first, her factory was located between East Fifteenth and Sixteenth Streets, just across town from her house on West Thirteenth Street, between Sixth and Seventh Avenues. By 1887, her factory was much farther downtown, at 39 and 41 Park Place, the Graphic Building, between West Broadway and Broadway in an area known today as TriBeCa. At the same time, to ensure a steady income for her family until her business was established, she continued to work from her home as a decorator. As president of the Récamier Company, she earned $12,000 a year (approximately $275,000 today) once the business was established.[197] By September 1886, her success was broadcast in the *New York Times*:

> *A great deal is said about successful men, and often they deserve the credit afforded them. Our times are producing successful women as well, and among these none deserve higher commendation than a former leader of Chicago fashion and society. Mrs. Harriet Hubbard Ayer, whom rumor says is enjoying a comfortable income derived from the sale of her Récamier Cream at No. 27 Union Square, which is manufactured from a formula obtained by her during one of her sojourns in Paris from an old lady whose grandmother was a maid of honor to the Empress Josephine, and who assured Mrs. Ayer that it was the only "beautifier" Mme. Récamier ever used, of whom it was stated as a historical fact that her complexion retained its marvelous beauty until her death at an advanced age. Society people of Chicago will remember that Mrs. Ayer, too, had a beautiful complexion, which was probably due to the Récamier Cream, and she showed her genius when she turned it to account as the necessity arose for her to support herself and her children.*[198]

It is interesting to note the change in the origin of the cream from the chemist to royalty, and further embellishments included an advertising ploy Harriet utilized to give her product a more seductive cache. That she was blessed with beautiful skin helped her sell the "possibility of youth and beauty" to an eager clientele, many of whom met with her face to face in her shop. She invented a historic underpinning for her products, citing foreign royalty, as well as her own background and breeding, to which she added her need to work in order to support her children. Doctors, chemists and druggists named in her advertorials endorsed her creations, thereby providing authenticity and evidence of safety.

Summarizing her success, Harriet said:

> *American women can go out in the world and, upon their own resources take up the struggle and succeed as well as most men. When I first announced my intention to go into business my friends were very much concerned— everyone predicted some failure, and did everything to persuade me to take a position as governess or companion, or some other such position as is usually sought by women who have to support themselves, but having two daughters to educate I felt I would be unable to do them justice on any salary that I could earn and determined to branch right out into business (like a man), and the results prove that my judgment was correct—my success has been unprecedented. I have had a hard fight, and am now victorious.*[199]

The Récamier story, with some variations, was repeated in New York and Chicago newspapers:

> *One day in Paris, Mrs. Ayer, while suffering intensely from the scorching sun of a July journey across the English channel, was offered a pot of cream by an old French lady friend to be used on her face before retiring, being assured that it would do wonders in softening and beautifying the complexion. Its effects were so magical and so marvelous that Mrs. Ayer became anxious to possess the formula for the cream, which she learned was not an article to be bought. But the old French lady refused to give the recipe, which (so she told Mrs. Ayer) was the one used by her beautiful, famous ancestor, Julie Récamier, for forty years, and was the undoubted secret of her wonderful beauty, which as everybody knows, Mme. Récamier retained until her death.*

"Of course," Harriet continued,

> *the more I learned about the cream and the oftener I and my friends tested its merits the more anxious I was to possess the formula. Mme. C___ (I am pledged not to reveal her name) was, like most of the old noblesse, poor and likewise pious. One evening she came to me with a subscription-paper for some church affair. I offered to buy the formula for the cream.*

She refused at first, but finally consented on condition that I should not say I had purchased it from her. For years I made the cream for my own and my friends' use and only after my circumstance had so changed that I was struggling for my own and my children's support did I cease to supply dozens of my acquaintances gratis with Récamier Cream, which was then called, entre nous, *that French paste Mrs. Ayer makes. When I at last decided to put the cream on the market, I wrote to Mme. C___ about it and received her consent to my telling how I secured the formula, stipulating only that I should not make her name public. Many people have thought the whole history of Récamier Cream an invention; but such is not the case and I have no more doubt of it being the means by which the famous French beauty, Mme. Récamier, preserved her lovely skin than you can have of its marvelous efficiency.*[200]

Harriet underscored that her cream was not a cosmetic and that she also had for sale Récamier Balm and Powder, the ingredients of which were similar to the cream. These other products were created with the help of a chemist to treat freckles, pimples, redness and blotches and to help women achieve "delicate freshness." She always stressed that the ingredients were "positively harmless."

AN ADVERTISING GENIUS

In "An Open Letter to New York Girls," Harriet was purportedly responding to letters from young girls who wanted to use her products but were afraid to tell their mothers and fathers, who

are so prejudiced against all sorts of Cosmetics. *They are not Cosmetics in the common acceptance of the word—that is to say, they are not whitewashes or washes which cover up for a brief time the blemishes on your face only to increase the ill condition of your skin until you cannot do without these terrible and ghastly compounds. The Récamier Preparations are Curatives—not masks—and I have sworn in an affidavit that they contain neither lead, bismuth, nor arsenic to the extent of one grain. Récamier cream will soften a hard and rough skin and will cure all blotches and pimples…So, girls, please tell your mothers there is no reason why you should not use the Récamier Preparations, and no reason why your mothers should not also preserve a good skin or restore a bad one by their use. There is nothing to hide about them. They are neither paints nor whitewashes.*[201]

In response to her instantaneous success, Harriet bragged:

It seems incredible to me, and doubtless to you, but here are our books and they will prove to you that Récamier Cream and Balm—unknown until last September—are now selling in larger quantities and are in greater demand than any other toilet articles in the market.[202]

She then named Marshall Field's in Chicago and B. Altman Dry Goods in New York as some of the best wholesalers that carried her line. "To give you some idea of the demand for the Récamier Preparation," she said, "I have just made a special contract with Messrs. B. Altman & Co. to put up for them Récamier Powder in 50-cent boxes. Their sales of all Récamier Preparations are immense and are so important that they have special saleswomen for them alone."[203] Having unique counters and dedicated salespeople is certainly familiar today, but in 1887 it was novel. Of course, the Récamier line could always be purchased directly from her shop at 27 Union Square, and what is more, it was not only the ladies but also gentleman who found the products helpful after shaving.

So popular were the Récamier products that Harriet had difficulty keeping up with her orders and found that within six months she needed to expand her operation. Clearly, she had come up with a product that was popular, helpful and harmless, despite the inclusion of a corrosive element in the cream formula. She guaranteed that only she, or her "right-hand man," Mrs. Lutie Mason supervised the manufacture and that they personally weighed, prepared and tested every ounce of the ingredients. Although there were twenty-five employees, only Harriet and Mrs. Mason knew the formula. She also acknowledged that the packaging was important and that her products looked artistic in their dainty jars and cut-glass bottles. These lovely objects may not be economical for the company, but then "I believe I never was accounted very economical."[204] A natural marketing genius, Harriet knew that beautiful packaging combined with her family crest and name on the label would provide a keen incentive for customers.

Harriet's stories appeared as if they were long news articles when in fact they were "advertorials." It was an innovative form of advertisement that had not been previously exploited. Articles covered the romantic origins of the company, the effectiveness of the product, the endorsements of well-known actresses and socialites, the popularity and demand for the items and the ingenious marketing. Harriet presaged modern American consumer culture and the identification of respectable women as consumers for whom shopping became a leisure activity and makeup a necessity. This was the beginning of a new identity for women as consumers to whom advertisers directed their promotions.

Even society women such as the Vanderbilts, Astors and Lorillards used Récamier Preparations.

> *Every society woman knows that Récamier Cream will positively heal the effects of sun and wind while at sea...It is simply marvelous for keeping the face soft and lovely under the most aggravating exposure to the elements. Récamier Cream, Récamier Balm, and Récamier Powder are for sale by druggists and fancy goods dealers everywhere and by the proprietor and manufacturer, Harriet Hubbard Ayer, No. 27 Union Square, New York City.*[205]

Other beauty products existed previously, but none was marketed as brilliantly as Récamier Preparations.

Vita Nuova

Not too long after Harriet introduced Récamier Cream, a new product was teasingly mentioned but not described in a March 1887 ad headline. The rest of the month saw multiple articles in the *Brooklyn Eagle* about "Ayer's Vita Nuova (New Life), the name signifies a health restoring and life renewing tonic. It has been tested by scores of persons and has effected most marvelous cures." Harriet had expanded her products to include this general tonic that supposedly treated nervousness, dyspepsia, indigestion, flatulence, sleeplessness, etc. Harriet maintained that a leading doctor had given her the formula three years before.[206] She said that this was an exhilarating drink that left no depressing effects when taken according to directions. It was pleasant tasting, not harmful and cost only one dollar a bottle. She claimed that the sales were very large, and everyone, including gentlemen, was satisfied. This product "was not intended solely for ladies, but for overworked merchants, bankers, lawyers, physicians, and all other persons requiring a tonic and whose digestion is impaired in the slightest degree."[207] Then she described her other products, asking how could any woman risk her beauty and physical health when it cost only twenty-five or fifty cents for proper care. "Mrs. Ayer spoke with a good deal of pride of the credit she had established and impressed the reporter with the belief that her statements were to be relied upon." As usual, the article contained her contact information for the direct purchase of Récamier products.[208]

What exactly was this cure-all liquid? Oleson, in his *Secret Nostrums*, found it to be port wine, containing 18 or 19 percent alcohol, and cocaine—ingredients that could make anyone feel good regardless of their infirmity.[209] Vita Nuova was described in advertisements as

> *a life giving and health renewing cordial and tonic. Unsurpassed in excellence as a restorative, effecting, marvelous cures in all cases of mental exhaustion, general debility, nervous prostration, insomnia, dyspepsia, hysteria and its many forms, neuralgia and congestive headaches, etc., etc.*

The symptoms replicated some of those from which Harriet frequently suffered: sleeplessness, insomnia, mental exhaustion and general debility. It was further claimed as a positive cure for the habits of opium and alcohol, and it left no craving. The dose was half a claret glass or about three tablespoons three times a day. If we can trust this book's analysis citing cocaine as a component of Vita Nuova, it reveals that Vita Nuova was similar to countless other patent medicines that were sold legally. Cocaine, an opium derivative extracted from the opium poppy, was a drug readily prescribed by physicians and sold over the counter in drugstores during the nineteenth century.

Yet another advertorial in the *New York Times* on July 3, 1887, gave testimonials of people who wrote defending and praising Vita Nuova, ending with Harriet saying she would return money to any dissatisfied consumers. One letter, written by DeLancey Nicoll, who was New York's assistant district attorney from 1885 to 1888 (and who was elected attorney general from 1892 to 1894), testified to the confidence he had in the potion and how it had helped him. "It has not only added to my physical vitality, but has clarified the mind and stimulated its action."[210]

As to the marketing of Vita Nuova, Harriet was again ingenious, saying that a doctor might charge twenty dollars for a prescription, but a person could buy her tonic for only one dollar—and it was blessed by leading physicians. She also advertised that she would supply free samples at her uptown office at 27 Union Square to anyone with fatigue, dyspepsia and mental or nervous exhaustion. She claimed that over two hundred people a day appeared. In order to help the poor and the infirm, she planned to continue this good deed indefinitely so that the indigent, some of whom returned multiple times, could benefit. "Of course, this has increased the sales of Vita Nuova fourfold, so you see it is a somewhat charitable act and a fine advertisement combined."[211] In answer to any negative press for her products, she defended herself by blaming her accusers of jealousy and false allegations, warning readers not to be fooled by substitutes sold by unscrupulous dealers.

In her defense, an advertisement on June 12, 1887, stated:

> *Harriet Hubbard Ayer is no charlatan. She has gained the confidence of the people of the United States by her honorable business methods, and her elegant Récamier Toilet Preparations to-day are used in almost every elegant home in America. A woman of birth, education, and breeding, she has stepped from her parlor into the whirlpool of commercial life.*[212]

In just one advertorial, she managed to set herself up as virtuous, dependable, respectable and admirable to counteract evident criticism and innuendos about both the efficacy of her products and her integrity.

Harriet argued that the highest medical authorities approved of her tonic and went on to name gentlemen who had written laudatory letters from all over the United States, including Delancy Nicoll. "You will find that it tastes like a wine thirty years old, while positively free from alcohol or narcotics, and purely vegetable, and without the reactionary effects which render many tonics worthless." Could Oleson's analysis be wrong, or was Harriet using false advertising? Offering her line at druggists and retail dealers in Boston, as well as at a wholesale price directly from her company, Harriet was connecting her products to health as well as beauty, and druggists and merchants who sold her products attested to not only her honesty and integrity but also her sound business practices.[213]

The most covert advertorial was titled "Theodore Houston's Death." It related the death of a successful man to anxiety and overwork, which could have been prevented had he taken Vita Nuova to cure his nervous troubles. Harriet mentioned a general, several politicians and a minister as endorsers and continued to offer free samples at 27 Union Square so that the balm's merits could be thoroughly tested before purchase. And, of course, the balm sold well despite any negative press she may have received.[214] Such advertorials, including one called "Practical Charity," consisted of testimonial letters of approval and thanks for donating the product to the poor.[215] Harriet began what has become common practice today: the offer of free samples to advertise products and convert recipients into consumers.

Another marketing ploy touted "the phenomenal success of Mrs. Harriet Hubbard Ayer as a business woman…the sensation of the drug trade." The reporter interviewed a number of druggists, who verified that her products have become standards. "Mrs. Ayer is an honest, straight-forward, energetic woman, whose statements can be depended on. Mrs. Ayer conducts her business just as a man would."[216] This was high praise for someone only one year in business, praise that compared her favorably to men. It reads as if a reporter wrote it, but it was another of her self-planted reports.

It was the projection of Harriet Ayer herself that was central to her sales strategies, and she changed her story, both about herself and the discovery of her cream, to suit the market. She was smart and consistently reinvested her earnings into newspaper ads all over the United States and Canada, bringing her immediate, colossal national success. Harriet was quick to call attention to the health benefits to differentiate her products from other lesser toilet articles. She appealed to women to look their best for men with the use of her products.

INTERNATIONAL FAME

Récamier products were sold in England at the American Exhibition and Wild West Show in London in the summer of 1887. The fair was three years in preparation and ultimately attracted about one million visitors to view the displays of American products and ingenuity. After only one year in business, Harriet had the wits to participate in this fair, thereby promoting her company abroad. The main attraction at this fair was Colonel F. William Cody, known as "Buffalo Bill," who was featuring performances by American Indians. There were naked Indians in war paint and beads, charging horsemen, lasso throwing exhibitions and sharp shooting at moving targets. The *London Times* reported that the Prince and Princess of Wales and other royalty attended the hour-and-a-half performance, which was producing "an instantaneous electrifying sensation."[217] It may have been there that the princess first encountered Récamier Preparations. Of all the product displays,

> *the most beautiful was that of Mrs. Harriet Hubbard Ayer's Récamier preparations and they seemed to sell like hotcakes too. There was a very strong discussion before the committee of the American Exhibition as to whether or not the first award should be given to Mrs. Ayer, because the committee claimed that it was utterly impossible to give an award to "cosmetics." Mrs. Ayer's agents were then compelled to have the preparations analyzed and to demonstrate to the satisfaction of the committee that they were not "cosmetics," not injurious, but absolutely beneficial. After this was done the committee gave the award to Mrs. Ayer.*[218]

The exhibition was said to have brought America closer to England and promoted a more intimate understanding between the two nations.[219]

Since the firm's letterhead claimed "Manufactured by Permission to H.R.H., The Princess of Wales, the Récamier Toilet Preparations with offices in London, Paris, Montreal and New York, with a laboratory in New York," it is likely that Harriet sold Récamier products abroad.[220] Advertisements for Récamier products appeared in newspapers and magazines all over the United States and in Canada, along with replications of articles.[221]

CELEBRITY ENDORSEMENTS

In addition to using her name and her family's crest on her products, Harriet also incorporated the names of such well-known endorsers as Sarah Bernhardt and Lillie Langtry in her newspaper advertisements. While some people ostracized Harriet, she was able to maintain respect because of her upper-class background. Actresses, no matter how successful, were still thought of as déclassé, yet Harriet had entertained people in the performing arts as a young hostess in Chicago and respected and admired their talents.

At first, Harriet used a cropped print of Baron François-Pascal Gerard's 1805 painting of Madame Récamier in her advertisements.[222] When exhibiting Récamier products at the American Exposition in London, Harriet found that English women were impressed with the celebrity endorsement of actresses like Lillie Langtry (1853–1929). Throughout the late-nineteenth century, manufacturers actively used testimonials from popular actresses for products from cosmetics and corsets to soap and patent medicines. Lillie Langtry had first used her public profile to endorse Pear's soap in 1882 and was the first woman to advertise a commercial product, for which she was well paid.

Born in England in 1853, Langtry had many notable lovers, including the Prince of Wales. She was also friendly with aesthete Oscar Wilde and the American painter James Abbott McNeill Whistler. Her debut as an actress in 1881 was at the London's Haymarket Theatre. She traveled to the United States in 1882 and likely met Harriet in Chicago. On a succeeding trip to New York in 1883, Harriet temporarily loaned or rented Lillie her house on Thirteenth Street. A newspaper article denied the rumor that Harriet paid Lillie for her endorsement, but she probably did.[223] In an ad entitled "The Four Cleopatras," Lillie's letter of August 14, 1888, was quoted:

> *As I wrote you some months since, I use the "Récamiers" religiously and I believe them to be essential to the toilet of every woman who desires to retain a fair skin if Heaven has so blessed her, as well as to her less fortunate sisters, who need not despair so long as you continue to place within easy reach these remedies for all imperfections. Yours most sincerely, Lillie Langtry.*[224]

Harriet was able to enlist the services of other actresses, including Lillian Russell, Cora Urquhart Brown Potter, Helena Modjeska, Fanny Davenport and the internationally renowned French actress Sarah Bernhardt; surely she paid them each in cash or kind for their services. The "Cleopatra" ad included Cora Brown, the "Divine Sarah" and Fanny Davenport. The ads served the dual function of publicizing actresses and their careers and broadcasting Harriet's products. Throughout the 1880s, testimonials for Récamier products were accompanied by the images of the endorsers, asserting:

Crafting Récamier Preparations

Récamier Cream is used daily by fashionable women and prominent actresses all over the world. It is the only preparation of its kind whose merits are attested to by physicians. It will preserve your youth, remove blemishes, and not only make but keep your face smooth and fair.[225]

Adelina Patti (1843–1919) was another celebrity to endorse Pear soap early on. She appeared so frequently for Pears, Récamier and others that she was dubbed "Testimonial Patti." A contemporary of Jenny Lind, she was one of the most highly regarded and highest-paid classical opera singers of her day. Although she was born in Madrid to Italian parents, both of whom were singers, the family moved to New York and lived in the Bronx, where Patti was trained professionally. She sang for the Lincolns at the White House after the death of their son Willie in 1862 and subsequently all over the United States and Europe. This beautiful, ingénue-like opera star was an excellent actress, and she demanded $5,000 in gold per performance, paid in advance. Her sharp business sense must have appealed to Harriet, who paid Patti for her endorsements. In 1888, Harriet publicized a letter from Miss Patti saying that she had Récamier products express mailed to her when she had run out of them. Accusations that Harriet paid her endorsers persisted, but Harriet vehemently denied them.[226] Still, newspapers continually claimed that she had spent a fortune, about $50,000, on testimonials.[227]

The endorser most remembered today, and one of the greatest actresses in history, was Sarah Bernhardt (1844–1923). Because of her tendency to fabricate, her exact date of birth and early history are cloaked in uncertainty. She had a number of husbands and lovers, such as the Prince of Wales, a man who seems to have had affairs with several of Harriet's endorsers. Bernhardt's career as a serious dramatic actress began in 1862, and she worked in France and England but also traveled to the United States. The publicity surrounding her served Harriet's purposes well. The divine Sarah wrote, "The Récamier preparations are the perfection of toilet articles. Please send me, without fail, tomorrow, two dozen assorted for immediate use." In the case of Lillian Russell, the ad reproduced an image of her side by side with a facsimile of her letter praising Récamier Preparations.[228] Such statements were broadcast in various newspapers.

Récamier products were advertised in magazines such as the *Century* and *Harper's*. The magazine ads were often longer than those in newspapers, except for the advertorials. One included a poem showing a sailor sitting on a box of

Récamier soap trying to hoodwink the natives with a substitute, but they knew better and would only accept the Récamier brand. Under the poem and the image of the sailor with the natives were answers to questions about why people should use Récamier Preparations. Again, it included affidavits by all those named above and one additional American opera star, Clara Louise Kellogg. Another deceptive ad started with Kellogg's trip to Europe and then went on to say that she would not travel without Récamier products.[229] Testimonial advertisements were apparently successful because Harriet's business grew exponentially. Her timing was excellent given the fact that middle-class women were just beginning to experiment with cosmetics during the 1880s and '90s and that she disguised her products as medicinal creams.

OTHER PRODUCTS

After Harriet expanded her products to include a balm, soap, powder and lotion, she created a pamphlet listing various scents of concentrated odors for the handkerchief; scented waters for the toilet; sachets; bath accoutrements; hair tonics and shampoos; toothpastes and mouth washes; hand creams; sponges; brushes for the hair, clothes, infants, hats and teeth; manicure goods; and objects of art for the toilet table. She also increased her advertisements to street railways, billboards and walls.

In launching a new product, her advertorial titled "The Largest Sign in the World, Récamier Sarsaparilla; An Open Letter to the Trustees of the Brooklyn Bridge from Mrs. Harriet Hubbard Ayer" was attention-getting. The letter begins:

> *Gentlemen: I desire to use the Brooklyn Bridge for the purpose of advertising my Récamier Sarsaparilla, and will pay you any reasonable price you may name for such privilege…the best household remedy for the ills that attack poor and rich alike through impure blood, bad digestions, and torpid liver.*[230]

Sarsaparilla is a trailing vine that grows in the tropics. Its root has been used in folk medicine to cure multiple ills, including abdominal problems, debility, skin conditions, impotence, etc. The helpful chemicals in the bitter root are distilled and mixed with sugar water. *Secret Nostrums* revealed the contents to include stillingia, yellow dock, May apple, iodid of potassium and iron, in addition to the sugar and sarsaparilla. Thus, Harriet promoted yet another tonic, different from her Vita Nuova, and thought boldly about using the only bridge in New York. Her published request to do so was surely just another advertising ploy, as she was competing with Dr. J.C. Ayer (no relation), who also produced sarsaparilla.

Another ruse Harriet used was to make it seem as though people were questioning the efficacy of Récamier products and Vita Nova, claiming they were cheap and dangerous. Harriet retorted that it was "the most colossal humbug in the country…I shall publish your reply as my answer to all cranks and blackmailers" and those who sell fraudulent reproductions. She obtained a statement from Dr. Thomas B. Stillman, a chemistry professor from Stevens Institute of Technology, who scientifically analyzed and then defended her products. He stated that all of her creams were made of ingredients appropriate for their stated purpose and that the secret was in the manufacture. He also claimed that Vita Nuova was not just "wine of coco" but a fine grade of wine mixed with other substances that gave it its unique qualities and medicinal value at a price lower than what a druggist would charge. Stillman and two others, Henry A, Mott, PhD, and Peter T. Austin, professor of general and applied chemistry at Rutgers College and New Jersey State Scientific School, signed the letter.[231]

Harriet's retort to criticism of her products was to get doctors and scientists to sanction them. She reported that Mr. William Allison of the Druggists Circular Co. had circulated false information about her Vita Nuova. After consulting her lawyer, she decided not to bring suit but instead asked the druggists to prove their erroneous statement or else retract it. They only needed to visit her factory to see that her products were not harmful. She again repudiated the druggists' claim, saying that as a struggling woman she was being maligned and falsely accused. Dr. E.P. Fowler allegedly responded:

> *I do not recommend your preparations; I never give my name to recommend any kind of preparation. In reply to your note I will only say that preparations made according to the formula you have submitted to me for your "Récamier Balm" and "Vita Nuova," and used as per directions, contain nothing detrimental to health.*

While this testimonial was not a glowing reference, it seemed professional, especially because it underscored that Dr. Fowler did not usually endorse products.[232] There were no government controls over products such as these until the passage of the Pure Food and Drug Act in 1906, so the public never knew the contents of these potions.

The periodical called the *Chemist and Druggist* had a paragraph about another of Harriet's accusers, specifically a disgruntled former employee, Lutie Mason, Harriet's once-trusted assistant, who alleged that she was fired without cause and that it was she who had invented Récamier Cream. The article printed the contents of the cream and the fact that it was sold for a price much higher than the actual value of its ingredients. It ended saying that Vita Nuova was similarly profitable and even more dangerous than any of the other Récamier products, "the cocaine in the preparation producing a temporary exhilaration."[233]

We must assume from all Harriet's disclaimers that there were people who accused her of being a charlatan. Somehow she was able to get reputable doctors and people in important positions to testify to the authenticity and value of her products. Articles typically ended with a strong sales pitch:

> *That most women do need preparations to cure and remove pimples, spots, redness and roughness of the skin, blemishes of all kinds, and blackheads, is without question; that no dainty woman can endure these things without a feeling of mortification goes without saying; that they create a feeling of disgust in the minds of men who see them is an accepted fact; that they can all be cured by the use of Récamier Preparations has been amply proven; that it is important to preserve a good complexion is self-evident...Refuse substitutes and insist upon the genuine with the trademark of Harriet Hubbard Ayer. Send for a sample of Récamier Powder to Harriet Hubbard Ayer, 62 and 64 Park Place, New York.*

Her use of the phrase "disgust in the minds of men" is revealing of Harriet's attitude about the appeal of women to men. Women, according to Harriet's principles, needed to keep themselves looking good in order to attract and keep a husband.

Harriet Hubbard Ayer's Book: A Complete and Authentic Treatise on the Laws of Health and Beauty, published in 1899, tells the story of a woman who had let herself go, "growing fat and dumpy and indolent." She noticed that her husband spoke glowingly of younger, more attractive women. Afraid of losing her man since she was "just as much in love with him as [she] was the day [they] were married," she lost weight, improved her hygiene and bought "the prettiest gowns and negligees for home and the most elegant wraps and waists for the theatre. You never saw any one so astonished and delighted as my husband," who on one occasion called her "a regular peach."[234]

SUPPORTERS

One of Harriet's ardent defenders was Mrs. John Sherwood (1828–1903), the author of a popular etiquette book first published in 1884 called *Manners and Social Usages*. Mary Elizabeth Wilson Sherwood's book was written to help the nouveau riche, the lower classes and the immigrant population, "the vast conglomerate which we call the United States of America." Books such as this helped outsiders fit in with the establishment; they served as part of the leveling process of democracy. "America of the eighties was etiquette-conscious and anxious to improve, reading the books surreptitiously, but earnestly."[235] Books on etiquette proliferated, and many of the articles on the women's pages in the newspapers dealt with the subject.

In her article "Mrs. Harriet Hubbard Ayer's Struggles and Honorable Successes Taken as Text," Sherwood admonishes society for finding it unacceptable for women to work and hiding it when they did. "This is a poor form of pride, and aggravated self consciousness…and a shameful scorn of that noblest of all things, 'work'—so honorable in men; why not in women?" She uses Harriet as an example, writing that while the word "cosmetic" is repellent, Mrs. Ayer boldly advanced: "What it must have cost her, what poverty costs any woman, what publicity and wrong impressions and ignorant criticism costs a reduced lady—who shall ever write this book which shall tell the story." Sherwood went on to tout Harriet as having "the French talent for the exactitude of the medicinal and chemical science." She defended her endorsers as being the best class of actresses and singers and said that it paid for women to study chemistry and science. "Mrs. Ayer is a model of what wealth and success can bring." Such praise by an author of a book on etiquette for a woman who violated high society's rules of moral decorum was evidence of both Harriet's popularity and the creeping advance of women's status.[236] Sherwood underscored Harriet's appeal for sympathy, her compassion for others and her bravery in the face of adversity as part of her brilliant advertising campaign.

Work Ethic

Harriet's work routine was strenuous:

> *Early every morning in the crowd of working men and women waiting for the train at the Eighteenth street station, on the Sixth Avenue L road, can be seen a pretty woman quietly dressed, with a well-rounded figure, short yellow hair in tiny curls all over her well-shaped head, and straightforward laughing eyes. It is Mrs. Harriet Hubbard Ayer on her way to her office. Her mode of life as a businesswoman is in striking contrast to the life she led as a society woman. She is at her office in dull, dingy, depressing Park Place at 8 o'clock every morning, rain or shine, and she generally sees the porter out in the evening. On every weekday, except Saturday, she is the last one to leave the office, and on Saturday she takes a half-day holiday, which she usually spends in "hustling the advertising." I served a long apprenticeship as a society woman, and I know well that life of endless excitement, frivolity, and fatigue, with nothing to show for it at the end but heartaches and the gratification of petty vanities. And I also know the somewhat wearing existence of daily, hourly labor, but had I my choice as between the two; I could not hesitate an instant. I would not change my present position in the world for any social height within the reach of woman.*

Harriet truly enjoyed the accomplishment, the recognition and the independence her business brought her. Since it was mostly women whom Harriet employed, there was a look of femininity to the office. Her desk was in the corner, where she could see the whole room. A glass cabinet with samples of her products was always in view. "Instead of going to lunch, Mrs. Ayer saves time by having a 'beefsteak and trimmings' or something of that sort cooked in the factory, and with her stenographer as her guest she eats her lunch at her desk." A model for her employees, Harriet was efficient, hardworking and frugal, and these characteristics were part of her success.[237]

It was deduced that she earned between $10,000 and $15,000 a year from her interior design business after she left Sypher's and $12,000 annually in salary from her Récamier company, which would equal approximately $150,000 annually in today's dollars. When Récamier was at its zenith, it is possible that she was grossing over $1 million a year. Annual reports from

1890 to 1896 reveal that the company retained its stock value at $50,000 and that its liabilities were between $2,500 and $4,200, with assets between $14,500 and $17,000. Even after her disastrous incarceration in 1893, the company retained its stock value.[238] Récamier Preparations stimulated the American quest for beauty, prompting a new major industry in the United States. The cosmetics industry eventually evolved from nonexistent into one of the top ten industries in the twentieth century. Harriet's success brought her not only new wealth but also admiration and concomitant problems.

11

Trouble Behind the Scenes

The more successful Harriet became, the more she expanded her cosmetic business and the harder she had to work. Although she visited her children in Stuttgart during business trips to Europe (and even took them on holidays), she began to feel as though she was losing them. She became suspicious of Blanche Howard and questioned some of the charges for Margaret, since Blanche had promised that Margaret's expenses would be minimal. With Hattie returning to New York in 1888, Harriet's expenses would soon decrease, yet she sensed that Blanche was not being entirely honest with her.

Harriet was excited when her elder daughter was ready to return to New York after several years in Stuttgart. She met Hattie in Europe, and on their trip home Hattie surprised her by announcing that she planned to marry Lewis Seymour. Since Harriet's association with his father had deteriorated, this revelation came as a shock. Harriet had hoped that as a result of their long separation the young couple would have cooled their ardor, but apparently they had not. In part, Harriet was to blame. Feeling indebted to Seymour for his initial help, she had taken the ailing Lewis to see doctors in Europe on one of her trips in 1886 and left Lewis with Hattie in Stuttgart while she traveled for work.

Harriet tried to convince Hattie that this was a passing infatuation, but to no avail. Hattie was twenty-one and insisted on marrying this young man who was so like his father. When they arrived in New York, Harriet found that she had no allies, for even Madame Hubbard, swayed by the

Seymours, approved of the match. Caroline Seymour, James's wife, came to call on Harriet. Reminiscent of when Elida Ayer had called on Madame Hubbard to discuss Herbert's marriage to Harriet, the two women had little in common.

Harriet then decided to talk to James Seymour face to face about breaking up the romance between Hattie and Lewis. She went to his office to persuade him to help her end the liaison. Instead, she was met head on with the astounding and insulting request for her to become his mistress. She, of course, vehemently rejected his proposal. One would think she would have been suspicious of his motives all along for sponsoring her business and ingratiating himself with her children. Perhaps she was as wily as he and thought she could defuse his amorous advances, but instead she was faced with a persistent and powerful enemy. Rebuffed, he vowed to seek revenge.[239]

And so Seymour did, for no one is as vengeful as a spurned suitor. As soon as Harriet returned from Europe, she went to her office and found it disorganized, with many unfilled orders. The first sign of insubordination was when her long-term assistant, Lutie Mason, thwarted her authority, telling Harriet that she was now acting on orders from James Seymour. Harriet dismissed her immediately but then had to do her assistant's work. Although she had a large staff of salespeople, administrators and factory workers behind the scenes to fill orders, this pressure and stress resulted in a decline in her health once again.

In the spring of 1888, Harriet was about to send for Margaret to come home, but the nine-year-old child had developed scarlet fever. Before the discovery of antibiotics, scarlet fever, a streptococcal throat infection accompanied by fever and rash, could cause heart and kidney disease and ultimately death. Although Harriet had planned to go to Stuttgart, she collapsed from the strain of her work and anxiety about her elder daughter's forthcoming marriage. Dr. Schrady, Harriet's regular doctor, sent her to the nursing home of Dr. J.W. Pinkham in Montclair, New Jersey, to recuperate over the summer. Blanche wrote to Harriet, assuring her that she was giving Margaret the proper care and attention. At the same time, Blanche was intimating to Margaret that General Grubb might be her real father because she was tall, with dark curly hair like his, while both her parents were small with straight hair. She also insinuated that Harriet had many gentlemen friends when they lived in Chicago. "She [Margaret] has the uncertain choice between Grubb and McCullough for presumptive fathers," Blanche wrote, insinuating that Harriet had slept with Grubb and the actor John McCullough.[240] In a concerted effort to brainwash Margaret, Blanche withheld Harriet's letters and failed to remind Margaret to write regularly to her mother. Blanche, who did not want to lose Margaret, had a hypnotic effect on the girl and convinced her that the stories about her mother were true. In later years, Margaret's son Hubbard noted, "Blanche Howard was a real weirdo. She constantly reminded little Margaret that she was 'Unstable as water.'"[241]

Hattie continued with her wedding plans, and she was married on a cold day on November 12, 1888. The wedding took place at St. Luke's Church in Montclair, New Jersey, and was officiated by Reverend Dr. Rainsford of St. George's Church in New York, assisted by Reverend Dr. Carter of St. Luke's.[242] Only the family and a few friends were in attendance. Harriet may have held a reception at her house in New York, which reportedly was decorated with masses of flowers. By this time, Harriet had paid off the $50,000 loan from James Seymour so no longer owed him anything. Although it was somewhat awkward, she could face him squarely at the wedding. Seymour paid for the penniless Herbert Ayer to come to see his daughter become the wife of Lewis Seymour. The young couple subsequently moved into a wing of the Seymour house in Orange, New Jersey. Thus, Hattie came under the Seymours' control and became her mother's adversary in the 1889 trials.

Soon after the wedding, Harriet, accompanied by faithful Lena, left for France, where she was to meet Blanche and Margaret in Paris. Instead, only Blanche turned up, insisting that Margaret wanted her mother to spend Christmas with her in Stuttgart. German winters were excessively harsh, especially in Stuttgart's hills and valleys. Although she had begun to cough up blood, Harriet felt compelled to go. She cabled Dr. Schrady, who recommended that before she left Paris she should see Dr. Jean Martin Charcot (1825–1893), the famous French neurologist whose insights into the nature of hysteria and nervous diseases influenced Sigmund Freud. Dr. Charcot warned Harriet not to go to Germany, but Blanche insisted that after the holiday she would see to it that Harriet went south to Italy, where it was warm.

When Harriet arrived in Stuttgart just before Christmas 1888, she found that the medicines Dr. Charcot had prescribed for her were missing. Blanche quickly offered the services of Dr. Teuffel. She put Harriet at ease and insisted that she rest. Margaret was excited to see her mother, but Blanche quickly sent her away so she could begin Harriet's treatment. She laced Harriet's liquids with sulfonal (sometimes spelled sulphonal), a hypnotic drug rarely used in the United States, and warned her ailing guest that other people were trying to harm her. Sick and exhausted, Harriet believed she could trust the people around her. Dr. Teuffel, who several years later was sent to a mental institution, was put in charge of her treatment, and she proceeded to get worse. While her own doctor had given her small doses of sleep-inducing drugs, Dr. Teuffel prescribed large doses of sulfonal, harmful when cumulative and ultimately lethal. Harriet succumbed to the drugs and fell into a drug-induced coma. Only Lena surmised what was happening, but because she was a mulatto servant, she did not receive much respect and had little power to help. Margaret was completely under Blanche's spell and believed the lies she was fed that her mother was an alcoholic and a drug addict, evidenced by her current stupor.

Lena sent a telegram to Hattie for help, and the reply came that Dr. Schrady agreed with the treatment Harriet was receiving in Germany. Hattie, who was now under the control of her husband and her father-in-law, had heard the same innuendos about her mother that Margaret was now hearing. James Seymour exerted power over everyone and was not above bribing Blanche, who needed money to support her sister, nephews and nieces.[243] Furthermore, Blanche had become attached to Margaret and thought of her as her own child, and she definitely did not want to lose her—or her tuition money. Blanche wrote:

> It would break my heart to give the child up. No one understands her as I do. No one who does not understand that she is the child of opium and lies and some other vices of which you do not know, can make a good woman of her, for her mother's blood runs freely in her veins.[244]

She also claimed that Harriet was an alcoholic and that when she could not obtain liquor, she would drink perfume. Margaret did not want to leave and wrote:

> Please tell Papa to do all he can before he lets me go to that awful woman [Harriet]. She surely won't let me stay with Wawie anymore. I won't go on a ship until I am dragged, and I will run away if I get the chance. If I lose Wawie I lose all the good in me.

Blanche had all of her students call her "Wawie," the Indian word for white. And in a letter to her grandmother, Madame Hubbard, Margaret wrote that she was glad to hear from her but reiterated that she wanted to stay with Wawie forever: "She has done more for me than anyone else has. She has improved everything from my soul to my toes."[245]

Finally, after days of unconsciousness, with the help of Lena, Harriet was able to recover partially. Lena had put herself in charge of dispensing the medication and was able to substitute chalk powder for sulfonal. As soon as Harriet could walk, she escaped to Paris, where she had friends like Madame Duval, her former French teacher. When she was well enough, Harriet realized that a telegram from General Grubb asking her to stay in Paris was bogus since it was signed Grubb and not "Ginger," as he was affectionately known in her family. In fact, it was sent by one of Seymour's henchman to keep her away from the board meeting at which Seymour planned to appropriate her company.

Before returning to New York, Harriet wired her lawyer, Stephen H. Olin, to meet her at the pier. With great resolve, she made up her mind to take James Seymour to court and prove that Blanche had aided him in debilitating her, action that took tremendous courage in a male-biased society and in male-dominated courts.

PART III
Trials and Tribulations

The Trials of Mrs. Ayer

Never outside the realms of romance was a more dramatic story told than was set forth in the affidavit read before Judge Daly in the Court of Common Pleas yesterday. A woman whose success in business has made her name familiar in every town and city from the Atlantic Ocean to the Pacific charged a stock broker, a man whose wealth is estimated at many millions, with a crime that appears almost incredible in this century. She implicated in the alleged conspiracy against her, the broker's son, the young man's bride who is her own daughter, a famous authoress and a noted German physician. In order to rob her of her money these people, according to her sworn assertions, wished to have her declared insane and placed in an asylum. Their scheme was not to have two venal doctors pronounce her demented and then to bury her out of the sight of the world, but to actually deprive her of her senses through the use of a terrible drug administered in such excessive doses that to continue them for any length of time would mean death.[246]

During the year 1889, Harriet Hubbard Ayer was sued or brought suit against others five times. The multiple lawsuits she instituted were not only against James Seymour, her son-in-law, Lewis and her own daughter Hattie, but also against her former employer Obadiah Sypher. Adding to her distress was the seemingly frivolous suit against her by a trusted former employee, Lutie Mason Frenzel, and last but not least, one for the custody of Margaret brought by her irresponsible former husband, Herbert.

Out of necessity, Harriet had become successful as the first woman ever to create her own cosmetic business, and now she was being publicly penalized by two of the principal men in her life. Unfortunately for her, this was the same year that her paramour, General Edward Burd Grubb, was running for public office, so it is no wonder that he had recently severed his relationship with her (or she with him).

AYER V. SEYMOUR

Just three years after James Seymour financed Harriet Hubbard Ayer's company, Récamier Toilet Preparations, Inc., and soon after she had returned from Stuttgart, where her daughters were studying with the "famous authoress" Blanche Willis Howard, Harriet brought a suit against Seymour and his cohorts. In her absence, Seymour had appointed himself assistant treasurer of Récamier Manufacturing Company and his son, Allen Lewis Seymour, treasurer, and he gave Hattie a number of shares, thereby making her an accomplice. Together they had plotted to drug Harriet in order to keep her in Europe while they took over her business. Harriet sued them for the recovery of 498 shares of the Récamier Company's stock that she had issued and given to Seymour as collateral for the $50,000 he had loaned her. That number of shares would have given him almost half ownership of the company's stock, but since Harriet had repaid the loan by August 1888, she insisted that the stock be returned to her. Apparently, the Seymours, in addition to withholding her stock, were stealing money from the company's funds. Harriet also brought a suit against the Récamier Company for the recovery of $20,000 she alleged was stolen.

Before dealing with the return of her shares, Harriet's attorney, Stephen Olin, asked the court to take immediate action to prevent the shares from being voted on and appropriated at a forthcoming shareholders meeting and to prevent further funds from being pilfered.[247] Of course, Seymour's lawyers fought that injunction, saying Harriet had no power to prevent the meeting. In spite of that, Harriet won the injunction, but this was just the beginning. She then had to produce affidavits to prove Seymour's wrongdoing.[248]

Olin's legal brief revealed that of the 1,000 shares in the company, Harriet owned 968 (498 of which were Seymour's collateral); her son-in-law owned 1 share, and Albert T. Watson, a telegraph operator in Seymour's employ, owned another. Harriet, perhaps all too casually, had dispersed a small number of shares to some of her employees. The brief also disclosed that the illegal meeting was to be held on May 15 to ratify the takeover planned in Harriet's absence.[249] The question put to the court was whether the president alone could authorize the date, time and place for meetings. Judge Joseph F. Daly, citing other similar cases, determined that under the current circumstances of wrongful diversion of company funds, Harriet had right on her side, and the motion by James Seymour et al. to hold a meeting without her was denied. This was a highly unusual decision, not only because Harriet was a woman suing a man but also because a majority of the board could indeed legitimately call a meeting.[250]

As soon as the judge determined that no meeting should be held without her, Harriet held her own meeting, and she, along with George D. Beatty and John E. Eustus, was elected a trustee for the year ending on May 1, 1890. William D. Leonard, representing Mrs. Ayer, presided at the meeting and voted her shares. Allen Lewis Seymour, her son-in-law, and Mr. Watson were present, and each voted on their own single shares. The 498 shares in dispute were not voted on. Of the shares belonging to Récamier firm members, Daniel G. Thompson represented a Mr. Robinson, who had recently transferred his 30 shares to Mrs. Lutie Mason, Harriet's former assistant, who was also present. None of these shares could be voted on as the transfers were too recent. The outcome of this court decision was that the old board, consisting of Harriet, Albert Watson and Lewis Seymour, was dissolved, and the Seymours were restrained from selling the company stock.[251]

While Harriet had already withstood the embarrassment of devolving from a fabulously wealthy Chicago matron into a sales clerk in a furniture shop and then finally evolving into a successful entrepreneur, she was now being accused of incompetence and disreputable behavior. The worst defamation was yet to come. It was difficult for her to maintain her equilibrium during the trials, yet she preserved her outer composure, especially in front of her adversaries, James Seymour and his son, by continuing to dress with great style and elegance, clandestinely using makeup to bring color to her pale cheeks and lips. In the face of the horrendous accusations that followed, she kept her sanity and controlled her anguish. Clearly, these trials and tribulations contributed to her already beleaguered physical state and ultimately led to accusations of insanity.

Harriet, with her lawyers, Stephen Olin and Austen G. Fox, confronted James Seymour in the New York Court of Common Pleas, charging him with not only conspiracy to defraud her but also attempting to poison her. She told about her departure for Europe in December 1888 to see her daughter and the plot to poison her with overdoses of sulfonal, proof of which she found when she returned to New York on February 25, 1889:

> *In May 1888, she believes James M. Seymour and Allen Lewis Seymour conspired against her to get possession of the stock, and also tried to have her rendered or declared insane and therefore unfit to manage her business. They gave her, she says, drugs in excessive quantities, bromide of Lithia and sulfonal (both hypnotic drugs), and tried to persuade her daughter that she was not sane. After she reached Europe, she declares, the Seymours were notified of her every movement, and by various means tried to prevent her return. After a meeting of the company, held June 2, 1888, of which she says she was not notified, James M. Seymour was elected Assistant Treasurer, she alleges that he went to her residence, 120 West Thirteenth Street, broke into a closet and trunks, and took valuable papers.*[252]

James Seymour, accused of trying to drug her with potions, claimed that Harriet's physician, Dr. George F. Schrady, had prescribed them. Under false pretenses, Seymour also had obtained her medical reports from Dr. William J. Pinkham, at whose sanitarium Harriet had stayed from June 25 to November 15, 1888. Harriet had chronic insomnia and intense headaches exacerbated by exhaustion and therefore was frequently under treatment by physicians.[253]

Sulfonal, a sleep-inducing drug used at the time to treat depression and urinary tract problems, was not commonly used in the United States, although Dr. Schrady said he occasionally gave it to Harriet in small doses. It was a new remedy of German origin and had been prescribed by Dr. Teuffel. Dr. Ransom Dexter, an outside American expert, maintained that he used sulfonal in cases of insomnia with uniform success. When this odorless, tasteless powder is administered in doses of fifteen grains, it brings on sleep within the hour with no side effects. Given more frequently or in larger doses, it is dangerous and can have fatal consequences. Although Dr. Teuffel prescribed this drug, it was Blanche who administered it in sizeable doses, the long-term effects of which were catastrophic.[254] Judge Daly wrote in his published opinion:

> *The amount of the dose and the frequency of its administration appears from one of the prescriptions as put up, and which was produced before me,*

*to be as alleged by the plaintiff, and thus to corroborate her maid as to the
actual doses given; and the evidence of the two American physicians now
before me is quite positive as to the injurious effect of such treatment, thus
corroborating the testimony of the maid as to the actual condition of the
plaintiff after taking the remedies prescribed.*

He went on to say, however, that foreign physicians testified that the treatment
by such a drug was beneficial and that he could not be sure of the complicity
of Blanche Howard, therefore he could not comment on it.

*The pertinent subject is whether the defendants intended to or believed they
could use Miss Howard and the means employed in plaintiff's treatment
while abroad to carry out their alleged scheme to keep plaintiff out of the
country for their own purposes. Upon this point there can be no room for
doubt, the most conclusive evidence against them being furnished by the
admissions of A. Lewis Seymour, and by oath of James M. Seymour, as
well as the circumstances already detailed.*[255]

The sensational story was carried in newspapers across the United States,
including New Jersey's *Trenton Times* on May 21, close to Seymour's home in
Orange, New Jersey, where he, his wife Carolyn and his sons James Jr. and
A. Lewis lived.

*Mrs. Ayer's counsel claimed that, in pursuance of a conspiracy to rob Mrs.
Ayer of her stock, to destroy her reason, place her in an asylum for the insane
and ultimately secure her entire property, her life had been endangered, her
health permanently wrecked and her business irreparably injured.*[256]

In his defense, Seymour's lawyers, General Roger A. Pryor and Edward
Hamilton Cahill, claimed that the stock Harriet had given Seymour was
not collateral, but that he indeed owned the stock and therefore had the
right to take over the business. He had given the stock to his daughter-in-
law and denied that he had tried to poison Harriet to keep her in Europe.
Lewis denied any wrongdoing as well, and Hattie did not appear in court,
as she was pregnant and unwell. James Seymour told so many lies that
Judge Daly was disinclined to believe his defense and trusted the testimony
of other witnesses.

Lena Raymond recounted how Harriet was drugged and rendered unconscious by Blanche Willis Howard and Dr. Teuffel, and she gave affidavits and testimonies on Harriet's behalf. Harriet's cook, Amelia Queen, swore that Seymour entered Harriet's town house at 120 West Thirteenth Street under false pretenses, broke into her closet and trunks and stole her company papers and private medical reports. Also, Mr. Henry T. Thomas told of falsifying the telegram from General Grubb to Harriet asking her to meet him in Paris and of James Seymour's connection to Blanche.

For the defense, there were letters from Dr. Teuffel attesting to the fact that Harriet was an alcoholic and letters from Harriet's younger daughter, Margaret, who was still in the clutches of Blanche Howard. Margaret wrote to her sister Hattie saying their mother was "an awfully bad woman" who had "a dreadful habit" and "makes everyone hate her. How I wish our mother was good. It's awful, and the only thing we can do is to try and make ourselves as much unlike her as we can. I think it was very mean of her to leave papa as soon as he lost his money." Harriet had actually left Herbert before the demise of his company and not because of his financial losses. The most damning evidence on behalf of the defense were letters from Margaret reiterating the lies that Blanche had fed her. Margaret said that she was glad when her mother departed for Paris because she was morally insane.

Letters from Margaret to her mother were published. They claimed that Blanche had tried to make her decent since she was an awful little girl who lied like her mother when she arrived in Stuttgart.[257] Blanche's own letters repeat that Margaret was not a nice girl. To her grandmother, Madame Hubbard, Margaret wrote that Blanche did not dictate the letters published in the newspapers. Letters from other girls corroborated that Harriet used coarse language, told low jokes, laughed loudly and was very excitable due to the excessive brandy she drank. When the brandy was removed, she drank perfume and became delusional. They also verified that she had become unconscious.[258] With all that is known about Harriet, she was not given to coarse language or unseemly behavior.

Blanche's letters underscored what the girls had written:

> She is cruel, selfish and ignoble. I have watched these traits for one month, in which she has not taken one drop of alcohol. I may be wrong in my prognostications, but I believe that only death would cure her excesses or her lies.[259]

She intimated that there was more to Harriet's ignoble behavior than addiction, possibly insanity or immorality. Blanche clearly had besmirched Harriet's image in the eyes of Margaret and Hattie. When the Paris edition of the *New York Herald Tribune* published a short paragraph about the trials, Blanche answered that she was hounded and insulted by the ruinous lies tarnishing her reputation. In her published defense, she continued to speak against Harriet: "A lady cannot reply in detail to a crazy, colossal falsehood, pathologically interesting no doubt…but beneath discussion." Blanche went on to call Harriet "a careless and indifferent mother, several degrees baser than a hired murderer."[260]

The words of each witness were described in detail. Amelia Queen reiterated that Mr. Seymour appeared at Harriet's house not once, but twice. The first time, she withheld from him the contents of the closet, and he only saw a box. The second time, he broke into the closet and removed the papers he wanted, leaving others scattered on the floor and on the bed. Lena Raymond told the dreadful tale of how Blanche fed the drug to Harriet several times a day until she became unconscious. Harriet was unconscious and delirious for twelve days, from December 29, 1888, to January 10, 1889. Recognizing the danger of her mistress's condition, Lena assured Blanche that she could dispense the medicine and was duly instructed how to administer it. She then began to substitute a chalk powder instead of the lethal one, and Harriet began to recover. Every once in a while, Blanche slipped Harriet the drug, and she took a step backward, but she slowly became lucid enough for Lena to make her understand what was being done to her. Harriet then refused to see Dr. Teuffel, and another doctor, who was in touch with Dr. Schrady, was called in. Dr. Pinkham also described how Seymour had tricked him into revealing Harriet's medical history. All of that information, combined with Henry Thomas's description of the deceitful telegram, made for a strong case against the Seymours.

Blanche Howard was in constant contact with the Seymours. She provided them with information about Harriet's health and treatment and censored Harriet's private letters to Margaret.[261] She implored Harriet to allow Dr. Teuffel to treat her for her insomnia and cabled the Seymours that treatment was to begin on December 26. Blanche gave Harriet fifteen grains of sulfonal every half hour. She insisted that she was in touch with Dr. Schrady, who authorized this treatment, which claim Dr. Schrady later denied. It was then that Harriet thought she might die and told Lena to contact General Grubb to take care of her children should that occasion arise. She told him that she was planning to sail home on the *Umbria* on February 2. It was at this moment that the Seymours sent Harriet the false telegram informing her that Grubb would be coming to Europe to meet her. Of course, the Seymours denied these accusations.

Harriet reportedly had originally been under the care of Dr. J.B. Madison of Brooklyn for her long-standing addiction to morphine. In consultation with Dr. Schrady, she was sent to Dr. Pinkham's sanitarium in Montclair, New Jersey, in June 1888. Dr. Pinkham allegedly cured her of her morphine addiction but substituted alcohol instead.[262] Under the influence of her new habit, she may have behaved boisterously and exhibited the behavior Margaret referred to in her letters, in contradiction to other reports that Harriet was suffering from hemoptysis insomnia; that is, coughing up blood in addition to not being able to sleep. Judge Daly reviewed the affidavit of Henry T. Thomas regarding misleading cablegrams sent to Mrs. Ayer and damaging admissions made to Mr. Thomas by Seymour:

> *This evidence clearly establishes, as I have said, that the defendants, James M. Seymour and A. Lewis Seymour were engaged in the efforts to keep the plaintiff out of the country, and away from the management of the business, which was entirely in their hands and under their control. The plaintiff has shown satisfactorily that of the 1,000 shares of the stock of the company she is the owner of 968, while the defendant A. Lewis Seymour owns but one share, and the defendant James M. Seymour none, that she is excluded from management of the company by the claim set up by them to the 498 shares and by the transfer of such shares, and that injury is to be apprehended to the plaintiff's stocks and interests by the alleged acts of the defendants, James M. Seymour and his son. The injunction is continued and receiver pendente lite will be appointed,* [that is, pending the time the litigation is settled].[263]

By the end of May, Judge Daly appointed a receiver, Richard M. Henry, to hold the shares until the legal contest was over. The receiver had to give a bond of $25,000. On June 5, 1889, the Supreme Court upheld the election of new trustees held on May 27, 1889. Harriet remained as president, John E. Eustis was trustee and George D. Beatty was the new treasurer. All of the shares were returned to her and the monies cleared up, with Mr. Seymour receiving $6,000 from Mrs. Ayer. Lutie Mason Frenzel still owned thirty shares. Allen Lewis Seymour retained his one share, as did former trustee Albert Watson.

Hattie issued a statement saying she had not wanted to sue her mother; in fact, she had offered to return the stocks her father-in-law had given her even before the trial. She said that this litigation had brought her grief and mortification but that her father fully approved of all her actions. In fact, her father wanted to represent her and her shares in the trial, but the judge rejected him as a substitute.[264] Harriet was not only fighting the spurned and avaricious James Seymour but also the covert manipulation of her rejected husband. The newspapers finally announced, "Mrs. Ayer is the Victor, She Defeats and Ousts the Seymour Family."[265] The judge said he could not rule on the medical treatment or the private arrangement Harriet made with Seymour for the loan, but clearly the intent was to defraud and appropriate Harriet's rightful property. The defense had focused on the alleged addictions that led to Harriet's pitiable mental state, rendering her unable to manage the Récamier Corporation.

For Harriet, however, it was another Pyrrhic victory. The next day, the papers reported that she had to sell all she owned to pay the legal fees. Not one to forget her audience, she sent a public thank-you note to the more than twelve hundred people who sent letters and telegrams of support, sympathy and congratulations: "In the darkest hour of my life the quick response to my position as a mother battling for her children came to me as a benediction and will remain with me always." It was signed "Harriet Hubbard Ayer, Hotel Victoria, New York City, Friday, June 7, 1889."[266]

Why did James Seymour, a multimillionaire, resort to such deception and thievery? Why was he so desperate to gain control of the Récamier Company? After several fraudulent schemes in which all investors lost money while he walked away with millions, he was casting about for something new for himself and Lewis. Seymour's financial trouble regarding the Phoenix Mine was exacerbated in December 1888 when the stockholders decided to investigate him and found bogus charges amounting to $12,000. These and other liens and claims added up to $20,000. The sale of the mine was advertised to satisfy these claims, and a committee was appointed to straighten out the company's affairs. Other people took over in order to save the mining company. James Seymour's Phoenix Mine shares were sold to "the poorest classes, elevator operators and shop girls for a dollar. It was called the 'cruelest swindle ever.'" The article went on to say:

> *The Government committee of the stock exchange made an examination, withdrew the stock of the mine from its list, and made things so unpleasant for Seymour that, last November* [1888] *he retired from business.*[267]

Therefore, James and Lewis Seymour needed to find a new business, and they thought they could seize the Récamier company from Harriet.

Seymour and his associates were forced to close their offices in September 1889. It was a serious situation for Seymour, who did not even list an office address in the 1889–90 New York city directory. In fact, the United States marshal levied a writ of attachment on his property because of a suit brought against him by his former engineer, Mr. Treadwell of Brooklyn. Treadwell wanted an account of the stock transaction profits of the Phoenix Mine operations. With all Seymour's financial and business problems, it is no wonder that he tried aggressively to take over Harriet's company, which reportedly was earning over $1 million yearly.

> *Foreseeing the necessity of retiring from Wall Street after the bursting of Phoenix, Mr. Seymour looked around for some occupation for his son Lewis, whom he had trained strictly after his own financial methods. Mrs. Ayer had made some little headway with her Récamier preparations and Seymour jumped at the project of putting his son with the business.*[268]

Some people insinuated that Harriet attached herself to Seymour hoping for an alliance with this multimillionaire. She agreed to take his son Lewis to Europe with her for some surgery he needed and also for him to see her daughter Hattie, even though Mrs. Seymour did not "countenance the marriage." The relationship between Harriet and James Seymour was friendly until he took unscrupulous steps to drug her, steal her papers, lie about her and try to appropriate her business.[269] Despite the judgment against him, in May 1889, Seymour and his cohorts held on to Harriet's office at 52 Park Place. Seymour physically took over Harriet's office, "garrisoned the place with a number of detectives and hired employees, and prepared to resist any attempts made by Mrs. Ayer to gain possession."[270] Her lawyer, Stephen Olin, said he would apply for an order to vacate. In the meantime, Harriet, ensconced at the Victoria Hotel, was reported to be ill, and her condition was critical. "She is troubled with hemorrhages and insomnia."[271] Harriet bided her time until the Supreme Court ordered Seymour to leave in June.

LUTIE MASON FRENZEL V. HARRIET HUBBARD AYER

Still reeling from the lawsuit against the Seymours, Harriet was sued one month later in July by her former "right-hand man," Lutie Mason, now Mrs. Arthur B. Frenzel. The complaint was summarized:

> *Mrs. Lutie Frenzel yesterday secured an injunction in the supreme court from Judge Andrews, restraining Mrs. Harriet Hubbard Ayer from selling 470 shares of the Récamier Manufacturing Company. Mrs. Frenzel was in the employ of the Récamier Company when she was Miss Mason, and alleges that she is entitled to an interest in the business and owns some of the recipes. Mrs. Ayer says that she discharged her when she resumed sway at the Récamier Manufacturing Company's office, and that the action is the most diminutive order of Blackmail. She turned the papers over to her lawyers, Olin, Rives & Montgomery, and doesn't intend to lose any sleep over the matter.[272]*

The *Chicago Tribune* kept track of Harriet's affairs even though she and her former husband had, by and large, left the city by 1883. "Mrs. Frenzel says it was she and not a kind old countess who concocted the toilet cream." Quoting from an affidavit, she said that Harriet gave her the idea that there were enormous profits to be made in cosmetics and that she would find the capital if Mrs. Frenzel would invent the formula. Mrs. Frenzel then took Harriet's French-made cream to a chemist, who analyzed the contents, and she, with apparatus borrowed from Professor Thomas Stillman, succeeded in making the compound and devising the attractive containers. She even found a less expensive ingredient for Harriet's powder and urged Harriet to cease making false claims about the origin of the products. Mrs. Frenzel went on trips to other cities, including to the American Exhibition in London, to promote the products. Harriet allegedly assured Mrs. Frenzel of a yearly salary of $5,000 if she could acquire the patronage of the Princess of Wales or other royalty. Mrs. Frenzel also accused Harriet of being "extravagant in her management of the business." She knew that Harriet received financial support from James Seymour but insinuated that not all of it was used for the business but rather for her "personal convenience."

It is possible that Harriet's personal and business accounts were intermingled, but she surely used most of the money to advance and advertise her business. Not only was this a nuisance suit, but it was also a great disappointment in human relations for Harriet. Lutie Mason had known Harriet in Chicago and went to work for her in 1884 before the advent of the Récamier Company. She had even testified on Harriet's behalf at her divorce proceedings in 1886. As her personal secretary and confidante, and one of the few people who were trusted with the formula for Récamier cream, Mrs. Frenzel turned against Harriet under the influence of James Seymour, which action led to her being fired. Perhaps this frivolous suit was filed in retribution for being fired, or perhaps her new husband saw it as a way to make some quick money. But the worst damage that Frenzel caused was to place doubt among consumers about the origins of Récamier products and the romantic connection of French royalty. The much-publicized trial, while it temporarily damaged Harriet's commercial reputation, could not erase the sympathy people felt for Harriet's personal hardships as a deserted single mother trying to support her children.

The ingredients of Récamier Cream and Balm and Vita Nuova revealed in the newspapers were similar to those listed in Oleson's *Secret Nostrums and Systems of Medicine*. For the cream, they listed the following ingredients: rice flour, cocoa butter, lard and mercury chloride, in addition to the contents previously mentioned. The cost of making a dozen jars was declared to be $4.80, which is only forty cents per jar, which Harriet then sold for $1.50. Advertisements claimed that there was no arsenic, bismuth or zinc, but substantial amounts of zinc were found in many Récamier products. The last accusation by Frenzel was that Hattie Ayer Seymour did not owe her wonderful complexion to Récamier Cream, although her mother purports that she did.[273]

At first, Mrs. Frenzel's lawyer, B. F. Watson, asked Judge Andrews to placed a restraining injunction against Harriet's selling stock, but this suit was denied. Mrs. Frenzel and another lawyer, George L. Hoffman, filed an appeal on February 24, 1890. "During the course of this action, as well as in the other litigations above referred to, every possible effort had been made by

Mrs. Ayer's opponents to harass and annoy her, and deponent believes that this proceeding is instituted for the same purpose."[274] Harriet's retort was: "This petition is of the most primitive order of blackmail."[275] Ultimately, the court did not believe that the Frenzel suit had merit. On August 25, 1891, Mrs. Frenzel's motion was denied. But it took that long for this little thorn to be removed from Harriet's side.

AYER V. SYPHER

In June, Harriet instituted a suit against her former boss, Obadiah L. Sypher and the Sypher & Co., to recover salary and commissions she earned in 1883 and 1884. Olin, Reeves & Montgomery represented her again. "A motion will be made next week by the defendants on the ground of non-prosecution." This was possibly because of delay and inactivity on the part of Harriet.[276] That Sypher would have taken advantage of Harriet as a single mother and sole supporter of her children seems implausible, yet she had formerly been a wealthy client, and perhaps he thought he could get away with cheating her of her rightful salary. Or perhaps it was a mistake. At this moment, Harriet needed any monies due her to pay court and legal fees.

AYER V. AYER: CUSTODY SUIT

Only a few weeks later, on July 21, 1889, a suit was drawn by Herbert Ayer to regain custody of his daughter Margaret. This was the final blow. Harriet declared war. A reporter interviewed her in the parlor of her town house on West Thirteenth Street in Manhattan. With flashing eyes, stamping her foot on the carpet for emphasis, she told the reporter that if they wanted war, they should have it. Almost simultaneously, Herbert Ayer was reportedly on his way to Europe, a trip paid for by James Seymour, allegedly to take possession of Margaret. James Seymour was questioned as well, and he said that Herbert was merely going to visit Margaret, not to kidnap her.[277]

Harriet conjectured that it was at the instigation of the Seymours that Herbert was suing her, part of their grand scheme to ruin her morally and financially. James Seymour was endlessly vengeful. Herbert, having been divorced by Harriet, also seemingly wanted his pound of flesh. Harriet defended herself, saying that for the last seven years she alone had taken care of her daughters, and suddenly he is "seized with responsibility." She laid the greatest blame on Blanche Howard, who had tried to drug her into insanity or to death and had turned her daughters against her. She iterated that she had heard of Blanche through Reverend and Mrs. John Locke of Chicago, who sent their daughter to study with Blanche, and noted that they too were now dissatisfied with Blanche.

Things took a turn for the worse on November 14, 1889, when Judge Shepard gave custody of Margaret to Herbert until further order of the court and instructed Harriet to give up all claims for alimony and resign her position as guardian.[278] A referee was appointed to take testimony, and the hearings were held behind closed doors. It was rumored that Harriet was accused of having an illicit affair with a "famous Republican politician who ran a few years ago as a candidate for governor of his state and that other charges of a similar nature, connecting her with other men [actor John McCullough], had also been brought forth." The famous Republican was, of course, General Grubb, who ran for the office of governor of New Jersey in 1889, just as Harriet's notorious trials were being aired.[279]

The documents on file at the Superior Court of Cook County reveal a petition dated June 1889 by Harriet against Herbert. Here, Harriet resigned guardianship of Margaret to avoid litigation until Margaret was old enough to decide for herself which parent should retain legal custody. Harriet certified the actual petition in person on November 8, 1889. On that same day, Harriet swore before a notary public that she had never received alimony from Herbert and that she released him from any further claim for alimony. On November 14, Herbert filed a petition in court stating that he had recently visited Stuttgart but was unable to see Margaret. He also wanted to wait until she was of legal age to make the choice herself about her guardian. "The warm and natural relationship of father and daughter has always existed between them, and that it is the wish and desire of said child that your petitioner become the legal as he is her natural guardian, and the one to whom she must turn for the provision of her wants."[280] The petition goes on to say that Herbert, the petitioner, should be appointed guardian of the child and that previous decrees should be modified accordingly. It is surprising that the court would believe Herbert's petition when Harriet had been carrying the burden of child support alone since her separation from Herbert in 1883—explicit evidence of legal gender prejudice. Margaret was given over to her father's custody for a very short time. About ten days later, a settlement was reached in which Harriet retained possession of Margaret. Mr. Ayer withdrew his petition for custody, together with his charges that his wife was a morphine addict. In return, Harriet renounced any claim for alimony, current or future.[281] Once again, Harriet's competency and sanity were questioned, and once again she won in court.

On May 18, 1890, Harriet wrote a most revealing letter to Margaret informing her of the court's decision:

My Dear Child,

By the decision of the court you are at fourteen entitled to choose your own guardian. It is my desire you should know in case you wish to return to me I am ready to receive you. I know that in the past you have been influenced and your mind [has been turned] *against me but I find it possible to forgive in a child what I must not condone in a woman.*

If you decide to take upon your self the crime of repudiating your mother I have nothing to say. The condemnation and disgrace in this [illeg.] *alone, which will certainly follow you if you take this course will be a heavier punishment that I could wish ever to befall you. For my own vindication however you must know that in choosing to be dependent upon others you definitely renounce all claims upon me and from my estate. My will has been most carefully drawn up, a copy of this letter with a complete and authentic record of the events which make it necessary to write it have been attached to and are a part of my will and my attorneys and executors have been carefully and minutely instructed in the matter. When you kissed me and embraced me day after day in Stuttgart even at the station as I bade you goodbye I could not have believed that even when you had been taught to act so hideous a lie to your mother and that the hand so often and so lovingly about my neck had already written the terrible letters since published in hundreds of newspapers to the everlasting dishonor of the people who are accountable for them. You cannot realize how these letters have branded you. How all your life long unless you atone for the writing of them people of all nations will condemn and mercilessly denounce you as the woman who when a little child defamed her mother who bore her. The woman whom the world respects must stand by her mother. You will one day see how right I am. God grant you may not also some day when too late find yourself alone,*

*penniless and outcast and your life ruined through your own misguided
course. Should that day come I charge you to remember it has been through
no fault of your mother.*
Harriet Hubbard Ayer

There are few extant letters in Harriet's hand, and this one reveals not only
her hurt feelings but also that she could be dually forgiving and strong. She
threatened Margaret with expunging her from her will, a harsh punishment
for the young girl. Margaret had to choose between her mother and Blanche,
a parental substitute who was no longer kind and loving. The letter is torn in
pieces, which could mean that Blanche shredded it and never showed it to
Margaret or that Margaret tore it up after reading it and Blanche kept it.[282]

Conclusion of *Ayer v. Seymour*

It took from July to November 1889 for the case against the Seymours
and Blanche Howard to come before the United States commissioner,
Mr. Shields. A salesman for Harriet's company, John C. Stone, testified
further that at Seymour's request he had Mrs. Ayer's letters delivered to a
post office box under Seymour's control and that he saw Seymour reading
her mail. Another employee testified that Seymour had ordered him to
obtain copies of telegrams sent by Mrs. Ayer to "Dr. Peekinham [*sic*] of
Montclair, N.J." A typist swore that she typed a letter requesting Western
Union Telegraph Company to release copies of Harriet's telegrams to
Seymour. The Telegraph Company complied because the letters bore
Harriet's name.

The most damning testimony came from the publisher Henry T. Thomas.
Harriet had written to Hattie to come to Europe to fetch her and was told
falsely that Hattie was on the way. Hattie told Mr. Thomas that she could not
go because her husband was detained by a lawsuit. Harriet knew nothing
about her daughter's inability to rescue her. Seymour told Mr. Thomas
that Harriet was "not mentally responsible" and that "no reliance [should]
be placed on anything she said or did." Harriet told Mr. Thomas that she
wanted to return home and that she was going to contact her lawyer. Lewis
Seymour told Mr. Thomas that he did not want her to return and that if she
did, he would not allow Hattie to see her because Harriet had accused him

of tampering with the books before she left. He also said that her physical illness was feigned and her mind was not right. At another time, Lewis admitted that Harriet might not return because he "had taken care of that." He admitted that he had sent a telegram to Paris and signed it Grubb, which he thought was very clever of him. He said he had not told anyone of this, not even his wife. He continued that Miss Howard would not relinquish Margaret to Harriet and would fight to keep the girl. When confronted, Lewis did not deny any of Thomas's statement. And with this, Judge Daly definitively decided that the Seymours "were engaged in the effort to keep the plaintiff out of the country, and away from the management of her business, which was entirely in their hands and under their control."[283] So it seems that Lewis was equally as involved as his father.

While Harriet's reputation was sullied by public accusations that she was a morphine addict and alcoholic, a negligent mother and unfit to run her business, amazingly there were no repercussions for James and Lewis Seymour other than negative publicity. They were not fined or incarcerated for attempted murder, disparagement of character or loss of business. They had to close their office and desist from their brokerage business because of other fraudulent scams that had occurred before the trials.

Harriet may have won all these legal battles against James Seymour and his entourage, but this unscrupulous man was relentless in taking further revenge.[284] The repeated lawsuits in 1889 not only debilitated Harriet mentally and physically, but they also depleted her financial resources, further alienated her children and affected her business negatively. Given her determination to maintain her independence and control of the Récamier Company, Harriet still had to contend with this persistent enemy.

AFTER-THE-TRIAL TRIBULATIONS

Harriet was not only totally alienated from her daughters, but also, once again, she lost her house and belongings in order to pay the lawyers' and court fees. Although she had periods of depression—and with good reason—her pluck and perseverance somehow endured. Even while she was busy with court appearances, she continued to advertise Récamier products. *Harper's Weekly* had a very long advertorial that repeated many of the endorsements mentioned previously.[285] It included letters from actresses,

Harriet's discovery of the cream's formula, doctor's assertions about the reliability of her products and her remarkable success.

Meanwhile, Harriet's furnishings were offered for sale in twelve hundred lots that included antique furniture, bric-a-brac, Japanese and Oriental hangings, valuable paintings and china. Bidding among fashionably dressed women was spirited, yet objects sold for much less than their actual value. Among the items sold were a piano, a carved oak desk, oil paintings, a watercolor of an Arab by Fortuny and a fine collection of china, including Dresden, Royal Derby and Meissen. Everything sold except the portraits of Harriet. The contents show that Harriet had once again accumulated valuable antiques and paintings.[286] The termination of her town house on West Thirteenth Street and her belongings represented a second forced sale for Harriet (the first having been when her Chicago home and its contents were sold to pay Herbert's debts). The New York City directory between 1890 and 1893 listed Harriet Ayer as resident at 305 Fifth Avenue, corroborating her move. That area was bursting with upper echelon apartment houses full of potential cosmetic customers. Her new apartment above her store on Fifth Avenue was reportedly luxurious.[287]

Yet an article in April 1890 about events in Washington, focusing on the opulence of houses, dinners and jewels, devoted a paragraph to Harriet's jewels. It claimed that although she owned them, she did not wear them at that time:

> In her collection were fifteen necklaces of pearls, each pearl as big as a filbert; and there was a necklace of rubies set in diamonds. One of those rubies was an inch long, three-fourths of an inch wide and an inch thick. It had belonged to an Indian rajah, and had never been cut. She had several pear shaped diamonds, and one of these, she said, had belonged to Cardinal Mazarin, and had been worn by him 200 years ago as buttons on his gown. A number of her diamonds were worth $5,000 a piece, and she had $200,000 worth of jewelry which she was carrying around in her trunk.[288]

One has to wonder whether this summary of her jewels was grossly exaggerated, given that she had just sold her house and other belongings to pay for her court and legal fees. Another explanation may be that she invested in historic jewelry for resale to her clients, and these were impermanent business assets.[289] Nevertheless, she was back at work by June, proclaiming, "On Tuesday, June 4th, 1889, I resumed entire control and management of the above named company [Récamier]. All mail and matter of a personal nature should be so marked." She then listed her name and her title. Although Harriet revived after her legal ordeals and continued her business, the trials took a toll on her health. She had suffered extreme distress, which had physical and mental repercussions, necessitating her periodic removal to quiet places in Long Island for rest and recuperation. She also traveled abroad, leaving on June 4, 1891, for Liverpool on the *Teutonic*, a White Star ocean liner, and arrived back from Liverpool on board the *Majestic* on July 8, 1891.[290]

After the trials, Harriet apparently stopped paying Margaret's tuition and board. In a letter to Hattie, Blanche wrote that James Seymour was angered, and he, too, stopped paying for Margaret. Blanche tried to get Hattie to pay Margaret's tuition for old times' sake: "I hold you guilty of a wrong towards Margaret and towards me." She accused Hattie of poor judgment and childishness. "How can you wear one jewel while your sister is supported by others?"[291] Blanche ended by saying she would support Margaret on her own if she had to. But by this time, Blanche had little patience for Margaret. In letters to her niece, Marion Stuart Smith, circa 1891, Blanche wrote that Margaret was "a treacherous lying gaudy person who loves food better than Wawie Howard." And in another letter she said, "It is simply a thing for me to bear Margaret."[292] So Blanche, too, was upset by the trials and accusations against her that were published in the newspapers. It surely affected her ability to attract new students but not her long-term relationship with Dr. von Teuffel, whom she married in 1890.

Somehow, despite all the trauma, hard work and anxiety in her life, Harriet managed to find the time to translate from French Baroness Staffe's *My Lady's Dressing Room* in 1892. The French Harriet had learned in 1872 while recuperating in Paris from the death of her daughter still served her. Baroness Staffe, who was an arbiter of elegance and beauty, wrote this book about social etiquette, dress, domestic skills and beauty, with an underlying theme of courtesy and mutual respect.[293] Harriet both translated and annotated it, presaging future articles she would write about health, beauty and manners that were eventually incorporated into a book of her own. According to an undocumented article of the 1880s:

Mrs. Ayer found time to add a graceful volume to the literature of the manners of this epoch. Her book, "My Lady's Dressing Table," will not be overlooked by the historians of the future who wish to know how we looked and walked and talked in the latter end of the 19ᵗʰ century. Mrs. Ayer's style is piquant and—rare combination—graceful and sententious at the same time. It charms and while it seems light and tripping, it is really serious. Mrs. Ayer's book is like herself, endowed with delicacy, point and grace. That she could make a treatise on the toilet acceptable to men, is as paradoxical as that the writer herself should have earned a claim to celebrity by success as a business woman.[294]

For the next year or so, only advertisements and advertorials bearing her name appeared in the news. The only sad occurrence was the death of her mother, on October 22, 1892. Madame Hubbard had been quite ill with endemic dysentery and chronic albuminuria, a kidney ailment. Her death certificate specifies that she was buried at Rosedale Cemetery in Chicago, but that cemetery has no record of her.[295] Harriet's life was in order after her recuperation, and her business was still running well, until the Seymours, aided and abetted by Herbert Ayer, began their next assault in 1893.

Figure 1. Photograph of Harriet Hubbard Ayer, 1870s. *Collection of the Chicago Historical Museum Library.*

Figure 2. Harriet Hubbard Ayer (1849–1903), wearing a Worth gown in a
photograph from circa 1872. *In Margaret Ayer and Isabella Taves,* The Three Lives of
Harriet Hubbard Ayer *(Philadelphia: J.B. Lippincott Company, 1957), following p. 64.*

Figure 3. *Harriet Hubbard Ayer* by William Merritt Chase (1849–1916), 1879. Signed and dated "Wm. M. Chase 1879" at lower right. Oil on canvas, 48 ¹/₈ by 32¼ inches. *Parrish Art Museum, Southampton, New York, museum purchase from Ayer's great-granddaughter.*

Above: Figure 4. Wood engraving of Chase's *Portrait of a Lady* (before the bottom was cut off) by Frederick Juengling (1846–1889). *In Marianna G. Van Rensselaer, "William Merritt Chase,"* American Art Review *2, no. 1 (January 1881), facing p. 92.* Negative #84160d, Collection of the New York Historical Society.

Opposite, bottom: Figure 6. *Feet* (cut from *Portrait of a Lady*) by Chase, 1880. Oil on canvas, 14 by 38 ³/₈ inches. (See p. 43.) *Graham Williford Foundation for American Art, Fairfield, Texas.*

Figure 5. *Portrait of a Lady* (Harriet Hubbard Ayer) by Chase, 1880. Oil on canvas, 27¼ by 22¼ inches. Originally signed "Wm. M. Chase" at lower left of the canvas, but the painting was cut down. Though he resigned it, the signature was inadvertently removed. *California Palace of the Legion of Honor, Fine Arts Museum of San Francisco, gift of Henry K.S. Williams.*

Figure 7. *Harriet Hubbard Ayer* by Eastman Johnson (1824–1906), 1881.
Signed and dated "E. Johnson 1881" at lower right. Oil on canvas, 72¼ by
38 ⅛ inches. *Corcoran Gallery of Art, Washington, D.C.; gift of Harriet Ayer Seymour
Macy (Mrs. Valentine E. Macy Jr., granddaughter of Harriet Ayer).*

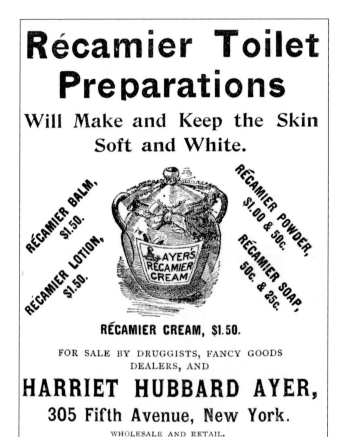

Récamier Toilet Preparations

Will Make and Keep the Skin Soft and White.

RÉCAMIER BALM, $1.50.

RÉCAMIER LOTION, $1.50.

RÉCAMIER POWDER, $1.00 & 50c.

RÉCAMIER SOAP, 50c. & 25c.

RÉCAMIER CREAM, $1.50.

FOR SALE BY DRUGGISTS, FANCY GOODS DEALERS, AND

HARRIET HUBBARD AYER,

305 Fifth Avenue, New York.

WHOLESALE AND RETAIL.

Send for Circular and Free Sample Powder.

Mention SCRIBNER'S MAGAZINE.

Right: Figure 8. Advertisement. *In* Scribner's Magazine *13 (June 1892).*

Below: Figure 9. Advertisement, 1886.

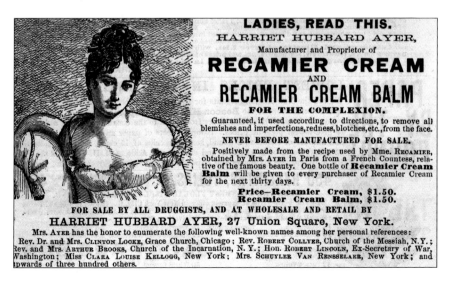

LADIES, READ THIS.

HARRIET HUBBARD AYER,

Manufacturer and Proprietor of

RECAMIER CREAM

AND

RECAMIER CREAM BALM

FOR THE COMPLEXION.

Guaranteed, if used according to directions, to remove all blemishes and imperfections, redness, blotches, etc., from the face.

NEVER BEFORE MANUFACTURED FOR SALE.

Positively made from the recipe used by Mme. RECAMIER, obtained by Mrs. AYER in Paris from a French Countess, relative of the famous beauty. One bottle of **Recamier Cream Balm** will be given to every purchaser of Recamier Cream for the next thirty days.

Price—Recamier Cream, $1.50.
Recamier Cream Balm, $1.50.

FOR SALE BY ALL DRUGGISTS, AND AT WHOLESALE AND RETAIL BY

HARRIET HUBBARD AYER, 27 Union Square, New York.

Mrs. AYER has the honor to enumerate the following well-known names among her personal references:
Rev. Dr. and Mrs. CLINTON LOCKE, Grace Church, Chicago; Rev. ROBERT COLLYER, Church of the Messiah, N.Y.; Rev. and Mrs. ARTHUR BROOKS, Church of the Incarnation, N.Y.; Hon. ROBERT LINCOLN, Ex-Secretary of War, Washington; Miss CLARA LOUISE KELLOGG, New York; Mrs. SCHUYLER VAN RENSSELAER, New York; and upwards of three hundred others.

Figure 10. Photograph of Harriet Hubbard Ayer, circa 1890s. *In* Harriet Ayer's Book,
facing p. 26.

Part IV
Insanity and Incarceration

In the Matter of
Harriet Hubbard Ayer, a Lunatic

After the trials, Harriet remained estranged from her daughters and was probably an embarrassment to her friends and family since the proceedings were broadcast publicly. With her mother dead, she was left without anyone to rely on. The fall of 1892 was also the prelude to a countrywide economic breakdown and financial failure that culminated in the depression of 1893, circumstances that must have affected her business. Harriet always had periods of mental depression, but given the extreme stress she had suffered, she began to exhibit more severe symptoms. On February 8, 1893, Dr. William James Morton, a specialist in nervous and mental diseases with an office at 10 East Twenty-eighth Street, went to see Harriet.[296] He examined her at the request of her former husband and her elder daughter. This was not the first time father and daughter had teamed up to look into Harriet's deteriorating health. Whether feigning interest or out of genuine concern, they insisted that Harriet visit this alienist rather than her own doctor, Dr. A.A. Smith.

Dr. Morton claimed that they had called him as early as October 1892. Dr. Smith stopped seeing her when she was placed under Dr. Morton's care. Since that time, Dr. Morton checked on her frequently, but it was not until February 8 that he called another specialist to verify his diagnosis. That psychiatrist, his longtime friend Dr. Graeme M. Hammond of 58 West Forty-fifth Street, had never seen Harriet before. Nevertheless, he signed the lunacy certificate for her commitment to a Bronxville asylum.[297] Dr. Morton claimed she had fixed delusions and heard voices that said improper things to her, and those voices led her to become suicidal. He ascertained that she was not under the influence of alcohol or morphine. While Dr. Hammond, a young professor of nervous diseases who was just beginning his career, confirmed Harriet's condition on the certificate of lunacy presented to Judge David McAdam in the New York Superior Court the next day, he did not appear in court.

With his colleague Dr. Hammond, Dr. Morton verified that Harriet was suffering from "melancholia and no longer capable of running her cosmetic business." Addiction to morphine and alcohol were also cited as habits that had "unsettled her mind."[298] He described her symptoms as depression and mental excitement, with a propensity for suicide. He said, "Her facial expression is that of acute misery, and her tears flow constantly. Although the doctors draw a picture so pitiable that, if their diagnosis may be relied on, there is seemingly small doubt that the career of this remarkable woman, sensational as it was romantic, may now be ended."[299] Dr. Morton's prognosis was that Harriet's condition was not "hopeless," and he was sure that with proper treatment she would be restored to full mental and physical health.

Harriet's condition might have been called a nervous breakdown after 1900. These terms cover all kinds of emotional collapses, from severe mental difficulties to milder ones, and are often a code for severe depression—or psychosis. Neurasthenia, or melancholia, inclusive of any number of nervous symptoms, was the term used in Harriet's day. It was a vague enough term that could mean anything, a catchall diagnosis that could be used by the layman as well as psychiatrists.

Thus, on a cold February morning in 1893, this well-known woman of a certain age was clandestinely abducted from her apartment on Fifth Avenue and Thirty-first Street. Accompanied by Dr. Morton and her housekeeper Lena Raymond, Harriet was removed to a private insane asylum in Bronxville, New York, a suburb north of Manhattan. The kidnapping took place quickly and quietly so that reporters could not leak the news of her incarceration. Despite all efforts to keep her commitment secret, word spread. Within two weeks, newspapers across the United States confirmed that the famous Harriet Hubbard Ayer, "known on two continents as a shrewd business woman, proprietress of a widely advertised cosmetic, and formerly a prominent social leader of great beauty," was insane.[300]

Dr. Morton maintained that Harriet went along cheerfully to the asylum, but subsequently Harriet reported that she was tricked.[301] Harriet willingly entered the carriage believing that she was going to see her daughter Hattie and her grandchildren in New Jersey. At that time, doctors did not explain diseases and treatments to their patients, and Harriet was never informed about her forthcoming incarceration. Dr. Morton believed that Herbert Ayer, who was paying him, had "only kindly motives" and was worried about the welfare of his children. He "thought with the systematic care of an institution being exercised she would mend more rapidly."[302]

As the carriage made its way up Fifth Avenue from Harriet's home, past the new department stores and shops, including her own, she looked out the window. When they arrived at Central Park, although in a depressive stupor, she noticed the skaters on the pond near Fifty-ninth Street and realized that this was not the way to Orange, New Jersey, where her daughter lived with the Seymours. As she passed the park, Harriet was able to see the skating pond, since the London plane trees that had been planted around the perimeter when it opened in the late 1850s were leafless in winter. During the first decade, the park drew more visitors for the novelty of ice-skating than in the warmer months.[303] Although she knew they were headed in the wrong direction, Harriet was too weak to protest and probably just closed her eyes or cried, as she was quick to do in her depressed state.

Only seven short years after becoming the founder and president of Récamier Preparations, Harriet Hubbard Ayer's astounding career as an independent entrepreneur came to an abrupt end. Suffering from extreme exhaustion after many legal battles to retain control of her cosmetic company and custody of her youngest daughter, she had been deceived into believing that her elder daughter had sent for her. What Harriet did not know was that her beloved Hattie and her husband, Lewis Seymour, protégé of her worst enemy, were among those who had signed the lunacy papers attesting to her aberrant behavior. It was through the machinations of James Seymour and Herbert Ayer that the plot to commit her to a mental institution was finally accomplished. As revealed in the trials, they had tried several years before to drug her and to drive her insane in order to steal her lucrative company, but they had failed. This time, their nefarious goal was achieved.

The Vernon House Retreat for the Insane in Bronxville was a handsome three-story stone house set on sixteen acres. It was built in 1863 by Robert Masterson and bought by Dr. William Granger about 1890. Having graduated from Phillips Academy and Williams College, Granger received his medical training at Harvard Medical School and Bellevue Hospital.

As a psychiatrist, his intent at Vernon House was to provide private care for a limited number of wealthy mental patients, which he did for the next twenty-six years. Vernon House was advertised in the 1898 edition of *The Medical Directory of the City of New York*, as a modern sanitarium for the care and treatment of mental and nervous diseases and cases of habit. It was touted as being only fifteen miles from New York City, "on a high elevation overlooking Long Island Sound and the Palisades, and surrounded by attractive grounds both open and shaded, beautiful scenery and charming drives." This meant it was equipped to administer moral treatment, a popular approach in the nineteenth century. Based on the concept of humane treatment and the possibility of rehabilitation of the insane, it advocated beautiful surroundings, including water, which was deemed therapeutic for the mentally deranged. Palatial manors were built in attractive settings to house the mentally ill. Dr. Granger's was the third most expensive of the eighteen private asylums in New York State at the time.[304]

After Harriet's commitment, Herbert Ayer petitioned Judge Andrews of the Supreme Court on February 27 to appoint a commission to legally declare Harriet a lunatic, the term used for the mentally ill:

> *I am not moved to this step by any personal or selfish considerations. I desire no interest in her property. I have taken this action for the purpose of protecting and guarding the name and reputation as well as to secure the peace of mind of my daughters, and that of their mother, whose failings are entirely those resultant from and attributable to her mental condition, and not from any lack of moral attributes.*[305]

Herbert claimed that when he went to her apartment at 305 Fifth Avenue, he found her "dying from the effects of morphine and other stimulants, with no one to restrain her."[306] Was his testimony believable, since he was influenced by and financially dependent on James Seymour? Was Harriet Ayer mentally ill? Was she addicted to drugs and alcohol? Should she have been sent to an insane asylum or to a sanitarium for rest and detoxification under a doctor's care?

In today's world, Harriet would have been taken off any drugs so that her condition could be properly evaluated. Then she would have been given an antidepressant and psychotherapy to alleviate the symptoms that were consistent with severe depression. Whether a propensity for mental illness was inherited, given her mother's long-term depression after the death of Harriet's father, or whether the propensity was aggravated by the unending stress in her life, there is no doubt she was depressed.[307] Having been treated for headaches and insomnia with various forms of opium—laudanum, morphine, cocaine and the like—her depression may have been exacerbated by drugs.

The use and effects of morphine, the drug perennially prescribed by Harriet's physicians for anxiety, insomnia and headaches, was widespread during the nineteenth century. Morphine, an analgesic, is effective in suppressing pain. Most opium consumed in this country during the nineteenth century was legally imported and manufactured. It was easily obtainable over the counter at pharmacies, groceries and general stores. Countless patent medicines contained opium or its derivatives, including Harriet's Vita Nuova tonic. Although these drugs were used for soldiers wounded in battle during the Civil War, opiate consumption in the United States during the nineteenth century was mainly used for relief of "female problems," such as painful menstruation. There were no moral implications in its use as there are today.

Symptoms associated with prolonged use of opiate derivative drugs are numerous and varied, including anxiety, blurred vision, depression or irritability, drowsiness, constipation or diarrhea, nausea, tremors, sedation, weakness, hallucinations, dreams, agitation, headache and loss of appetite, among others. If indeed Harriet was being treated regularly with any of the opium derivatives, her symptoms of hallucinations, agitation, sedation and weakness were consistent with opiate addiction cited in the courts as mental illness. As for alcohol, the only mention of Harriet's drinking was an aperitif or wine. It is significant that the doctors in charge of committing her did not see evidence of morphine or alcohol abuse, for if her symptoms were drug induced, it is unlikely that she could be declared a lunatic.

Harriet's problems were caused by the interplay of diagnoses and cures suggested by her doctors for chronic headaches and insomnia. Her stress and exhaustion were treated with morphine in the United States and with sulfonal in Germany. Despite those drugs, until now, she had functioned well. Her innate intelligence and vigor allowed her to persevere energetically at her business, while the depression, caused by stressful external circumstances and medications, led to symptoms that allowed the doctors, acting according to sophisticated psychiatric treatments of the period, to commit her as a lunatic. Indeed, during her nondepressive states, Harriet demonstrated high accomplishment, elevated achievement, strong motivation and ambitious goal setting.[308] While these attributes made her a highly successful individual, her tendency to become depressed was the opposite pole.

The medical certificate of "lunacy" signed by Drs. Morton and Hammond stated that the onset of her problem was gradual. Harriet was "depressed with periods of moderate excitement, heard voices talking and singing all the time, called her dreadful names and kept her miserable, said she wanted to die and that death would be a happy release from her persecution. She said very little else as it was difficult to get her to speak at all." [309] The certificate also noted that she called for Hattie, whom she had accused of attempting to murder her only a few years earlier, and yet when she saw her she "received her with every expression of endearment. Begged her to protect her from the voices, became excitable, cried and moaned. Her facial expression was that of acute misery and the tears flowed constantly."[310] Harriet's estrangement from her daughters who had been turned against her was not just a figment of her imagination. When she left her husband, her main goal had been to provide for the girls in the manner to which they were accustomed. She was devastated by the malicious rumors that alienated them, as seen in the letters printed in the newspapers in 1889. In fact, she obsessed about their separation and desperately wanted to regain their love and respect.

The first stressful situation in Harriet's life was the death of her second child in December 1871. In that case, her mother, who knew the benefits of stress avoidance, took her to Paris to recuperate. Removal from the traumatic situation and distraction helped Harriet recover in 1872. Her more recent ordeals began in 1888, long before she was declared insane. Between James Seymour and Herbert Ayer, she was clearly brought to the brink of collapse. Her breakup with General Grubb also caused her anguish and despair. Indeed, the three men in her adult life all deceived and betrayed her. Although she was a very strong woman, she had a propensity for emotional responses: witness her inordinate fear of the dark; learned behavior from her mother who took to her bed in response to misfortune; or conventional behavior for nineteenth-century women.

In 1888, Harriet sought the help of Dr. Shrady, who sent her for a rest cure to Dr. J.W. Pinkham's sanatorium in Montclair, New Jersey. When in Europe in 1888, she sought the help of the famous neurophysician Dr. Charcot in Paris. In 1889, when Harriet had to go to court four times and then sell her belongings to pay court and lawyer fees, she again experienced tension and anxiety, and once more she went to rest in the country at Islip, Long Island, in 1891. It was about this time that Lena Raymond reported that she began to see extreme changes in her mistress's behavior that were much more severe than she had seen during the last nine years. By the end of 1892, Harriet apparently suffered her most critical depression, possibly exacerbated by the death of her mother, and these extreme symptoms finally gave her family cause to place her in an asylum. The voices she was hearing, while not consistent with depression, could have been a concomitant symptom from her long-term use of doctor-prescribed drugs.

Judge McAdam committed her to the care of Dr. William Granger's Sanatorium in Bronxville. Chapter 446 of the Laws of 1874, Section 1, printed on the lunacy certificate, maintained:

> *No person shall be committed to any institution, for the care and treatment of the insane, except upon the certificate of two physicians, under oath, setting forth the insanity of such person. But no person shall be held in confinement in any such asylum for more than five days, unless within that time such a certificate be approved by a judge or justice of the court of record of the county or district in which the alleged lunatic resides, and said judge or justice may institute inquiry and take proofs as to any alleged lunacy before approving or disapproving of such certificate, and said judge or justice may, in his discretion, call a jury in each case to determine the question of lunacy.* [311]

For all intents and purposes of the law in the 1890s, Harriet's case was correctly administered.

Section 2 had even more relevance in Harriet's case because it decreed:

> *It shall not be lawful for any physician to certify to the insanity of any person for the purpose of securing his commitment to an asylum, unless said physician be of reputable character, a graduate of some incorporated medical college, a permanent resident of the State, and shall have been in the actual practice of his profession for at least three years.*

Section 3 states that the certifying physician should not be the proprietor or superintendent of the asylum to which the lunatic is being committed. The

Lunacy Act of 1890 was in effect until 1959. It stated that private patients could not be committed without the order of a justice of the peace and that they had to be informed of their imminent incarceration. As will be seen, it was because of a technicality about the doctors' qualifications and the fact that Harriet was never informed about her commitment that Harriet eventually claimed she was unjustly committed.

Harriet was delivered to Vernon House on February 9, 1893, and remained there until March 10. She was placed under the care of the proprietor, Dr. Granger, who had never seen her until she arrived at his sanitarium. The investigation in March was conducted by a commission, consisting of Dr. Matthew Chalmers and John H. Judge, who were appointed by Judge Andrews on the application of Herbert Ayer. Charles W. Brooke represented Herbert. Stephen Olin once again represented Harriet, not by prior arrangement but because he had been her legal advisor during her past trials and cared about her.

During the lunacy trial, Dr. Morton, Dr. Granger and Lena Raymond were interviewed. Dr. Morton said he found the patient's condition grave, but there were no signs of alcoholism or morphine addiction, only melancholia. He heard from Harriet's friends, colleagues and acquaintances that she had suicidal tendencies. She had all the comforts at home but no one to compel her to obey her doctor's orders. He believed that Harriet's main preoccupation was her estrangement from her two daughters, even though he had seen Hattie with her at least twice. Mr. Olin questioned him and ascertained that Hattie and Herbert had hired him, therefore he was beholden to them to have Harriet put away. He mentioned the fact that Hattie did not accompany Harriet to the asylum.

Dr. Granger testified that when she arrived at his sanatorium, "her colored maid," Lena Raymond, and a friend accompanied her. He said that at first Harriet would not eat, and he thought he would have to force-feed her. After a short time, however, she began to eat. However, she did not always obey the orders of attendants. When visitors came to Vernon House, she often cried and sometimes even refused to meet with them because she did not want them to see her in this condition. He insisted that he saw some improvement during the month, that Harriet now slept soundly, answered questions more readily, read books aloud and seemed brighter. Nevertheless, she was still depressed and did not speak unless spoken to. Dr. Granger further testified that Harriet was still hallucinating but that she was taking long walks and was considerably improved. When asked if she was competent to manage her business, Dr. Granger said he did not think so. The legal rules defining the rights, privileges and obligations of individuals assumed a degree of mental capacity sufficient to manage one's daily activities and affairs. The doctors agreed that Harriet was not in a condition to do so. When he asked his patient if she wanted to choose someone to disperse her belongings, she answered that she did not care, an answer consistent with her state of depression.

Lena Raymond Tooms was asked to testify, and she stated that Harriet's illness began on April 18, 1892, and that Harriet constantly called for Hattie.[312] Lena mentioned that she and a nurse had taken Harriet to Islip, Long Island, during the summer of 1891 to recuperate from the strain of her business. Lena thought that Harriet had changed considerably during the last year. She said, when questioned about Harriet's use alcohol, that her mistress occasionally drank claret and champagne but not whiskey or brandy.[313] Harriet did not linger in the courtroom to hear the testimonies. In her depressed condition, sequestered against her will in an unfamiliar environment, she no longer cared what was happening around her and to her. She was so physically and mentally beleaguered that she could not fight these insanity charges as she had in 1889. A jury decided that Harriet Hubbard Ayer was "insane at the present time, and incapable of caring for her own interests."[314]

Dr. Granger, into whose care Harriet was now entrusted, had published a book titled *How to Care for the Insane: A Manual for the Insane Asylum Attendants* in 1887. This book was used to train nurses and attendants and directed that patients be treated kindly and given exercise, useful work, diversion and entertainment, according to the principles of moral treatment. He advocated the wearing of adequately warm clothing and good shoes, along with weekly baths. Patients were to have private rooms, nicely decorated with pictures and flowers, if possible. He encouraged patients to dress well and keep their rooms in order.[315] He also wrote that the asylum dining room should be attractive and the food warm and palatable. If the patient refused to eat, attendants were, however, allowed to use force. Many a patient had cracked teeth as a result of force-feeding.[316] Attendants were to give kind and intelligent care and assist in the recovery and well-being of patients, and they were to report any new aberrant behavior to the attending doctors. Harriet's experience was quite different.

On the day she arrived at the asylum, Harriet was assigned to a bare, dark room. An attendant ordered her to undress. Some food was brought on a tray, and when Harriet did not eat it immediately, the woman pinned a soiled towel around her neck and poured some indescribable liquid down her throat faster than she could swallow it. The attendant told her frightened, weeping patient that she had better learn to eat what she was given.[317] For fourteen months, Harriet had to obey the orders of ignorant, poorly trained attendants. When she could not sleep, she was drugged; when she did not eat, she was forced to do so. No matter what personal function she was in the midst of, the attendant was present, and the doctor often barged in unannounced. She had to beg for her own comb and brush to be returned, and baths were given only once every two weeks.[318]

Harriet's environment, while unpleasant and below her standard of living, may not have been quite as dire as she dramatically described after her release. We know from a list of her effects that her room was furnished with objects from her home that included lamps, vases, candlesticks, bisque figurines, photographs of family and friends, china, silver flatware and even a silver tea set. She had a picture of her great-grandfather (more likely her grandfather Judge Smith), photographs of Hattie and her children, two pictures of Margaret, pictures of some friends and some other small objects. No articles of clothing were mentioned, so we can assume that she did indeed endure fourteen months wearing the same clothes in which she arrived, with only a thin sweater to keep her warm in all types of weather.[319]

For a person who sought light because of her fear of the dark, life was so unpleasant that she wanted to die. The shutters on the windows were kept closed, and she had only a foul-smelling kerosene lamp for light.[320] Brought up to be compulsively clean, this woman who later preached cleanliness, fresh air and exercise as panaceas was forced to live in abominable conditions. Yet, this private sanatorium was surely better than the public facilities then available. After pleading for some books to read, she was eventually given a Bible. For diversion, a crude needle and thread with a broken thimble were provided so that she could do some meaningful work mending the coarse sheets.[321] A few months later, however, she began to take an interest in the other patients, just as she had done when she was hospitalized in Chicago during her first pregnancy. As her health improved, her compassion for others returned.

At $350 a month, her quarters, food and treatment should have been better than what she described. A state law required that patients committed to private institutions had to pay for their own care, thus everything in her apartment had to be sold to pay for her internment. The court, in addition to committing Harriet, also appointed someone to oversee the sale and dispersal of her estate. Her entire family, including her two sisters, Jule Lockwood and May Wetherill, and her daughter Hattie Seymour were opposed to the court-appointed overseer. They put forth Henry T. Cutter, a successful businessman and president of Hegeman's and Hudnut Drugstores. Two friends, employees of the Récamier Company, and Stephen Olin, Harriet's lawyer, objected to the family's selection.[322] Miss May Morrow, secretary of the Récamier Company, who for four years acted as private secretary, stenographer and Harriet's confidante, testified:

> *The peculiar loneliness of Mrs. Ayer's position and the nature of her malady, which permits her to recognize those around her, make it cruel to suggest that her friendships should be wholly ignored and forgotten in the appointment of a custodian of her person. To [e]ntrust the property or person of Mrs. Ayer to those who had made unsuccessful attempts to deprive her of her property and who have attacked her reputation and rendered her life miserable would be a very great wrong.*

But Charles Brooke, the lawyer for Herbert Ayer, charged that Miss Morrow was merely acting as a dummy for Frank J. Sprague, vice-president of the Récamier Manufacturing Company, who sought to obtain full control of Harriet's stock and had perpetuated an "outrageous and atrocious system of frauds." Mr. Sprague countered with a letter to the editor of the *New York Times* on March 29, 1893, denying that he sought control of her company or that he was involved in any fraudulent activities.[323] He insisted that Mr. Olin, Harriet's trusted attorney, was on the board of the company and had access to all its activities and its books. He promised to cooperate with whomever was appointed to conserve Mrs. Ayer's estate. Somerville P. Tuck was the referee appointed by the court to select the proper person, and he submitted his report to Judge Patterson of the Supreme Court. After much discussion about who would most appropriately and fairly represent Harriet's estate, the court appointed Alfred Bishop Mason, a director of the Cotton Oil Trust. Mr. Brooke, however, claimed that Alfred Mason was in fact a partner of Sprague's. Mr. Olin opposed everyone except Mr. Mason, whom Harriet knew, since no one but him and Olin had Harriet's best interests at heart.[324]

Mason's official title was committee of the person and estate of Harriet Hubbard Ayer, a lunatic. Ultimately, he seemed to do a good job, obtaining appraisals for Harriet's estate and selling her effects in an organized fashion and without prejudice.[325]

In addition to needing $350 a month to pay for Harriet's internment, there were various other claims against her estate amounting to $4,483.90. Doctors' bills, expenses for the inventory of the estate and legal fees from Olin, Reeves & Montgomery had to be paid. Stephen Olin, while befriending her, still charged for his services. Judge O'Brien of the Supreme Court objected to some of the charges. Olin's bill was $1,275, but the judge decided that $500 was sufficient. Dr. Morton asked for $145, and the judge asked him to itemize his charges. The three commissioners who heard the lunacy testimony wanted $100 each for just one day's work but were asked to take half. The court protected Harriet's assets when she could no longer do it herself.

Stocks from her corporation were included in the sale, along with all of her furnishings, jewelry, clothing and personal effects, including the portrait by William Merritt Chase. Her unfinished house in Florida was now valued at $5,000 when only two years before it was on the market for $15,000.[326] Each classification of objects had a separate appropriate appraiser; one of them noted that such a forced sale would not bring more than a third of the real value.[327] Mason apparently had Harriet's entire estate valued at $55,000, the amount Tuck had determined was necessary to pay her expenses.[328] Unfortunately for Harriet, the 1893 economic depression diminished her chances of recouping the real value of her property.

This was the third instance of Harriet's belongings being sold under duress. The first was in 1883, when Herbert lost his business and needed to pay his creditors, and their house and its contents were put up for sale for less than their value. The second was in 1889, when Harriet had to sell the contents of her West Thirteenth Street house below market price to pay the legal fees for the lawsuits. And now, only four years later, she was required to sell her company stocks and other assets in order to pay for her forced internment in Vernon House. Compounding this sense of loss must have been the memory of her very first house in Chicago, which was destroyed by the Great Fire in 1871. Yet, each time, her indomitable spirit allowed her to survive and recover.

Escape and Recuperation

After about a year in the asylum, Harriet met a young man who was self-confined, therefore, he had the freedom to come and go. He was a Freemason who had read about Harriet in the newspapers and offered to help by sneaking a letter out, since letters to and from the asylum were censored. Speaking in French so that the attendant, who watched Harriet day and night, would not understand, they made a plan for him to get a letter to her lawyer. Harriet secretly wrote a note and slipped it to the Freemason without the attendant noticing. Hope can lead to defiance, and Harriet was ready to risk being caught in the hope of being rescued and released.

The Freemason, whose identity Harriet never divulged, was part of the oldest and largest worldwide fraternal organization dedicated to the brotherhood of man. Among the many rituals and obligations, Freemasons promise not only to uphold the rules of their particular lodge but also to act in a civilized manner and, most important for Harriet, give aid or charity to those in need. Since this man presented Harriet with his thirty-second-degree Mason's pin, it can be assumed that he had completed the requirements for his own intellectual and moral development. Degrees, or steps, ranged from four to as high as thirty-three degrees.[329]

Harriet's letter reached Stephen Olin, and the procedure for her release from the asylum began within forty-eight hours. As soon as Dr. Granger received Olin's letter, life in the asylum improved for Harriet. She was given a better room, invited to eat with Dr. Granger and allowed small privileges.[330] Because signs of her recovery had appeared before her release, she already had more concessions than the other inmates. Yet when Frank Sprague visited, he found her

> *brokenhearted and neglected in appearance, whereas she had formerly been fastidious in that regard; she was physically weak when she was discharged* [and] *she could scarcely walk, her shoulders were bent, her hair had become gray, and she seemed to have aged twenty years.*

Regardless, her two brothers-in-law could now attest to her mental coherence.[331]

Justice Truax of the Supreme Court signed an order releasing Harriet with the report that she was sane on April 8, 1894, and simultaneously discharged Alfred Bishop Mason. Since she was deemed capable of handling her own affairs, Harriet immediately took over the management of what was left of her company and seemed perfectly competent to do so, as confirmed by a number of her relatives and friends. Her application for release was supported by Dr. William A. Hulse of Bay Shore; her former physician, Dr. A. A. Smith of 40 West Forty-seventh Street; her brothers-in-law, John L. Lockwood, Jule's husband, and Captain A.M. Wetherill, May's husband; Frank L. Sprague, vice-president of her company; Alfred Bishop Mason, the court-appointed committee; and John T. Montgomery, an employee of her company.[332]

If she was depressed, Harriet was restored to health. If she was addicted to drugs, she was cured of her addiction. She had no expectations of what the future held for her, but once again she demonstrated her extraordinary resiliency in the face of tragedy. She weighed only eighty-six pounds when she left Vernon House. Her blond hair had turned gray, her skin was sallow and, what's more, she had on the same clothes she had worn when she had arrived, except now they were ragged. She no longer had any place to live, for her apartment over the store on Fifth Avenue and almost all its contents were sold to pay for her board at Vernon House. Her daughters, who had been set against her by Blanche Howard, were still estranged. Society remembered only the sensational newspaper reports of her insanity.

Despite her recent horrendous experiences, Harriet was not vindictive. She was willing to accept help until she got back on her feet. Stephen Olin gave her some financial assistance. She welcomed the support of her sisters, whom perhaps she had brushed off in the past. At first, she went to stay with Jule in Elberon, New Jersey, for several weeks.[333] The sea air must have been somewhat restorative after her "imprisonment," as she referred to it. In fact, she attributed her incarceration to an absurd blunder. She was so forgiving that she did not believe her former husband would have committed her were it not for his being inflamed by James Seymour. But she did accuse the doctors who signed her lunacy papers of arrogance and Dr. Granger of being too eager to acquire and retain patients. She only stayed with Jule for a short time because her brother-in-law was so dictatorial. Always a difficult man, especially when drunk, he worked long hours selling bottled distilled water in Manhattan, commuting from New Jersey. Still plucky, Harriet removed herself from the unpleasantness of John Lockwood, and on January 5, 1895, she stopped in Chicago on her way to see her younger sister, May.[334] Harriet went to Kentucky where Captain Wetherill's regiment, the Sixth Infantry, was stationed at Fort Thomas in Campbell County. The fort was located on a beautiful hilltop overlooking the Ohio River. The Wetherills remained there until 1898, when he received orders to go to Cuba. The United States had declared war on Spain in April 1898, and Captain Wetherill was sent to the armed intervention to drive the Spaniards out of Cuba. Wetherill, along with Theodore Roosevelt and his Rough Riders, fought in the Battle of San Juan Hill, in Santiago de Cuba, on July 1, 1898, the bloodiest battle of the Spanish-American War. He was killed in action.[335] The Wetherill family maintained a summer house near Jamestown on Conanicut Island in Narragansett Bay, Rhode Island, where Harriet later spent time with her widowed sister.

While in Kentucky with the Wetherills, Harriet was determined to recapture her former stamina and worked hard to recuperate by exercising daily, eating healthy food and getting plenty of rest. Eventually, she regained the pounds she had lost and reached her original weight of 136 pounds. What she did for herself, she later prescribed for others: "Scrupulous cleanliness, air, light, diet, exercise."[336] Having experienced maltreatment in the insane asylum, she now proved that "a woman whose beauty had vanished, if she were willing to do so, could be made over again, could get back her physical loveliness, and that she could be made strong and charming, buoyant and blithe by hygienic and common sense methods."[337]

So it was in Kentucky that she set about righting herself, once again overcoming adversity. It is interesting to note that while Harriet was determined to recover more than just her health and beauty, in her books and articles she did not encourage other women to seek the intellectual or commercial objectives that she had attained. She did, however, believe that beauty and goodness equipped a woman "for the highest duties that may devolve upon her."[338]

It took about a year or more for Harriet to recuperate fully and for her to find a new vocation in order to support herself. Upon regaining her health and spirit, she embarked on a new crusade to expose the horrible conditions in insane asylums and the ease with which people could be wrongfully committed. She made up her mind to fight for improved laws governing the examination and confinement of the insane.[339] Absent her business, which she sold after her release, Harriet focused her energy on revealing the horrors of asylums and wrongful institutionalization. She realized that she had spent much of her life in pursuit of selfish goals and vowed to work for better laws and conditions for the insane and to rectify current state laws. She did not wallow in self-pity but rather assessed her life's accomplishments and decided to alter her course once again.

With the help of her loyal friend, Mrs. John Lyon, she was invited to give a presentation before the Women's Club in Chicago at Central Music Hall on April 15, 1896. The Women's Club was the perfect venue for Harriet's presentation. It was founded in 1876 to work for self- and social improvements. By the 1880s, it focused on social reforms, establishing facilities for orphans and women prisoners. Typical of the period, it comprised an elite group of women but Harriet was never a member; she did not join any groups until later in life. Mrs. Lyon paid for the lecture titled "The Cause of the Living Dead." Harriet dramatically portrayed the hardships to which the insane were exposed at the hands of physicians and attendants. She began her story with an account of the change in doctors ordered by her daughter and former husband. She admitted that her health had deteriorated and that she displayed many symptoms of melancholia. Although ill, she claimed that there had been no need for her to be committed to an insane asylum. She explained how her daughter Hattie had deceived her into believing that she had sent for her to come to New Jersey.[340]

When speaking of the indignities she endured, Harriet dramatically changed from a beautiful black gown into the ragged one she wore for fourteen months during her confinement, messing her hair to further approximate her pitiable former state. While she was changing, her accomplice, a "Judge Carter[,] read a number of depositions referring to her mental and physical condition before, during and after confinement in

Bronxville."[341] He explained the current system for ascertaining the mental status of the insane and how the doctors who signed her certificate of lunacy were not qualified according to law. Dr. Morton was one day short of certification. Using her former training in amateur theatricals, Harriet vividly described how she was made to wear the same dress in both winter and summer and had to beg for some string to replace broken shoelaces. She told of her escape through the good offices of the Freemason. "No one would believe, she said, how easily and quickly people, supposedly insane, are imprisoned in asylums and how difficult, almost impossible, it is to secure their release once they are adjudged insane."[342] She wanted to organize a society in every state for the protection of both the mentally ill and those illegally deprived of their liberties and to change current laws that made possible experiences such as hers.[343] There were two doctors who alone had sent eighteen hundred people to Bellevue Hospital in New York each year, revealing that people could be easily committed without substantial medical and psychological examinations.[344]

Harriet claimed that she constantly took notes and drew pictures of her surroundings, collecting data for a book, which she vowed to publish. She said that she had thirty-five hundred pages and was slowly progressing with it. A letter to John Townsend, Esq., a lawyer versed in lunacy law, written on her stationery on February 12, 1896, regarding her arguments exposing improper and involuntary commitment reads as follows:

> *I have been told recently that physicians committing a patient to an insane asylum must examine the patient on the day the certificate is signed...Now according to Dr. Graeme Hammond's own statement, he saw me only once which was the examination made on the 7th day of February when I was also examined by Dr. Morton, that is to say, the two together. Dr. Morton's certificate of qualification, which has to be certified by a judge of a court of record, was not even filed in New York until the 8th and on the 9th, the day of my actual commitment. Dr. Hammond did not see me at all and Dr. Morton did not come into my apartment.*[345]

She underscored that she was never informed that she was being committed to an asylum for the insane, nor was she told that she would have to pay for her care. On these technicalities, and the fact that one of the doctors was a day shy of having the proper psychiatric qualifications, Harriet was able to have the courts rule that she was improperly incarcerated—indeed, "kidnapped"—against her will, without knowing where she was being taken and why. Harriet supposedly repeated this lecture at other venues, but I have not found any others. No record of the book she was writing has been found. The laws regarding the insane were not changed immediately, but Harriet had ignited public awareness about the ease with which people could be declared insane and committed to an asylum, and so she had accomplished part of her goal.

THE DEMISE OF THE RÉCAMIER COMPANY

By February 1896, Récamier Manufacturing Company had become insolvent. Harriet and Frank Sprague claimed that the liabilities were $126,334, of which $15,068 was due on notes, $10,274 on accounts payable and $2,256 for merchandise, with $1,200 contingent and the balance for advertising contracts. The advertising contracts were with newspapers all over the United States and also for street railway, billboard and wall advertising. The total amount of these contracts was $97,534, with $13,110 in dispute. Of the liabilities, $6,924 was due to Harriet as salary and money advanced. Assets were fixtures and accounts receivable. That Harriet spent a lot on advertising is made clear by these figures. The assets amounted to a mere $7,858 of goods, fixtures and accounts receivable and cash.

Justice Lawrence of the Supreme Court appointed Charles M. Sprague (no relation to Frank) as receiver on the application made by Harriet and Frank J. Sprague, who was still vice-president of the company. At this point, Sprague owned 313 shares, and J.H. Montgomery, another employee, owned 100 shares; F.W. McLanathan, 30 shares; and F.R. Williams, 1 share. These stocks may have been sold when Harriet's appointed commissioner was raising money to pay for her confinement at Vernon House.[346] Thus came the poignant end to the first cosmetic company created, organized and managed by a woman. It did have an afterlife, however. At a receiver's sale in October 1896, all the corporate assets, including the trademark and the good will, were sold for $4,000 to a former employee, Maria E. Rinn. Miss Rinn continued the business under the trade name Récamier Manufacturing Company, using Harriet's signature on the products. In

1897, Harriet brought suit to end the use of her name, but an agreement with Miss. Rinn was reached, and the suit was dropped.[347]

Herbert Ayer and James Seymour, with the aid of Blanche Howard, had accomplished their long-term goal of defeating Harriet, but to little advantage. Without her leadership and advertising genius, Récamier Preparations was not the same. Harriet sold the business that had made her a household name and once again reinvented herself.

PART V

Harriet Hubbard Ayer, Journalist

A Reporter for the World

After recuperating from the hardships she experienced in the insane asylum, after bringing to public attention legal aspects of false incarceration, after exposing the intolerable conditions in asylums and after dissolving her cosmetic company, Harriet was at a loss for another vocation. Without family for moral support or a source of income, she was totally alone and needed a way to sustain herself. Following a short period of despondency, she contemplated a career as a journalist. After all, she had written advertorials successfully. This next period from 1897 to 1903 would bring her contentment bolstered by accomplishment and satisfaction.

In 1896, after closing her office on West Thirty-first Street, Harriet was living in Harlem, at 141 Lenox Avenue. In anticipation of the subway opening there in 1898, the Lenox Avenue area was in the midst of constructing new apartment buildings. One day, after reading about the newly created women's pages of the *New York World*, Harriet decided to pay a visit to the twenty-story World Building. Joseph Pulitzer (1847–1911), the newspaper's owner, had commissioned this early skyscraper in 1890, designed by the well-known architect George Browne Post (1837–1913).[348]

As Harriet approached the Renaissance palazzo-style building constructed of a buff- and red-colored mix of sandstone, yellow brick and terra cotta, the imposing entrance adorned with sculpture symbolizing the arts and the humanities must have made an impression on her. She entered the lobby and asked to see the editor. Although she had no formal journalistic experience, she had written long articles about herself and her products for the *New York Times*, the *Chicago Times*, *Harper's Weekly*, the *Boston Globe* and the *Brooklyn Eagle*, among others.[349] Her name had dominated the headlines and advertisements for many years, and now she yearned to be the one writing the news instead of being the subject.

If timing is everything, Harriet's was perfect. A tradition of hiring women had already been established, and the paper was launching a special woman's section. Arthur Brisbane, a syndicated columnist, was the paper's new editor in 1896, and Harriet was brought to his office; not surprisingly, he had recognized her name. [350] Since she was not known as a writer, he tested her by having her write a piece on the spot. If she failed, he would be rid of her immediately, but she passed the editorial test, and Brisbane hired her straight away. He realized that her name would sell newspapers, and he was not disappointed—although it was risky for him to employ a woman the public remembered as insane. The articles declaring her sane were much less conspicuous than those that had proclaimed her a lunatic.

The *New York World*, founded in 1860, was not a successful paper until Joseph Pulitzer purchased it in 1883. Pulitzer, best remembered today for establishing the Pulitzer Prizes, bought and sold newspapers all over the United States and was successful because of his commitment to serving the common man.[351] In response to the growing market for a working-class newspaper, he was able to increase the *World*'s circulation from 11,000 to 250,000 by 1895. The paper, in addition to its morning and evening editions, published a Sunday edition, a diversion for people who did not have the time to read during the week. The Sunday edition was divided into separate sections featuring special departments that included news reports, editorials, sports, advertisements and women's topics. Pulitzer built the circulation by printing human-interest stories, some of which were sensationalized, and he enlivened the text with illustrations, advertising and entertainment. The colored comic strips were a big hit, and the name "yellow journalism" came from one of the characters: the Yellow Kid. Yet Pulitzer was committed to raising the standards of journalism, and although he was not physically on the premises, he kept tight editorial control and would not let Brisbane take credit for editorial content.

Pulitzer had recruited the famous investigative reporter Nellie Bly in 1887. While there is no record of Harriet's contact with Nellie Bly, they shared an interest in exposing the evils of insane asylums. Nellie's first assignment for the *World* in 1887 was to investigate the brutality and neglect at the Women's

Lunatic Asylum on Blackwell's Island (now Roosevelt Island). She described the sordid conditions in the Blackwell asylum while an undercover agent for the paper. In addition to her article for the *World*, she published a book, *Ten Days in a Madhouse*. Bly was sure to have read about Harriet's incarceration and her vivid description of that horrible experience. And Harriet likely read Bly's account about the lunatic asylum and was possibly drawn to the *World* because of her. As a "stunt" reporter, Bly was still working at the paper in 1896, the year Harriet began. Stunt reporters took on dangerous and entertaining challenges to attract attention to their feats.[352]

There were several other women writers, including plucky Kate Swan, who also provided stunt reporting; Ella Wheeler Wilcox (1850–1919), the poet-journalist; and even Eunice Beecher (1813–1897), abolitionist, reformer, suffrage advocate and wife of the famous preacher Henry Ward Beecher.[353] Many of the stunt articles focused on perilous physical pursuits achieved by women, such as "Kate Swan Scales the Harlem River Bridge."[354] On the other hand, there were the more conventional types like Wilcox, who believed "it is better for a woman to fail in an effort to be womanly than succeed in an effort to be masculine."[355]

The *World* valued the new modern woman, a woman who was energetic, self-reliant and interested in a vocation outside the home and Harriet was an ideal representative. Her articles advocated self-improvement for the purpose of making a woman more attractive to men. Her writing satisfied a diverse audience, the very people Pulitzer wanted as readers. Hoping to attract the emerging middle class, many of whom were women, the paper was full of articles about women such as Helen Keller, Susan B. Anthony and Lillian Russell. After a while, Harriet was assigned to write feature articles of interest to both men and women, yet she is not mentioned in most books about women journalists. There existed a network of these writers at the time that Harriet began to write. In 1889, the Women's Press Club of New York was formed because they were excluded from men's organizations. Although the clubs supported women journalists, Harriet was not a member.[356] Throughout her life, she resisted membership in women's organizations and yet accomplished much that those organizations advocated. Harriet was given a desk and a secretary in the newsroom dominated by men. Her articles on health and beauty, as we shall see, proved to be so popular that she eventually had two assistants. Her first article, "Beauty and Health," appeared by November 22, 1896. It was introduced by the following paragraph:

Mrs. Harriet Hubbard Ayer, the most famous authority in the world on feminine beauty and how to preserve it, will not only conduct this department in the Sunday World, *she will also answer regularly in the* Evening Edition *of* The World *such questions as may be addressed to her regarding the proper treatment of the complexion, the hair, the teeth, etc.*

Initially, her job was to answer questions dealing with physical appearance, health and grooming; however, it was later expanded to include etiquette and other things.

By her second article, Harriet was already apologizing for not having answered all the letters she received, promising to respond to them all as soon as she was able. The second beauty and health article dealt with hair care, freckles and bad breath, for which she described care, cures and formulas for treatment. It also included some of the letters she had received and already answered. Those letters dealt with freckles, facial care (including treatment of blackheads) and large joints. Along with that article, there was one called "The Doctor's Advice." Its placement on the same page as her column gave her suggestions efficacy. On December 6, 1896, she answered questions about the reduction of hips, bust size and weight loss. She recommended a careful diet with lots of walking—ten miles was not too much for a healthy woman, and she did not mean walking around a "shopping promenade."[357] By December 3, she had two articles. One, under "Other Topics to Interest Women," featured "Mrs. Ayer's Hints on Beauty, Helpful and Practical Talks to Women by an Expert in the Modern Art of Beautifying," which dealt with dandruff and the thinning of hair, eyebrows and eyelashes. The other, longer article was about the famous French singer Yvette Guilbert (1865–1944).

The headline read, "Mrs. Harriet Hubbard Ayer, the Beauty Expert, Makes a Study of Yvette Guilbert." Harriet interviewed Guilbert in her New York apartment at the Hotel Savoy. This hotel, located at Fifth Avenue and Fifty-ninth Street, was an apartment house for wealthy tenants. Harriet wrote about Guilbert's background, her day-to-day experiences and how she preserved her remarkable physical freshness. Perhaps Guilbert, recognizing a kindred spirit in Harriet allowed Harriet to observe her toilette while she narrated her life's story, a tale that had similarities with Harriet's childhood. Guilbert was an ugly child whose mother and father did not believe she could succeed in life. Nevertheless, she could sing and act. Guilbert, who had a unique physiognomy, started singing at the age of five, was a model at age sixteen and then went on to become a famous chanteuse at the Moulin Rouge in Paris. She is best remembered as a favorite model of Henri Toulouse-Lautrec, who immortalized her in his many portraits and caricatures, emphasizing her rather distinctive nose. She had to work hard under difficult circumstances to become the famous chanteuse she was at the time of Harriet's interview. Like Harriet, she went from an ugly duckling to an unconventionally attractive, curvaceous, cultivated and talented woman. To protect her voice and her figure, she did not drink alcohol and was careful about her diet. Most poignant in her story was the fact that she was now taking care of her ailing mother, who had been unkind to her. Harriet ended her article by telling how Guilbert's unusual facial features conveyed the very uniqueness that attracted artists such as Toulouse-Lautrec. The message to readers was twofold: do the best you can with the features you are born with, for success can be attained if you take good care of your health (read beauty).[358]

During this initial period, Harriet was writing her articles on health and beauty every other week. Another article dealt with wrinkles, their cause, prevention and treatment. The answer for many of these problems was a healthy diet, cleanliness, proper massage and skin moisturizers. At the start of her articles, she would mention by initials only those whose questions she was answering, stating that she received so many letters that correspondents had to be patient until she could get to their queries. The regular health and beauty articles were interspersed with interviews. "Mrs. Grover Cleveland Analyzed" appeared on Sunday, December 2, 1896.

Frances Folsom Cleveland (1864–1947) was twenty-one when she married President Grover Cleveland, who was twenty-seven years her senior. They were married in the Blue Room of the White House, the only president to be married while in office. As the youngest first lady ever, Mrs. Cleveland was a very popular hostess during Cleveland's two nonconsecutive terms of office, from 1885 to 1889 and then again from 1893 to 1897. Harriet wrote about Mrs. Cleveland at the end of her second White House term, after she had three children (she had two more after she left the White House). The article in the *World* was not political; in fact, it was a health and beauty article in disguise. Harriet wrote, "The face of each woman is the outward symbol of both mental and physical development. It changes from girlhood to the perfect maturity of thirty gradually but surely." Thirty seems to be the cutoff point at which life's troubles appear on the face, according to Harriet. Yet she attributed Mrs. Cleveland's new Madonna-like look and increased weight as normal—"that pink and ivory opulence of the firm, beautiful flesh of health…of a typically beautiful and normal woman in the zenith of her loveliness." Mrs. Cleveland was only thirty-two, while Harriet was already forty-seven years old when she wrote this article.[359]

Following the article about Frances Cleveland was one that criticized Susan B. Anthony, the civil rights leader who fought for women's suffrage in the United States. "The Political Woman, The Strangest Product of '96," appeared in the *World* on December 27, 1896. Once again, it was not a piece about Anthony's battle for women's suffrage, but rather one about her physical and personal appearance. Harriet bore witness to the widespread prejudice against the suffragists and drew attention to a stereotypical prototype: "a lined face with thin-lips and narrowed eyes, the result of unhappiness, strain, and the hopelessness of women in politics, especially unmarried ones." While focusing on Susan B. Anthony and Elizabeth Cady Stanton, both suffragettes, she named several women in the United States who held office. She felt their strong public stands and protests had changed their looks.[360] Interestingly, she did not use as an example her own experience and its concomitant ill effects on her own countenance. Her looks had actually suffered greatly after fourteen months at the Vernon House; she was living proof for other women that facial changes due to adversity could be alleviated with proper care.

Harriet's opinions were not necessarily those of the *World*. On February 16 of the same year, Nellie Bly reported more affirmatively on another famous suffragette, Mrs. Stanton. Bly wrote about her intellectual activities at the age of eighty, her piano lessons and her efforts to write a Bible for women. In her preface to the *Woman's Bible*, Stanton wrote, "The object was to revise only those texts and chapters directly referring to women, and those also in which women are made prominent by exclusion." This was true for only about one-tenth of the scriptures. Bly did not mention Stanton's social activism in leading the fight for woman's rights. Unlike Anthony, Stanton was married and had six children, all of whom arrived according to plan, except for one unplanned menopausal baby. She refused to use the word "obey" in her marriage vows where it was expected that a woman would obey her husband. It was Stanton's experience as a housewife that galvanized her to action:

A Reporter for the *World*

The general discontent I felt with woman's position as wife, housekeeper, physician, and spiritual guide, the chaotic condition into which everything fell without her constant supervision, and the wearied, anxious look of the majority of women, impressed me with a strong feeling that some active measures should be taken to remedy the wrongs of society in general, and of women in particular.[361]

Even when she had limited financial backing, Harriet had a housekeeper and governess, therefore she had been spared the household drudgery that most women endured. She fought for her own rights and did not openly sympathize with, or promote, the women's suffrage movement. Her articles underscore her consistent effort to teach women how to be more appealing to men. During the earlier entrepreneurial phase of her life, she believed that when a woman was downtrodden, she could disguise her weariness by using the proper creams and makeup and by drinking the cure-all Vita Nuova. As a journalist, she advocated a healthy lifestyle through exercise, proper diet, cleanliness and attention to facial care, dress and etiquette. Frequent bathing was formerly considered dangerous to health, but with the gradual introduction of indoor plumbing, personal standards of cleanliness improved. Bathrooms that contained sinks, tubs and toilets with running water were often found in most middle-class urban housing.

Harriet promoted the link between cleanliness and physical appearance as a sign of upward mobility. Her articles were helpful to the waves of immigrants that doubled the city's population during the 1890s. These were people who wanted to improve their lives instantly. Many were hardworking and literate and wanted to assimilate quickly. Her advice to women was especially welcome, as attested to by the enormous number of letters she received. Clearly, she had honed her skills as an interviewer, but her reporting was hardly objective, biased by her own experiences, upbringing and period attitudes. According to Harriet, women under the age of thirty did not need to use cosmetics. "Cosmetics and youth should be strangers."[362] When the ravages of age begin to take their toll, a woman must take action to repair the damages. As for men, no matter how much they protest that they love a plain, simple woman, they always go after the pretty ones. Over and over again, her book affirms: "The pursuit of beauty has been aided and abetted by man, if indeed, it does not owe its origin to the male. The best man in the world, the worst man in the universe and all the others in between, succumb to the charm of beauty in women."[363]

Is this the summation of her experiences with men? Were the men in her life only attracted to her beauty? Certainly she was an unattractive teenager when Herbert married her, but she was a beautiful woman when General Grubb first met her, although he withdrew his love for a younger woman and because of her unconventional behavior. James Seymour, however, was the epitome of the men she wrote about, men who took advantage of beautiful women. He wanted Harriet only as his mistress. One wonders what would have happened if he had offered to leave his wife and marry her? They had much in common, and there was probably a strong physical attraction between them.

Modifying her earlier commercial advice, when she made money by selling products to young and old alike, she wrote:

> *During the years I studied chemistry and cosmetic art and manufactured so-called cosmetics, I labored faithfully, both here and in Europe. And the longer I remained in the laboratory manufacturing these articles, the less I felt the average woman needed them or should use them, and the more respect I had for scrubbing brushes, soap, and water, without other aids, at least for women under thirty.*

Now she offered free advice to young women who wished to preserve their beauty and to older women who wished to restore a semblance of youthful beauty.[364] With letters pouring in, Harriet's new career as a journalist was launched triumphantly during its first month and a half, from November 22 to the end of 1896.

16

The Women's Pages

The next year saw many more articles about physical and social care for women. By January 3, 1897, just a month after Harriet began her journalistic career, her byline was writ large at the top of the page. She composed a full page about the proper way to massage the face, accompanied by many illustrations. She advocated Swedish massage as the best treatment, especially for the eradication of lines and wrinkles. While this, of course, was appropriate for women over fifty years of age, she wrote, there was no harm in beginning earlier in life. In another article, she answered questions about the removal of unwanted facial hair. She wrote that electrolysis can be effective but is costly and painful. Instead, she suggested a depilatory, for which she provided a formula, but recommended that readers purchase it at a pharmacy rather than concocting it themselves. Another letter asked about how to keep a child's hair light; Harriet counseled that peroxide should not be used on a child. Many of her answers would hold true today since her advice was highly practical.

"Mrs. Ayer on Aids to Beauty, Suggestions About Face Blemishes and the Care and Growth of the Hair" was the next subject she addressed about two weeks later. Again, she mentioned the initials of those who had written to her about these subjects. She described blackheads, or flesh worms, correctly writing that pores have to be unclogged. She prescribed an ointment to be rubbed into the skin to provide friction.[365] In answer to future letters, she admonished her readers to use their real names instead of fictitious ones, such as "Constant Reader," so she could answer in a more personal way and not confuse one admirer with another. She was asked to repeat her regimen for overcoming obesity. Again, her answers would be relevant today:

> *Avoid starchy and sweetened food; all cereals, vegetables containing sugar or starch such as peas, beans, corn, potatoes, etc. Have your bread toasted; sprinkle it with salt instead of butter. Milk, I regret to say, if it be pure and good, is fattening. Hot water is an excellent substitute for other liquids. Add a little lime or lemon juice to it, if you choose. Limit your sleeping hours to seven at the outside; no naps. You must take exercise."*

Then she recommended walking (at least five miles a day) or wheeling (bicycle riding).[366] She was asked to recap her information on facial massage, which she did in another article. In various ways, her readers asked her to repeat or give more details on previous articles. Over the next few months, "Mrs. Ayer" continued to answer queries in "Advice on Health and Beauty." On other pages in the paper, there appeared articles on wheeling, which had become a major form of transportation and recreational exercise. Harriet offered advice on that, too.

On Sunday, June 13, 1897, Harriet deviated from health and beauty topics to report on the work of Rose Hawthorne Lathrop (1851–1926), the daughter of the famous author Nathaniel Hawthorne. Rose Lathrop went on to found St. Rose's Free Home for Incurable Cancer on the Lower East Side of Manhattan in 1899. She had separated from her husband before he died in 1898, and in 1900 she was named Mother Mary Alphonsia in the religious order that she originated, known as the Dominican Sisters of Hawthorne. Harriet compared Mrs. Lathrop to Madame Jeanne-Françoise Garnier, founder of Les Dames du Calvaire in France, a group of women who helped care for the sick and poor and who were the inspiration for Lathrop's group. The article ended with a request for donations to support the work of the American version of Les Dames, the Daughters of the Cross, who voluntarily donated their time to caring for people suffering from incurable cancer and related illnesses. With several poignant accounts about how Mrs. Lathrop saved poor children in New York's East Side slums and how she devoted her life to charity, Harriet wrote this piece similarly to her brilliant advertorials. After reading the article, readers could not help but sympathize and could hardly refuse to support these women and their cause. Unlike her articles about Susan B. Anthony and Yvette Gilbert, Harriet did not analyze Lathrop's facial features or refer to her looks; she focused on the good deeds Lathrop performed.[367]

While Harriet's life was no longer that of a glamorous socialite with a large expense account, as a workingwoman she still had time to go on vacation. In July 1897, although the weather had been unseasonably cold and rainy, she went to Patchogue, Long Island, where she stayed at Raulah House, a small hotel. She was no stranger to Long Island, as in the summer of 1891 she spent some time in Islip recuperating from illness and exhaustion. Since her next article was spread across several issues, some appearing while she was away, most likely she completed them before going on vacation.

Harriet's next big story was a case study: "Restoring a Woman's Lost Figure." She weighed and measured Mrs. Martha Baker before, during and after a specified regime of diet, exercise and massage. She explained the causes of obesity, as well as the proper diet that would lead to weight loss. The articles appeared in the *Sunday Magazine*, from July 7 to August 13, 1897. Weekly articles were written so that someone who had not read the previous week's edition could easily understand the recommended regime. The articles were illustrated with pictures of Mrs. Baker before and after the weight loss regime. The headlines in the magazine section of the *World* boasted of Mrs. Baker's loss of fifteen pounds in just three weeks, without medication, and of the wonderful improvements in her health. Proper exercise and correct diet were responsible for effecting the desired change. Facial massage treatments were used to prevent wrinkles. Harriet then answered questions about weight loss. She ended:

> *In conclusion it may be repeated that the treatment and regimen applies to women and men alike, and can be tested by the poor as well as the rich, and I feel that I may be pardoned when I say that it is the duty that we owe to ourselves, our families and even to our friends to keep in a normal, healthful and non-offensive physical condition, especially when that object can be accomplished by the observance of a few simple rules pertaining to diet, exercise and sleep.*[368]

Hundreds of letters poured in for Harriet to answer, so she knew she had discovered a subject of great human interest, as it is even more so today. It was said that she received twenty thousand letters a year in response to her articles.

On Sunday, August 29, 1897, the *Sunday World* announced that it would "receive photographs of women, young and old, who desire suggestions and criticism for their personal improvement." The paper would print before-and-after photographs, but names would be withheld. The pictures of four women were shown, and Harriet gave suggestions for improvement. On September 19, nine images of women were shown, identified only by their initials. Hairstyle and teeth improvements were recommended. This form of before-and-after images, accompanied by advice for physical improvement, appeared intermittently throughout the year.

The following week, Harriet tackled the matter of appropriate dress for outdoors. Printed as two tablets, one reading "Is It Right" and the other "Is It Wrong," the tablets provided her advice for both proper dress and etiquette. What is the correct behavior when visiting someone, when seating people at a dinner and so on? The "wrong" list is even more interesting. For example, "It is wrong to live in homes so grand that one's manners are too small for them."[369] Another article was captioned, "Puzzling Questions of Etiquette Answered by a Society Expert." Readers were encouraged to write to Mrs. Ayer.[370]

During October 1897, she wrote several articles about correct etiquette while also writing about beauty and health. Letters were to be addressed to the Beauty Department. In one case, she referred to good breeding, while another is headlined, "How to be Polite: Perplexing Questions of Deportment, by Harriet Hubbard Ayer."[371] The article answered readers' questions about all kinds of health and beauty issues. So, for several weeks in a row, she continued to write about etiquette. The last article was about gifts for children and parents for Christmas and even included suggestions for gifts to housemaids.

Following was an enticing article entitled "How to Read your Sweetheart's Character," with the subtitle, a quotation from Shakespeare's *Macbeth*: "Your Face is a Book Where Men May Read Strange Matters." This time, she analyzed the various parts of the face: nose, eyes, mouth, ears, chin and forehead. She wrote, "It is not fair to condemn or exalt the subject because one feature is bad and another beautiful. The face should be considered as a whole. There are certain well-defined features that infallibly stand for well-recognized characteristics." There are, for example, the conceited mouth and a gossip's mouth, but beware of a rosebud mouth, because the women who possess them are vain, frivolous and untruthful. Such analysis is given to all facial features.[372] Thus ended her first full year as a journalist. She wrote nothing during the holiday season, resting until the second week of the New Year.

The year 1898 saw increased activity on her part and even more letters from loyal readers devoted to her articles. On January 9, 1898, she wrote two articles, one on how to be beautiful and how to behave properly and another with pictures of women for whom advice for improvement was offered. A reader asked a question about improper or violent behavior by men toward women, a problem that women did (and still do) conceal. "It is inconceivable that a human being who calls himself a man should treat his wife in the manner you describe," Harriet answered. "She may be 'only a woman' in his opinion. If a man to whom you are engaged shows the slightest inclination to kindred brutality, you would certainly do well to break with him."[373] Harriet knew from experience what it meant to get rid of a difficult man.

The same day, January 9, the case study of Catherine Lane appeared.[374] The article recounted the story of how Catherine's mother wrote about her emaciated daughter's nervous dyspepsia, a disease that prevented her daughter from pursuing her acting career. The poor girl ended each day in paroxysms of pain and could not sleep or eat. She had been a successful actress but could no longer work because of her illness. Harriet wrote:

> *The sufferer's story was not a common one. It was the history of a singularly bright and pretty girl. Gifted with dramatic talent which found expression when the time came for a daughter to aid a mother in earning a living for the entire family whose head had suddenly been stricken with paralysis.*[375]

Harriet was so moved by the letter that she approached the editor of the *World* for funding to move this girl from her home in Philadelphia to live with Harriet in New York, where she could administer daily treatments. She consulted with various physicians, all of whom claimed that they could not cure Catherine of what we would today call functional dyspepsia but who thought that Harriet's suggestions were worth trying. Harriet made no promises to cure Catherine, but she was willing to try. Catherine's symptoms were similar to those of stomach ulcers or reflux. She experienced spasms, pain and the inability to eat, which led to extreme weight loss, mental anxiety and physical weakness. At the age of twenty-four, she had become, in her words, "a complete wreck." None of the treatments previously prescribed by the doctors had worked. Catherine agreed to try Harriet's therapy, the price of which was exposure in the newspaper.

Slowly, Harriet fed Catherine small portions of bland foods every two or three hours and made sure she had lots of rest, accompanied by daily massages, electric baths, oxygen and, finally, physical exercise. Little by little, her spasms subsided and her diet became less restricted. Catherine lived with Harriet for six weeks, until she was totally cured and could return to work.[376] Her grateful mother wrote a letter of appreciation, which was published. About a year later, Catherine herself wrote to allow Harriet to disclose her true identity. In a theatrical manner, Harriet revealed that her patient was none other than the famous actress Lillian Daily. Two years later, Lillian wrote to say that she was still healthy and was now acting in the best parts; she sent Harriet a picture to verify how well she looked.

This was not the first time that Harriet had taken a poor suffering girl into her home. Once before, she had taken in a beleaguered girl as a companion for her daughter Margaret. Maggie Morris, a seventeen-year-old girl, had accused a police sergeant of assaulting her in the winter of 1884–5. Sergeant Crowly was sentenced to seventeen and a half years in jail for this offense. The poor girl, who worked in a paper box factory, could not go out on the street without attracting curiosity seekers in her neighborhood because of the publicity. It was then that Harriet offered to take her into her home as a companion for Margaret, with the consent of Maggie's mother. However, the girl began to steal jewelry and lace from Harriet. When Harriet called the police to look into the matter and to examine her trunk, they found a letter stating that Maggie had been married at the time of the Crowly trial; therefore, she was not an innocent, guileless virgin, as had been reported in the newspapers. According to Harriet, the letter was one of many fictional stories that Maggie wrote as an attention-getting device. Her letter was immediately seized upon by the defense in order to free Sergeant Crowly. Harriet declared the letter bogus. Her jewels and knickknacks were returned. There was no further word about when Maggie left the Ayer domain, but all told, she probably spent a year or two there.[377] Harriet's aid to Maggie was not just a publicity stunt but a sign of Harriet's genuine empathy for the poor and the suffering.

Following were articles in the *World* about etiquette, namely the need for and definition of a chaperone, as well as articles on what to wear, how to act in a social setting, what to give as an appropriate gift for a wedding, manners related to shopping and behavior in the street and further answers to questions of health and beauty. On March 6, 1898, Harriet wrote an article related to the holy season of Lent entitled "The Etiquette of Lent, How to Conduct Yourself During the Solemn Season." In it she declared, "God's poor and God's afflicted alike look forward to this holy month of the year when, with special tenderness, they see the hands of the beautiful and great, these fairy-like ladies, stretch warmly toward them," speaking of some wealthy women and Episcopal parishioners who ministered to the poor and sick. Lent, in the Christian community, is a forty-day period of fasting, prayer, penitence and alms giving to prepare oneself for the event of the Passion of Christ. While Harriet did not describe the religious reasons for these charitable acts, the article did reveal her religious orientation.[378]

As the months passed, Harriet continued to answer questions from her readers about the perpetual problems of the face, hair and body care. She had a separate byline for her weekly articles: "Harriet Hubbard Ayer's Hints to Beauty Seekers." Harriet answered every letter graciously, as if she had not addressed the problem previously, because she felt that it was personally meaningful to each individual who wrote to address the same issues anew. By the end of 1898, the title of Harriet's articles changed to "Timely Hints: Health and Beauty or Hints for Beauty Seekers, Wise Counsel Upon THE TOILET" and other similar titles. Her byline was usually Harriet Hubbard Ayer, but on occasion the prefix "Mrs." was used.[379] The paper carried various articles about theater, dance, fashion, interior design and other subjects, written by other women, but articles by men predominated. There were stories about the very women Harriet had enticed to endorse her products, for instance, Adelina Patti, the opera singer, and Lillian Russell, the actress. In the following years, Harriet continued to write articles similar to those mentioned above almost every other week.

By 1899, she was writing one article a week on health and beauty. In addition, she periodically produced longer articles, including "In What Country Do Woman Have the Best Time?"; "The Child's Toilet"; "How to Make Your Own Cosmetics"; "Parisian Institute of Beauty"; and "Recipe for Vegetarians," followed by several in 1903 with Asian influences: on Buddha, yoga and Hindu concepts, mostly written by the Hindu savant Yogi Ramacharaka.[380] In July 1900, Harriet had taken over as editor of the women's pages with a large-print byline at the top of the page reading, "THE SUNDAY *WORLD* HOME PAGE EDITED BY HARRIET HUBBARD AYER." The *World* continually redesigned and updated its pages because of its competition with Hearst's *New York Journal*. There were separate sections on politics, sports, entertainment and such, including the Sunday magazine in which were found many of Harriet's articles. Harriet hired others to write as she continued to produce her pieces on the usual subjects of obesity, fashion, etiquette and physical culture. According to Harriet, in which country a woman had the best time depended on a woman's dreams and desires:

> *Socially and intellectually, England undoubtedly offers great opportunities. Artistically, France and Italy. Musically, Germany, Italy and France. But the American woman who does not require the stimulus of a man's society to make her happiness can enjoy the best time procurable in any land, in delightful independence.* [381]

This advice surely came from Harriet's own experience, that of never having a man who stood by her for long.

Even before Harriet was formally named editor in July 1900, the name Margaret Kent appeared as a byline in articles such as "Hints Upon Life's Duties" and on other subjects. Kent's name first appeared on January 22, 1899, in the Sunday magazine section, soon after Margaret returned to New York. Her articles, like Harriet's, gave advice to women and appeared almost every week. On January 7, 1900, the name changed to Margaret Rathbone Kent. I am speculating that Margaret Rathbone Ayer, Harriet's daughter, was the same person. When Harriet became editor, Kent's articles were mainly "Rules on Etiquette."[382] The name Margaret Rathbone Kent continued after Harriet's death and throughout Margaret Rathbone Ayer's subsequent takeover of her mother's former position. It would stand to reason that Margaret had to have had some writing experience before succeeding her mother as editor at the newspaper and wrote under the pseudonym Kent.

In May 1902, Harriet wrote to Joseph Pulitzer requesting an assignment abroad to do a series of articles

> *showing to what extent the modern woman may be repaired and rejuvenated, and by what processes. I have made twenty-nine round trips to the other side so I am not suggesting the thirtieth for the sake of novelty. I am not writing mere words when I say that outside of my children I have no ambition paramount to my desire to be useful to the paper that has been so good to me.*

She signed the letter "Faithfully yours."[383] Although she was given the assignment to report on health and beauty methods currently used in Europe, she did have an ulterior motive. Margaret was studying music abroad at this moment, and having recently reunited with her daughter, Harriet wanted to be near her, as well as visit with some of her European friends. She spent some three months in Europe and wrote about Edward VII's health and cure, as well as about the latest Paris fashions, among other European news. She also managed to wheedle an interview with the notorious Florence Maybrick, the American woman convicted of murdering her English husband and imprisoned in London.

Harriet reported on the King's coronation held on August 9, 1902. She had had passing acquaintance with the Prince of Wales since she had not only copied the decoration of his yacht for James Seymour but had also worked with two of his mistresses, Lillie Langtry and Sarah Bernhardt, endorsers of her cosmetics. While others described the actual coronation, Harriet confined herself to writing, on August 10, the article: "The Countess Who Thinks She Cured King Edward VII by Absent Treatment." The king had developed appendicitis, and the original coronation date had to be postponed from June 26 to August 9. Countess Marie Borel, who had a gift for healing, allowed Harriet to interview her in her Battersea Park apartment in London. This was a coup for Harriet, for Countess Borel did not countenance interviews. Knowing the king, the countess was able to speed his recovery by what she termed "absent treatment." Her cures were brought about by the use of magnetic metal tubes that she first held and then passed on to the patient. So perceptive was she that during her interview with Harriet, she was able to discern that Harriet had pain in her hand and offered to help her.[384]

Florence Maybrick, the infamous American woman Harriet interviewed, was imprisoned for allegedly poisoning her husband. No one was allowed to interview her in prison, but through her connections and charm, Harriet inveigled a visit. The story of drugs, adultery, poison and deception was sensationalized in newspapers on both sides of the Atlantic, and Maybrick was convicted on unsubstantiated evidence. Her death sentence was commuted to life imprisonment because of reasonable doubt, but there was no possibility of appeal. Harriet interviewed her after she had already been incarcerated for thirteen years. Maybrick described the daily routine and food of the prisoners. She explained that there was a system of rewards for good behavior, and she was careful to follow the rules. Harriet described Maybrick's "deadly waxen look which long deprivation of light and fresh air inevitably produced."[385]

Having been wrongly committed to an insane asylum, Harriet showed great feeling for the prisoner and reminded her that she had thousands of friends in the world who had not forgotten her. In fact, as early as 1895, Harriet had written, "Mrs. Maybrick is an innocent woman. She has no more poisoned her husband, a well-known arsenic eater, than I expect to poison your dinner." The article in the *Chicago Tribune* went on to say that Mrs. Ayer was particularly interested in the workingwoman, particularly former women of wealth reduced to wage earning.[386] Harriet asked Mrs. Maybrick how she managed to survive in such harsh conditions and whether she had contact with her children. The woman's answer was that seven years before, all information about them had stopped, and when her mother visited, she was not allowed to touch her. The same was true for Harriet, who was not even allowed to sit near the prisoner. Although Baroness de Roques, Maybrick's mother, worked assiduously for her daughter's release, she was unsuccessful until 1904, the year after Harriet died. The article in the *World* drew sympathy and certain doubts about the conviction, but even the king of England was powerless to help Maybrick.[387] When she was finally released, Maybrick returned to America, lectured, wrote a book, worked as a housekeeper and ultimately became a recluse who died in Connecticut in 1941. Harriet's article brought the Florence Maybrick case back into the public eye which may have led to her eventual release. It also showed that Harriet had a nose for interesting stories, empathized with the downtrodden and could write about subjects other than health and beauty.

Pulitzer exacted payment for his largesse and gave Harriet the additional job of finding a servant and a governess for Mrs. Pulitzer, who was then in Lucerne, Switzerland. Harriet interviewed several women and checked all their references carefully; she then arranged for the two women she selected to travel to Switzerland. She wrote to Pulitzer's assistant, Alfred Bates, saying she had spent twenty pounds

> *in the governess and maid undertaking. I wish I could make the chief believe the truth in the matter, which is that I never received an assignment or request with greater pleasure than the one which you gave me the opportunity of doing ever so small a service for Mrs. Pulitzer personally.*

Pulitzer sent her a gift, and she asked if there was anything else she could do for him before she and her daughter left on July 28.[388] Such toadying was not in character for Harriet, but perhaps she felt indebted to Pulitzer for giving her a job when she was down and out; for allowing her to work in Europe; or perhaps it was just proper homage to one's "chief."

Harriet continued to write and edit the home page with her biweekly "Questions and Answers." Occasionally, longer articles appeared, such as "Newport X-rayed," which was solely a gossip piece accompanied by pictures of the notables who were vacationing in Newport, Rhode Island. She wrote another article about the right kind of corsets for stout women and yet another about the use of real babies for teaching nurses proper care. Her columns continued to advocate a proto-feminist doctrine of health, exercise and attention to grooming, which she asserted was attainable by everyone. While she criticized the use of artificial aids to beauty (like those she once promoted for Récamier Preparations), she underscored the importance of being physically attractive. In recommending that older women use cosmetics to camouflage their age, she was the precursor of the American obsession with youth and beauty. She provided homemade recipes for cosmetics where she had previously sold them. Women over thirty had to begin their skin care promptly, and those over fifty had to use beauty aids such as creams, delicate powders and rouge. With great certainty, Harriet counseled her readers that beauty brought women both entrée and power. And so it did for Harriet Ayer - along with hard work.

RAINY DAISIES

Never without fresh ideas, this energetic woman worked on other projects while editing the *World*'s women's pages until her death. She not only wrote a book on health and beauty but she also involved herself with a group dubbed by the press the "Rainy Daisies." There were several organizations devoted to dress reform during the second half of the nineteenth century. Harriet only belonged to the Rainy Day Club (RDC). In her articles, she advocated the same points the RDC did: lighter-weight clothing, less constricting corsets, shorter and less cumbersome skirts. Comfort, utility and health were the motivations for change. Sympathetic to the advances advocated by the RDC, which was founded in 1896, the year Harriet started working at the

World, she promoted shorter skirts while long skirts for women were still in fashion. Shorter skirts were especially important for working women on rainy days. Harriet was quoted:

> *For several years, says Mrs. Ayer, I have daily endured the nuisance of dragging my skirts after me or clutching them in a painfully wearisome effort to rescue them from the filth of elevated railway stations and from the mud and dirt of the city streets. For twelve years of my business life I have sat for hours each rainy day with damp, often soaking skirts about my ankles, and have suffered in health in consequence. Thousands of other women have done the same in this city alone.*

She said that she was glad to be a proponent of "the most sensible, practical, and proper dress movement ever in my opinion inaugurated." She publicized this organization founded by Mrs. Emma Beckwith and Mrs. Bertha Welby and proselytized its mission.[389] At the club's first annual meeting, Mrs. Beckwith presided as president, Mrs. Welby as secretary and Harriet as one of the vice-presidents. The stated purpose was "to effect such reform in dress as will secure for women health and comfort, while being genuinely artistic, graceful, modest, and inconspicuous, and to extend material aid to our less fortunate sisters along this dress reform." The dresses were to be not longer than four inches from the floor, and were to be worn with high boots, a modest, plain hat and suitable jacket. Any woman wearing this uniform was eligible for membership in the New York Rainy Day Club.[390] The group favored not only shorter skirts but also common-sense shoes, which Harriet championed in an article on November 1, 1903.[391] The new dress code was especially meant for "working women, clerks, saleswomen, factory girls—all of our sex compelled to go about the streets in all kinds of weather."[392]

The RDC, continued its fight into the 1920s. All they wanted was to wear their skirts short enough so as not to sweep the floor, yet men, and even some women, opposed the dress change, arguing that it was immodest. With the dual sanction of doctors and manufacturers, along with women athletes who began to play in less cumbersome outfits, the change slowly took hold. Harriet wore these shorter skirts to work, along with sensible blouses and jackets, nothing frilly. (See Figure 10.) One of her articles, "What Not to Wear for Walking," advised women to wear nothing ostentatious or fancy.[393]

On Sunday, March 20, 1898, Harriet wrote about the new, less voluminous skirt while her former physician, and by now old friend, Dr. George Shrady, advocated looser sleeves and bodices, as well as shorter skirts:

> *There are many reforms needed in this new fashion. Not alone are tight sleeves, waists, and skirts a menace to good health and the death knell to grace, but the long skirt also cannot be too strongly condemned. It is positively dirty. Sweeping along the streets it gathers untold quantities of dirt, filled with deadly microbes. I do not believe that there will ever be a sweeping reform in this matter. But women will gradually see what an injustice they are doing themselves, and a readjustment will be in order.*[394]

In other articles about manners and dress, Harriet continued to campaign for the shorter skirt, especially for walking and working.[395] Shorter skirts did arrive and with the passing years became shorter and shorter. Harriet continued to press her case about good health and proper care of the body as prerequisites for beauty that were accessible to everyone. She practiced what she preached and set an example in what she wore, as well as in what she wrote. Although in twentieth-century terms her advice seems familiar, it was radical in her day.

17

Recipes for Health and Beauty

$\mathbf{F}$or only a few pennies, all classes of women shared the secrets of health and beauty recommended by this famous former society woman. Most of her advice was common sense—suggestions for bathing, sleep, fresh air, exercise and healthy food—different from the earlier restrictive beliefs of limiting fresh air and bathing. By proffering rules of etiquette, proper apparel and correct behavior for various occasions, she benefited the emerging independent woman, as well as the upwardly mobile masses. So popular were her articles that Harriet was encouraged to compile the information into a book. *Harriet Hubbard Ayer's Book: A Complete Treatise on the Laws of Health and Beauty* was published in 1899 by King-Richardson Company in Springfield, Massachusetts. The *World* gave her permission to use previously published material, in particular the accounts of Catherine Lane and Martha Baker. She wrote in the preface: "The reason for writing this volume is found in the fact that for many years no single day has passed that I have not received letters from unknown women asking for a book that would give them practical advice on the subjects treated herein." [396]

The popularity of the book necessitated a second edition just three years later, in 1902. In the dedication to the second edition, she iterated that the book "would never have been written save for the repeated demands for such a volume"; therefore, she dedicated it to her countless correspondents. "I believe that good women can be more helpful, more uplifting, and wield a stronger moral influence if they are lovely to look at, graceful as well as gracious, perpetually young and beautiful." [397] That philosophy permeated

Harriet's writing. Unattractive as a youth, she was ridiculed and compared unfavorably to her more beautiful sisters. When she herself turned into a beauty at the age of nineteen or twenty, after marriage and children, she learned what a powerful tool it was to be attractive. She was sought after in Paris in the early 1870s and then envied in Chicago between 1872 and 1882, but it was in Paris that she learned how to dress and care for her appearance.

When she was compelled by circumstances to work, Harriet first used her good looks and her ability to create attractive settings and to entertain well. Her discovery of a face cream to enhance the complexion led to her promotion of the importance of caring for and improving one's physiognomy and body. This was equally important for other young women, especially those seeking social advancement. Her first avenue for proselytizing, Récamier Preparations, was one that made her a lot of money. Through her writing of long advertorials that appealed to rich and poor women alike, she practiced a skill that served her later in life. That writing talent and her ability to express herself clearly and elegantly is what she brought to the *World* and then to her book. She claimed that her only wish was that her suggestions would be of practical service to every woman who read them. She did not believe that beauty alone was the reason for her achievements; intelligence and perseverance played a major role, although she never wrote about the latter.

In the preface to the first edition, Harriet provided her qualifications for dispensing the information in the book: "For fifteen years I have been studying, experimenting, manufacturing and writing along the lines followed in this volume. I do not advance theories, but demonstrated facts in what I have to say." She then presented her philosophy:

> *I know that good women are happier and better if they keep their good looks, their youthful grace and elasticity, their girlish figures throughout life, than when through ignorance or carelessness, or both, they lose their personal charm and become old and bent, wrinkled or fat, or emaciated before they have reached the golden prime of life. I believe that good women can wield a stronger moral influence if they are lovely to look at, graceful as well as gracious, perpetually young and beautiful, than the reverse.*

She credited the numerous doctors and dentists who advised her and the people who provided photographs and illustrations. She was also influenced by the book she had translated and annotated in 1892, *My Lady's Dressing Room* by Baroness Staffe, as well as by the etiquette book of Mrs. M.E.W. Sherwood, which included beauty advice.

There are fifty chapters and five appendices in Harriet's book. Each chapter begins with a brief Shakespearean quotation, an erudite touch. Chapter one, called "The Will of the Wisp," is about the maintenance of beauty, a constant pursuit throughout a woman's life: "The pursuit of beauty is as old as the world—as old as the love of beauty. Do not let us blame the women who have learned, some of them in the saddest of all ways, that beauty is the supreme power of our sex." Beauty, she adds, is synonymous with purity and temperance.[398]

Chapter two, "The Art of Remaining Young," gives examples of well-kept beauties, some of Harriet's former endorsers. "It is the beautiful women of the world who have been most powerful…and who have largely made history. Beauty and goodness should walk hand in hand."[399] There are several ways to combat "the ravages of time in its impress upon our faces and forms"; one would be the hygienic method and the other the cosmetic branch, which may include plastic surgery.[400]

Chapter three, "The Sin of Dowdiness," asserts that dowdiness is not only a matter of beauty but also of dress and personal care. "There is a chance for every one of us to be attractive in appearance, and there is no such thing as a hopelessly ugly girl or woman."[401]

Chapter four, "The Well-Groomed Woman," promotes the importance of bathing and apparel. Here Harriet reveals her own stages of life, evolving from

"a gilded child of luxury," to a business woman at the head of an important enterprise, I have been a toiler working more hours in the twenty-four and harder than most men work, yet at no time have I seen the day when I felt that my appearance alone made, lost, or kept my friends, whilst the benefit I have received and the satisfaction I have enjoyed from the general observance of the hygiene hints herein given—hints which help to make the well-groomed woman in the best and truest sense of the term.[402]

Chapter five, "Cleanliness: The Handmaiden of Health and Beauty," gives the methods and formulas Harriet had been preaching. For example, she recommends a daily bath in luke-warm water, the use of pure soap made of vegetable oils and a scrub brush for the body, as well as a camel's hair brush for the face. The latter, she writes, is about six inches in length and five across and costs only $1.25.[403]

Chapter six is a continuation of the previous chapter about bathing. It includes a formula for an almond bath in warm water, which she said might be taken in the morning or at night.[404] She then prints formulas for perfuming the bath water.[405] The discussion ends with various forms of baths: Turkish baths, sulfur baths, electric baths, aromatic baths and more.[406] With the advent of electricity in the 1880s, new uses were found for it, as in stirring the bath water and treating hysteria with vibrators. The last line of this chapter reiterates her philosophy:

> *Beauty alone will cause a man to fall head over heels in love with a woman. But, personal cleanliness and perfect daintiness will preserve a man's affection and respect as no other attribute can, for even age is charming when clean and wholesome.*[407]

It seems that in Harriet's view, personality and intelligence have little to do with preserving a man's affection, thereby revealing a period assessment of men's devotion to women.

Chapters seven through eleven deal with "The Hair," where Harriet explains the anatomy of hair, heredity, cleanliness, massage of the scalp and coloring. She advises against bleaching the hair with peroxide to become or remain blond yet offers formulas for dying; however, she counsels readers to go to a professional for a proper job. Recipes for the treatment and prevention of dandruff, eczema and thinning hair follow. Within these chapters, she also discusses unwanted hair and electrolysis. She then suggests methods of curling the hair and ends with scalp massage. Hair was thought to be the crowning glory of a woman at the time, and it was, for the most part, worn long.

Nine chapters are devoted to the complexion. This was important because Harriet said that sixty out of one hundred American girls had poor skin, despite the fact that $20 million was spent annually on cosmetics, facial treatments and alleged cures.[408] The cause, in part, was the consumption of sweets. Harriet offers the formula for Fossati cream for pimples and sulfur soap. Once again, her advice boils down to healthy food and cleanliness. A whole chapter is devoted to freckles, the "offensive pigmentation" that plagued Harriet during her adolescence. She offers recipes for freckle cream, balm and ointment, some of which lighten pigmentation and others that remove spots. She also recommends creams and lotions for wind and sunburns, as well as other skin blemishes. For ugly, annoying blackheads, as well as acne, she supplies remedies and treatments. The next section deals with eczema and its treatment. The proper method of cleansing and steaming the face is another subject she writes about. She ends the complexion chapters by discussing the cause and treatment of wrinkles, a subject of interest to older women. Here, she does not forget to mention warts, moles, birthmarks and scars, ending by strongly recommending the Swedish facial massage as a way to strengthen facial muscles, firm tissues and nourish the skin. Writing about face skinning or acid peels, which were expensive and painful, she jests: "You takes it or you leaves it according to what you thinks."[409]

Chapters twenty-two through twenty-seven deal with the various parts of the face—eyes and eyebrows, nose, ears, mouth and teeth—while arms, shoulders, neck and bust are treated in chapters twenty-eight and twenty-nine. For these subjects, she again mentions what to strive for and how to treat and cure maladies or abnormalities.

Chapter thirty, "The Perfect Woman," cites the bodily requirements according to a German writer. Height should be eight times the length of the head and so on. Harriet then charts the good and bad points, ending with:

> *Better indeed than beauty alone, is the possession of a few of the foregoing technical requisites supplemented by cleanliness, neatness, fastidiousness, care in matters of the toilet, combined with engaging manners and gentleness of disposition.*[410]

Chapter thirty-one discusses the corset, a subject much written about in the *World*. Women coveted a twenty-four-inch waist and squeezed their bodies into tightly laced corsets to achieve that goal. Unless the waist was gained by exercise and inheritance, the average woman required a corset; therefore, Harriet advocated the boneless corset.[411] Harriet considered a well-fitted one a blessing and claimed that it was unhealthy and deforming to wear tight corsets.

Hands and feet are the subjects of the next few chapters. Chapter thirty-seven, titled "Late Hours and Dissipation," begins with a comment true to Harriet's personal experience. "When one considers how many women there are whose happiness and comfort have been destroyed through dissipated husbands…it is almost a wonder that everyone of the gentler sex is not a total abstainer."[412] She tells about women destroyed not only by alcohol but by drugs as well.[413] The message is "that excess is fatal to beauty and destructive of happiness and morality as well."[414] She then rails against excessive drinking of tea and coffee.

Physical culture—that is, the daily exercise of the muscles that "expands the lungs, and sends the blood tingling through the veins"—is something Harriet continually promoted. In her book, she devotes chapters thirty-eight through forty-one to the subject. She advocates proper breathing and exercises for different parts of the body, which were illustrated, as well as swimming. Chapter forty-three deals with sleep, and in it she recommends the proper position, bed, room and darkness.

Next, Harriet writes "Beauty and Health for the Business Woman," once again promoting her viewpoint that "the best looking of the business women applicants will get the position. It is scarcely necessary to say that a woman in business should dress with some severity." The woman who "dresses plainly will have more time and money to use in caring for herself, both physically and mentally…Keep your soul above the petty trials of life. Don't waste your strength in losing your temper over small things."[415] Again, she reiterates the importance of bathing and care for physical appearance, especially teeth.

Harriet even incorporates a chapter about the care and feeding of infants, including weaning from the breast. Then she repeats one of her *World* articles about "How to Read Character from the Features." She also deals with "Emaciation" and "Obesity." Within those chapters are found charts for proper weight according to height. She calls sugar and starch "the most formidable of flesh-producers."[416] In addition to a modified diet, she recommends exercise and cleanliness, as she does for most other problems. Her next-to-last chapter, forty-nine, is titled "Cosmetics," in which she repeats that she is not against the use of cosmetics in women over thirty but is "not an advocate of indiscriminate painting of the face, of hair dying or bleaching." Women should make up their own minds about those things "without masculine interference or dictation."[417]

By the time Harriet wrote this book, attitudes toward the use of cosmetics were softening. Max Beerbohm, the English parodist and caricaturist, in an 1894 article titled "Defense of Cosmetics," written while he was still at Merton College, Oxford, facetiously supported the use of cosmetics: "Many a husband, suddenly realizing that his wife was painted, sternly bade her to go up and take it off. On her reappearance, bade her with increasing sternness, go up and put it all on again." As the proprietress of Récamier Preparations from 1886 to 1893, Harriet had been timid about using the word "cosmetics." In London, she testified in 1887 that her products were patent medicines. But in her book and in her *New York World* articles, she declared unequivocally that after age thirty, the wear and tear of life, maternity and stress destroyed a woman's fine appearance. She provided formulas for rouge and for whitening the skin, for a pale skin was still the mark of gentility, signifying that the woman was not a toiler exposed to the elements. She waxed poetic:

> *Women are like flowers and beautiful out-of-doors pictures—all delicacy and grace, with an atmosphere of spring or summer or autumn emanating from them—each lovely at its appropriate time, that is, when they are as Nature intended them.*[418]

Harriet's last chapter is about perfumes. She recommends the odors of flowers because they are delicate. "I should always select violet or the most delicate heliotrope for a personal perfume. It is in far better taste for a woman to use but one odor at a time—for her handkerchief extract, toilet water, sachets, etc."[419] She then provides some formulas, but ends with a warning about the abuse of perfumes: women should not use strong scents, like musk.

Five appendices follow, including the complete stories of her cures for Catherine Lane and Martha Baker, mentioned previously. Harriet describes the daily treatment of Catherine, hour by hour, and ends with letters written by a jury of women who examined Catherine before treatment and after. Dr. Sarah A. French Battey wrote, "Catherine Lane had certainly improved greatly during the six weeks of hygienic living. She is apparently in perfect health."[420] These letters had, of course, been published in the newspaper along with the one from Catherine's grateful mother. For Martha Baker, there are detailed progress reports and menus. Harriet ends the chapter with a disclaimer saying that these were special cases, although most of her advice could be applied to anyone. Appendix C supplies remedies and toilet preparations, and Appendix D lists medicated soaps and their uses. The last furnishes a table of measures in pints, ounces, grams and such for the accurate measurement of the formulas provided.

Harriet's book underscored her beliefs and was helpful to the new modern woman, freeing her from old-fashioned ideas about health and beauty. Immigrant women and working-class girls, ignorant of the proper care of the face and body, let alone knowledge of how to enhance their looks, were therein advised. Harriet, who was touted by the popular press not only as an expert but also as an upper-class society lady, was to be emulated. She forsook many of the ideas in her Récamier advertorials and replaced them with common-sense suggestions, affordable by all.

Though true to her era in her acceptance of the role of women, she did provide an indirect means to help poorer women redefine themselves. She consistently advocated that women use their beauty and their feminine wiles to their advantage, asserting that looks were their ultimate tool in getting jobs and for catching and keeping husbands. Despite the disastrous gender discrimination she had experienced, she retained traditional attitudes. Nevertheless, a woman who felt she looked good—or at least better than she had before applying Harriet's advice—certainly had more self-confidence. Current thought corroborates the universality of flawless skin and healthy hair as being important to everyone's conception of beauty.[421]

Harriet's philosophy remained close to that of Baroness Staffe. The baroness promulgated the need for women to make themselves as attractive as possible for men, without ever letting them know at what cost beauty was acquired and maintained. Hide shortcomings and imperfections and never let a man see how it is done. "What is life," she wrote, "without some illusions?"[422] The popularity and ongoing relevance of Harriet's book is evidenced not only by a second edition three years later, but also by the Arno Press, in cooperation with the New York Times Book Company, reprint in 1974, seventy years later. More recently, in 2005, Main Street, a division of Sterling Publishing Company in New York, published a compendium of Harriet's advice and formulas. Titled *Bath and Beauty Splash: 100 Recipes for a Decadent Home Spa*, it included an introduction on women and beauty and chapters on the bath, the hair, the complexion, the hands and feet and perfumes, along with a glossary and online resources.

Throughout her life, Harriet was preoccupied with beauty. As a young Chicago socialite, she concentrated on her own improvement. In her business, she used her knowledge and experience to promote beauty enhancement for others, initiating and promulgating the American fixation on youth and beauty. And as a journalist, she focused on health and beauty affected by good hygiene, one of the steps to appearing fresh, natural and attractive. Other writers promoted much of what she did, but she was the one who brought these common-sense ideas to a wide public audience.

Death and Aftermath

H arriet's thriving career as a journalist ended with her unexpected death on Wednesday, November 25, 1903, at her home at 70 West Forty-sixth Street:[423]

> *She had been ill since last Saturday. The news of her death will bring grief to thousands of her friends in all parts of the world, and especially to many hundreds whose misfortunes she alleviated with kindly, cheerful, unostentatious benevolence. Mrs. Ayer was the most prominent newspaper woman in America. The achievements of her lifetime constituted a history of courage that misfortunes, no matter how severe or frequent, could never affect.*[424]

While the newspapers cited pneumonia, her death certificate verified that in addition to having pneumonia for six days, she also had an attack of acute nephritis for two days, a complication of the chronic nephritis that she had suffered from for the last two years of her life.[425]

Harriet was much loved by the staff of the *World* for her gentle manners and her sympathy for the suffering and hardships of others. "She was one of the most remarkable women in my experience and one of the best and cleverest. She had a heart as great as her brain and a beauty that age could not mar," wrote Albert Payson Terhune (1872–1942), who was on staff at the *World* when Harriet began and remained until after her death.[426] When the paper further honored her by flying its flag at half mast, some reporters asked Don C. Seitz (1862–1935), the business manager of the *World* since 1898, why the flag was lowered. After he told them it was for Harriet Hubbard Ayer, they were astounded that it was lowered for a woman. Seitz, a veteran journalist, told them that she was the best man on the staff.[427]

Harriet's obituary in the *World* noted:

> *It is seldom that one woman has so thoroughly commanded the respect and admiration of the reading public, as well as the love and friendship of all who came within the wide radius of her personal influence. For her to hear of a case of need was to relieve it…whether a friend or a total stranger.*[428]

This summary of her character is consistent with her behavior from the time of her first hospitalization and during the Chicago fire when she rescued neighborhood children along with her own. The *World* continued to list Harriet as the editor of the home page for several weeks after her death. The issue of December 13, 1903, finally announced that "the *World's* Magazine's Home Page will henceforth be conducted by Miss Margaret Hubbard Ayer, daughter of the late Harriet Hubbard Ayer."

Funeral services were held at Trinity Church on Broadway and Wall Street the next morning at 10:30 a.m. Reverend Dr. J. Hewitt Steele conducted the Episcopal service. Harriet's readers, colleagues, friends and family attended the crowded funeral service. Her daughters, Margaret and Hattie, were there with her grandchildren. She had outlived her former husband, her nemesis Blanche Willis Howard von Teuffel and likely her archenemy James M. Seymour. Much loved and admired by many, Harriet had exhibited heartfelt compassion for others while often displaying detachment from family members. Adversity softened her and in the end made her more appreciative of her relatives.

Harriet's body was cremated, and the ashes were shipped to Chicago by Margaret to be buried, not in the Ayer mausoleum, but in the ground on the Ayer family plot at Graceland Cemetery in Chicago. Her ashes were placed near her in-laws, John V. and Elida, whom she loved; her baby Gertrude; and Herbert's stepbrothers and their families. Many of Harriet's maternal family members were also buried at Graceland, but not her mother and father or her sisters, since they had all died elsewhere. Only Harriet, who had lived and worked in New York for twenty years, wanted to return to the city of her birth, probably to lay near Gertrude, whom she lost so traumatically in

Death and Aftermath

1871. Unprepared to die at age fifty-four after surviving so many tragedies, she left no will but must have informed her daughters that she wished to be cremated and buried in Chicago.

The *World* continued to publish Harriet's articles through December 1903, a month after her death. Some of her articles were syndicated, so verbatim copies also appeared in papers such as the *San Francisco Chronicle* in 1903 after she died. She had metamorphosed from a wealthy socialite into a business mogul, then into an inmate in an insane asylum and, lastly, into a popular newspaper columnist. She proved to be an extraordinary woman of great intelligence, energy and determination. After her escape from the asylum, she had reunited with her sisters and their families. She had even stayed with her cousin Mary Anne, Mrs. Gurdon Hubbard, in 1896 when she lectured in Chicago, revealing that any embarrassment due to her sensationalized divorce, business activities and incarceration did not vex her venerable relative.

Against all odds, Harriet Hubbard Ayer persevered and succeeded in a man's world. Her success was her downfall; the men in her life resented her genius, her persistence and her vigor in creating, managing and advertising Récamier cosmetic products. Although vulnerable to the machinations of men, each and every time she encountered adversity, phoenix-like, she successfully reinvented herself. Paradoxically, the men who sought to destroy her never profited from their malevolence, as the company failed without her leadership. Harriet facilitated the inauguration of the beauty industry and women's acceptance of cosmetic products that changed future grooming habits. She anticipated modern American consumer culture and identified women as customers for whom shopping became a leisure activity and makeup a necessity. Although her ambitions were circumscribed by Victorian traditions, she was both a successful entrepreneur and writer, two avenues of work open to respectable women. Her articles and book about women's health and beauty were in the vanguard, tapping into feminine desires that went beyond health and beauty to dreams of transformation and social advancement. Although she did not belong to the emergent feminist movements of her day, she epitomized the independent woman, played a part in the new mass journalism and was a prototype for later entrepreneurs in cosmetics.

Epilogue

After extricating herself from Blanche Howard's control in August 1897, Margaret arrived in the United States in 1898, ill prepared to take care of herself. She had been so isolated that for a time she even lost touch with her sister. As Margaret grew older, Blanche had become increasingly mentally disturbed and consequently disenchanted with her young charge, who she neglected and abused. Margaret, who had once admired and loved her more than her own mother, grew to hate and fear her. James Seymour paid part of her tuition, perhaps because of his daughter-in-law Hattie, or because of his fondness for Margaret. When he stopped sending money, Blanche turned against both him and Margaret.[429] Blanche needed the money which was why Seymour had been able to bribe her into indoctrinating the Ayer children against their mother. Just as Harriet had to escape from Blanche's clutches, so did Margaret ten years later. She sold a gold watch her mother had given her and with the money escaped to London from Guernsey in 1898, where she and Blanche were vacationing. Hattie had sent a ticket for her to sail back to the United States and left it in London with Marion Smith, with whom Margaret had become friendly in Stuttgart.[430] A short time after Margaret left her, Blanche died in Munich on October 7, 1898, at the age of fifty-one.

The nineteen-year-old young woman whom Hattie and Lewis met at the pier in New York in 1898 was nervous and fearful and spoke English with a faint German accent. Hattie offered Margaret a place to stay with her mother-in-law, Caroline Seymour, in New Jersey. By that time, James

Seymour had deserted his wife and disappeared. Margaret contacted Herbert, who was by then ill and penniless, living at the Palmer House in Chicago.[431] He was too ill to help her and told Margaret that Harriet was truly a good person. He advised her to contact her mother at the *World* to obtain a job.[432] Harriet then decided to bring Herbert east in 1898 so he could be near his daughters.[433] Caroline Kirkland, who knew Harriet, wrote in 1919:

> *Whether she was rich or in restricted circumstances, Harriet was always generous in sympathy and money to those with whom she came in contact. An evidence of this large-hearted tenderness was that after years of absence, when she heard that Herbert was alone, poor, mind gone, and body sick unto death at the Palmer House…she took care of him, paid all the many expenses of his last illness, and held his hand as he died.*[434]

Herbert died in a hospital in Newark, New Jersey, on January 12, 1899, after having being there for about a year. Newark was close enough to New York for the girls to easily visit him. Harriet, however, did not visit him; she merely paid his bills.[435] She had suffered so much herself that she felt sorry for Herbert, and although he had mistreated her in the past, he was still the father of her children. And what is more, she attributed much of his bad behavior toward her to the influence of James Seymour. Herbert was cremated, and supposedly his remains were flown to Chicago for burial in the family plot at Graceland Cemetery, but cemetery records reveal that he is neither there nor at Rosedale Cemetery.[436]

Margaret lived with different friends and relatives after a short stay with Mrs. Seymour. She even retained her childhood relationship with General Grubb, her adored "Ginger." In order to resolve the false idea Blanche had planted in her head about Ginger, that he was her real father rather than Herbert, Margaret confronted the general. He explained that he never met Margaret until she was four years old and that he had not seen her mother for six years before that. So another of Blanche's lies was put to rest. Margaret was now ready to face a reunion with her mother. With some trepidation, she had someone arrange a meeting with Harriet, who was then living in a small walkup apartment at 328 West 113th Street, overlooking Morningside Park in Manhattan, her address from 1897 through 1900. After a few awkward moments when the two first met, they embraced and vowed never to be apart again. However, it took a while before they truly felt comfortable together. It was sometime after this that Margaret asked if she could live with Harriet, and of course Harriet was ecstatic. She immediately bought a piano and a bed for her daughter.[437]

Margaret demonstrated some of the familiar behavior caused by trauma and stress—insomnia and anxiety. Harriet, well aware of the symptoms, called one of her doctors to help Margaret dispel memories of her last traumatic years with Blanche Howard and to help her adjust to her new life.[438] Harriet may have gotten Margaret the job writing for the *World* under the pseudonym Margaret Rathbone Kent. Rathbone was Margaret's middle name, taken from her grandmother's family.[439] If so, her first article for the women's pages appeared on January 22, 1899. Although the articles continued, she was able to go abroad for months at a time to study music and voice in Paris. Perhaps Harriet wrote the articles in her stead.

While living in Stuttgart, both Margaret and Hattie had studied at the Conservancy of Music in Stuttgart, which was under the direction of Professor Dr. Immanuel Faisst until 1894, when he died.[440] The conservancy offered classes for both professional and amateur musicians and also taught acting. When Margaret settled into her new life with her mother, she consulted with David Belasco, the successful playwright, director and theatrical producer, about the direction she should take in her career. He had taken an interest in her musical education and gave her lessons in stagecraft. Some of her mother's old theater friends, such as the opera singer Adelina Patti, were helpful to Margaret as well. Frau Cosima Wagner, wife of the composer Richard Wagner, who after his death became the producer of the Bayreuth Festival, also befriended Margaret and spoke highly of her talent. Margaret probably met Frau Wagner through Blanche, who was friends with the Wagners in Germany. They, along with Mrs. Stuyvesant Fish and other members of New York society, predicted a great future for Margaret, whose mezzo-soprano voice they thought had remarkable sweetness.[441]

Harriet sent Margaret back to Paris to study with the well-known singing teacher Mrs. Robinson-Duff. When Margaret returned to New York in 1900, she appeared in the chorus of Willard Spensor's *Miss Bob White* in 1901, a show that never made it to New York after tryouts in Philadelphia. Hattie and Harriet, however, attended the opening together, and after attending the performance, Harriet stayed in New Jersey to visit with her grandchildren. In 1902, Margaret returned to Paris for further study. That was when Harriet was able to convince Joseph Pulitzer to give her an assignment in London so that she could be with her daughter. Harriet and Margaret returned together aboard the steamship *Pennsylvania*, a Hamburg and American ocean liner. Reportedly, Margaret had performed in Paris and Germany but had declined offers to make her debut at the Opera Comique in Paris or at Covent Garden in London in order to make her musical debut in the United States.[442]

Margaret's first solo appearance in the United States came when she assumed the role of Mrs. Green Carnation in an operetta called *Tommy Rot* in October 1902. She was complimented for her ease and grace, but the part did not adequately allow her to show off her voice. She then played Lady Dope in the musical comedy *Fad and Folly*, which ran from November 27, 1902, to December 27, 1902. What was best remembered, however, was that she was the daughter of Harriet Hubbard Ayer. Soon after, in 1903, Margaret played a major role in the *Red Feather*, an operetta that ran for four months at the Lyric Theater and was produced by the famous impresario Lorenz Ziegfeld, remembered today for the famous Follies he launched in 1907. Margaret sang in the chorus of only one more musical comedy, *The Earl and the Girl*, which played from November 4, 1905, until March 10, 1906. Apparently, she was able to do this while working at the *World*. She had a short-lived marriage to a pianist, Harold Osborn Smith, in 1907.[443]

After the death of her mother, Margaret, for the most part, gave up her musical career to focus on her job as feature writer and editor of the women's pages of the *Sunday World* and the *New York Evening World*, which she did for about nine years. In 1913, she married Frank Cobb, editor of the *World*, a second marriage for them both.[444] Later, she switched to the *New York Journal*. She had two children with Cobb, Hubbard and Jane, whom she sent to the newly founded Dalton School in New York, where she taught music. Margaret profited from her mother's death. She not only took over as editor of the *World*'s women's pages, but she also sold her mother's name. Eventually, in 1957, she wrote a biography about her mother with Isabella Taves, a professional writer, ostensibly to make clear that her mother was not a lunatic. Without Margaret's book, little would be known about Harriet Hubbard Ayer, her family or her extraordinary achievements. Although biased and undocumented, Margaret's biography provides a starting point and a chronicle of events especially before the Chicago fire.

Hattie, who had married Lewis Seymour in 1888, had three daughters and a son. Lewis suffered financial reversals along with his father in 1888. He was also indicted in July 1894 for not answering questions put to him by the United States Senate Committee investigating the relation of the Sugar Trust with senators.[445] A chip off the old block, having apprenticed at his father's side, he too was accused of suspicious behavior. In 1897, the Seymour Brothers business, caught in a bull market, failed.

> *The Seymour brothers, who gave the name to the firm, are the sons of James M. Seymour who has been a prominent Wall Street operator for a score of years. He is a native of Texas, and came here many years ago with wealth and the prestige of a successful career on the Chicago Board of Trade. His success in this city has been almost uninterrupted, and the failure of his sons, who he started in business a few years ago, is a great disappointment to him. He said last evening that he did not care to discuss the matter.*[446]

Of Seymour's two sons, James Jr., probably because he was five years younger than Lewis, does not seem to have been involved in Harriet's life, although the brothers became partners. Sometime at the end of the century, James Seymour disappeared, taking with him whatever money he had and leaving his wife and extended family without an income. His disappearance confirmed for his family that he was the deceitful and malicious scoundrel Harriet knew him to be. Hattie finally realized what a rogue her father-in-law was and how he had wronged her mother. Lewis died sometime after 1900, leaving Hattie to support the children on her own.[447]

Afterward, Hattie moved to New York about 1909, where she was engaged in "a long period of strenuous teaching...including eleven years at the head of the piano department of the East Third Street Music School Settlement."[448] She gave high-quality music instruction to immigrant children and adults, who also received social services at this Manhattan settlement house. During and after World War I, Hattie discovered the uplifting nature of music for traumatic stress symptoms and used soothing music to help cure wounded soldiers. She then founded the Seymour School of Musical Reeducation and was for seven years chairwoman of the hospital music committee of the State Charities Aid Association. From her dual experiences at the settlement music school and with musical therapy, she wrote *What Music Can Do for You: A Guide for the Uninitiated*, published by Harper & Brothers in 1920. In the preface, she expresses a principle learned and practiced by her mother, "The failures of the past must become the means of leading us to a better future." She believed that the average person could know music by learning its connection with life. "Music is a necessity; it is for all."[449] In 1941, she founded the National Foundation of Musical Therapy, of which she was president.[450]

By the turn of the century, Harriet was reconciled with the daughters she loved so dearly, the daughters for whom she had worked so hard, the daughters for whom she had provided an elite education. Harriet's reaction to her own mother's indifference to her schooling and upbringing had furnished the determination to succeed as a single parent and to raise her daughters with care. While Harriet's letters reveal her affection, her total involvement with work and its concomitant problems distanced her from her children for reasons other than her mother's. Still, Harriet not only provided a musical education for them but also a positive model of a workingwoman.

As for Harriet's former company, Miss Maria E. Rinn, the past employee of Harriet's who had bought all the corporate assets, including trademarks and good will for $4,000 at a receiver's sale in 1896, continued the business under the name of Récamier Manufacturing Company. She used Harriet's signature until 1897, when Harriet brought suit to stop the use of her name. Rinn carried on the business until 1920, when she sold it to Miss Anna E. Reynolds. Miss Reynolds, too, had problems with using Harriet's name, but in a lawsuit on April 13, 1932, the claim against using the Ayer name and family crest was judged to be non-trademark use because no one by that time knew who Harriet Hubbard Ayer was. The 1886 trademark registration had expired in 1916 without renewal.

The 1932 lawsuit was between two companies, one using the name Récamier Manufacturing and the other using the name and signature of Harriet Hubbard Ayer. Even though Harriet had sold her business in 1896, Margaret had sold the use of Harriet's name four years after her mother's death to Vincent Benjamin Thomas (1868–1918), who became president of the Harriet Hubbard Ayer Corporation. He was married to Lillian Sefton, who knew Margaret since they had appeared together in a musical production. Thomas, whose company specialized in perfume and cosmetics, registered the script name in 1908 and used it uninterruptedly.[451] When Thomas died in 1918, his wife took over the business and, in time, became one of the highest-paid women executives in the United States, earning a salary of $100,000 per year in 1937, a fitting follow-up to Harriet's advances in the feminist workforce. By 1925, Sefton was remarried to the American artist Robert Leftwich Dodge, who became the art director of the company.[452] Lillian sold her Harriet Hubbard Ayer Company to Lever Brothers for $5.5 million in 1947. The company at that time was grossing between $6 and $7 million a year. While the two companies, both spawned from Harriet's original one, were in competition with each other, they did not infringe on each other's usage of the name. Since most people no longer remembered Harriet, these companies' reputations were largely self-created. Yet because of her earlier fame and achievements, they used the name Harriet Hubbard Ayer and Récamier Manufacturing into the mid-twentieth century.

Notes

Chapter I

1. Henry Edward Hamilton (1840–?), Gurdon Hubbard manuscript, Chicago Historical Museum Library, Chicago, IL (hereafter cited as G. Hubbard ms.). Hamilton was related to Gurdon Hubbard and Henry G. Hubbard.

2. Gurdon S. Hubbard (1802–1886), son of Elizur and Abigail Hubbard of Vermont, arrived in Chicago in 1818 and was quickly befriended by some of the local nomadic Indian tribes. He became the adopted son of Chief Waba of the Kickapoo Indians, who presented him with an Indian wife, Watseka. He lived contentedly with her for about two years, until they separated amicably so that, in 1831, he could marry Elinor Berry of Urbana, Ohio. Gurdon had been indentured to John Jacob Astor's American Fur Company for five years, during which time the company dominated trade in the region around the Great Lakes. He developed the American Fur Company after Astor retired and also became active in Chicago politics. By 1834, Gurdon had decided to make the Chicago area his permanent home. Elinor Berry died in 1838, and Gurdon married Mary Ann Hubbard, daughter of Serena Tucker and Ahira Hubbard (brother of Elizur) in 1842. By the time of this third marriage, he was involved in many other enterprises as well. He opened the first meatpacking plant in Chicago, and as his fortune grew, he also entered the insurance business, becoming the first underwriter in Chicago. Mary Ann (born in Vermont on November 2, 1820; died in Chicago on July 19, 1909) moved to Chicago with her family in 1836.

3. The Chicago city directory, however, listed Henry G. Hubbard at G.S. Hubbard & Co.'s warehouse only in 1839, after he had become Gurdon's partner.

4. A letter dated April 3, 1844, in Henry's hand about legal matters is found in the J.J. Hardin Collection, Chicago Historical Museum Library.

5. G. Hubbard ms. See also Joseph Turner Ryerson, "Gleanings from a Family Memoir" in Kirkland, *Chicago Yesteryears*, 69. Ryerson and Hank Hubbard hunted deer together south of Chicago.

6. Cyrus McCormick (1809–1884) patented the reaper, a machine that made harvesting grain easier and faster, and licensed factories to produce it in different parts of the United States.

7. H.G. Hubbard was born about 1809 in Middleboro, Massachusetts, and died on August 28, 1852, in Sandusky, Ohio. Juliet Smith Hubbard was born in 1817 in Edwardsville, Illinois, and died in October 1892 in New York.

8. No trace of his burial plot or obituary notice has been found either in Chicago or Sandusky. With such a contagious disease as cholera, the body was likely disposed of quickly in an unmarked grave.

9. Dr. Levi Boone (born in Kentucky on December 6, 1808; died in Chicago on January 24, 1882) was a doctor who became the seventeenth mayor of Chicago (1855–56). Stephen Francis Gale was born in New Hampshire in 1812 and died in Chicago in 1905.

10. Theophilus Smith (1784–1846). See Ayer and Taves, *Three Lives*, 21.

11. Because of the 1871 Chicago fire, records of births, deaths and marriages before 1871 are scarce.

12. Childbirth was a dangerous and life-threatening experience for women in the nineteenth century, fraught with complications. Doctors, who at the time were mostly male, were not allowed to examine naked females and therefore could not treat them properly. Instruments were not sterilized, and infection was widespread. Infants who survived frequently died before they reached maturity.

13. Ayer and Taves, *Three Lives*, 20.

14. Appignanesi, *Mad, Bad and Sad*, 101–02.

15. The rest cure, recommended for nervous diseases and hysteria, was first advocated by Dr. Silas Weir Mitchell (1829–1914) of Philadelphia and was subsequently adopted by the medical community as an acceptable form of treatment.

16. Sandweiss, *Passing Strange*, 190.

17. G. Hubbard ms; Ayer and Taves, *Three Lives*, 22. No trace of Henry was found in the archives or directories at the Montana Historical Society.

18. Ayer and Taves, *Three Lives*, 24

19. *Ayer's Book*, chap. 3, "The Sin of Dowdiness," 5.

20. "Harriet Hubbard Ayer," *Current Notes*, ca. 1888, 306; *New York Graphic*, ca. 1888, 242, collection of Bowdoin College Library, box 2, file 31.

21. Located on West Taylor Street at the corner of Lytle from 1858 to 1871, according to Andreas, *History of Chicago*.

22. Catherine Beecher, "To American Mothers," in *A Treatise on Domestic Economy for the Use of Young Ladies at Home, and at School* (Boston: Marsh, Capen, Lyon and Webb, 1841), as quoted in Goldsmith, *Other Powers*, 23–24. Catherine was the older sister of preacher Henry Ward Beecher.

23. Articles in *Harper's Bazaar*, July 7, 1888, 460; *Current Notes*, 1888, 306; and later in the *Chicago Daily Tribune*, April 10, 1896, quoting Harriet contradict the poor school record that Ayer and Taves described, stating that she graduated at the age of fifteen at the top of her class. Given her future successes, she probably did, especially since afterward she was remembered as one of the convent's most distinguished pupils.

CHAPTER 2

24. Ayer and Taves, *Three Lives*, 25.

25. While Herbert's birth and early years are clouded, his passport affirms that he was born on November 17, 1835, in New Orleans. He died on January 12, 1899, in Newark, New Jersey.

26. John Varnum Ayer, born on January 3, 1812, in Essex, Massachusetts, to Polly Chase Ayer and Samuel Ayer, died on April 30, 1877, in Chicago. One census records John's birth in 1813. Ayer and Taves repeatedly and incorrectly refer to him as John Vanessa Ayer.

27. For Sarah's version of the story, see Ayer and Taves, *Three Lives*, 29 who spell her name Sara.

28. There is some discrepancy of dates, but "Died," *The Bee*, June 12, 1833, 2, col. 3, notes the deaths of Sarah and her child, while Herbert's passport lists his birth as 1835. Perhaps he lied or was unsure.

29. "Herbert C. Ayer Dead," *New York Times*, January 14, 1899; "Herbert C. Ayer Dies," *Chicago Daily Tribune*, January 13, 1899, 1.

30. Ayer and Taves, *Three Lives*, 34, say he married a young farm girl from his home. See also "How Fate Made a Bigamist of John Ayer," *Chicago Daily Tribune*, July 11, 1909, G1; "A Very Curious History: The Story of John V. Ayer's Separation from His Wife," *Washington Post*, January 3, 1887, 3.

31. Ibid. See also *Chicago Daily Tribune*, 1909. "Capt. John A. Duble, the well-known old river man, who was an intimate friend of Mr. Ayer" was the source of this questionable story written well after the fact without documentation.

32. Ayer and Taves, *Three Lives*, 36.

33. "Fate Made a Bigamist."

34. Herbert did not seem to object to his removal from the Confederate army. After checking Louisiana and South Carolina, I could find no listing for Herbert Copeland in the Confederate army, only H. Copeland in South Carolina, the Seventeenth Infantry, Company G. I also checked the Confederate Relic Room in South Carolina.

35. Although Ayer and Taves, *Three Lives*, 43, does not specify, it is probably West Virginia, not Georgia.

36. Ayer and Taves, *Three Lives*, 32–35.

37. "How Fate Made a Bigamist" placed John in New Orleans in 1862 and his son in the Confederate army. Sarah had three daughters with Mr. Copeland, who apparently had adopted Herbert since he had no sons of his own. After the death of Mr. Copeland, Sarah and her daughters moved to Youngstown, Ohio, and John provided for them until her girls were married.

38. "Ayer Dead." Research in New Orleans found no trace of Planters' Hotel.

39. Sam Hale established his own company with his son George (Charles had died).

40. "Iron and Steel," *Chicago Times*, February 18, 1883, 7.

41. The three sons were George M. (1840–1914), who lived in Harvard, Illinois; Philip M. (ca. 1843–1875); John M. (ca. 1847–1898). See *Chicago Times*, February 18, 1883, 7, and Graceland cemetery records.

42. Elida Manney Ayer was born on January 1, 1802, in Poughkeepsie, New York, to John W. Manney and Elizabeth Collins Manney. She died in the summer of 1877 in Chicago.

43. Ayer and Taves, *Three Lives*, 37.

44. Ibid., 38.

45. Other Victorian women—for example, the artists Mary Cassatt and Cecela Beaux—lied about their ages at various times, perhaps to appear to be accomplished at a young age.

46. "The National Calamity," *Chicago Times*, April 14, 1865; *Chicago Daily Times*, April 17, 1865.

47. *Chicago Daily Tribune*, May 2, 1865; Ayer and Taves, *Three Lives*, 39.

48. Ayer and Taves, *Three Lives*, 40–41.

49. "Marriages," *Chicago Tribune*, October 3, 1866, 4; Herbert's obituary notices in the *New York Times*, January 14, 1899. Divorce announcements in the *New York Times*, September 21, 1886, cite the wedding on October 2, 1866, as opposed to the date of June 30, 1865, as cited in Ayer and Taves. *American Women of the Century* (1893) mentions that Harriet was just sixteen when she married, and the *Chicago Daily Tribune*, April 10, 1896, also records that she married at sixteen. Henry Hamilton wrote that she was born in 1850, not 1849, and that would account for age discrepancies, but he may have been subtracting from the repeatedly published age.

50. Ayer and Taves, *Three Lives*, 43.
51. Listed in the directory of 1870–71, but perhaps they likely moved in the year before the publication of the directory.
52. Ayer and Taves, *Three Lives*, 44.
53. Ibid., 49–50.

Chapter 3

54. Ayer and Taves, *Three Lives*, 54.
55. *Current Notes*, 1888, 306; *New York Graphic*, ca. 1888, 242.
56. Ayer and Taves, *Three Lives*, 56–59.
57. Ibid., 59, states that Gertrude died on the following day. Cemetery records reveal that she died on December 7, 1871, a month and a half later.
58. Annette Stott, "The Baby-in-a-Half-Shell: A Case Study in Child Memorial Art of the Late Nineteenth Century," *Art World Wide* 7, no. 2 (Fall 2008), www.19thc-artworldwide.org.
59. Ayer and Taves, *Three Lives*, 64.
60. Ibid., 66, records it as November, but Harriet would never have left Gertrude while she was dying. The baptismal font at St. James Episcopal Church, Huron Street, Chicago, donated by Harriet and Herbert as a memorial to Gertrude, records her birth and death dates on the base.
61. Ayer and Taves, *Three Lives*, 69.
62. Ibid., 72.
63. Ibid., 72–73.
64. *Current Notes*, 1888, 306.
65. Ayer and Taves, *Three Lives*, 73.
66. Ibid., 74.
67. The life of Kate Chopin (1850–1904) paralleled Harriet's in many ways. See Kate Chopin, *The Awakening* (Chicago: Herbert S. Stone & Company, 1899).

Chapter 4

68. Ayer and Taves, *Three Lives*, 77.
69. The Bible, in the collection of Margaret Garguilio, Harriet's great-granddaughter, is the only object the descendants retain of their famous ancestor.
70. Ayer and Taves, *Three Lives*, 80.
71. "Mrs. Ayer," *New York Times*, April 4, 1893, 6.
72. Andreas, *History of Chicago*, 782.
73. The first of such international fairs occurred in London in 1851, followed by Paris in 1867, and were repeated many times after.

74. Captain Wetherill died in 1898 and is buried at Arlington Cemetery, according to that cemetery's records.

75. Jule later had another son named Louis Lockwood.

76. Although Ayer and Taves, *Three Lives*, 87, say the Lockwoods lived in Elboron, a small, elegant resort town on the coast of New Jersey, they are not listed until 1887. The 1870 directory puts them in Elizabeth, New Jersey.

77. Ayer and Taves, *Three Lives*, 88–89.

78. Ibid., 89–90.

79. Ibid., 91.

80. *Chicago Daily Tribune*, April 23, 1882, 5.

81. "The Week," *Chicago Daily Tribune*, July 27, 1879, 11.

82. "Decorative Art," *Chicago Daily Tribune*, December 15, 1878, 10.

83. Ayer and Taves, *Three Lives*, 96, mentions *Scribner's*, which was not published until 1887.

84. Ibid., 97–98.

85. Graceland Cemetery records; Obituary, *Chicago Daily Tribune*, May 1, 1877, 8. His funeral was held at their home on Park Row, Reverend Edward Sullivan officiated. In her will, Elida left an estate of $50,000 to her sons, John and George. John's will left "his beloved wife" his "undivided half interest in property on Michigan Avenue and Lake Street." Her address in the 1877 Chicago directory had changed to One Lake Park Place, revealing a street name change.

John's will was much more complicated than Elida's, as it concerned his business, his debts and loans for his company. He made both Herbert and John M. the executors. Henry Higgins and Edward Warren Sawyer, along with Mr. Bonfield, a lawyer, witnessed the signing of the will. They attested to the fact that John was of sound mind when he signed. There had been a lawsuit against him by one Amorette Ayer Cooke. John owed her $27,441, and within months that debt was settled with interest. The bulk of the estate was left to "his beloved wife," Elida, and his three living sons. The appraisers included material objects such as beds, stoves, food, fuel and a sewing machine, in addition to hoses, one cow and two sheep, all of which were valued at $3,500 in total, $2,500 of which was for provisions for the widow and family for one year. Household furnishings and china and utensils were valued at $1,671.35. Other land and shares in various businesses were assessed, along with any outstanding debts. There were no debts or liabilities to be settled with Sam Hale's sons from their former partnership.

86. "Specimen Sales," *Chicago Daily Tribune*, September 19, 1880, 10.

87. Chase's *Keying Up: The Court Jester* was critically acclaimed and won a medal of honor at the fair. He also submitted *Ready for the Ride* to the

Society of American Artists (SAA) in 1878, along with such leading American artists as John Singer Sargent and Thomas Eakins. See also my article "Painting the Extraordinary Harriet Hubbard Ayer," *Magazine Antiques* (July/August 2010): 194–201.

88. Blaugrund, *Tenth Street Studio Building*, 119.

89. " William Merritt Chase," *American Art Review* 2, no. 1, 96. Mariana Van Renssaelaer was another example of a nineteenth-century working woman.

90. Juengling print facing page 92 in *American Art Review* 2, no. 1, 91–98; Keith L. Bryant, *William Merritt Chase: A Genteel Bohemian* (University of Missouri Press, 1991), 103.

91. The top portion of the painting, currently in the collection of the Fine Arts Museum of San Francisco, remained in the artist's collection and was sold at the time of his death for fifteen dollars. The lower portion was given to the art critic and reviewer Marianna G. Van Rensselaer and is currently in the estate collection of the Graham Williford Foundation, Dallas, Texas. By the fall of 1880, Chase was president of the SAA, a vehicle he used to advocate the importance of painting and his own talent. Over six thousand people attended the SAA's first exhibition in New York, and its popularity continued.

92. Johnson's painting was handed down in the Ayer family and was donated to the Corcoran Gallery by Harriet's granddaughter, Mrs. Harriet Seymour Macy, daughter of Hattie Seymour. The first painting by Chase was sold to the Parrish Art Museum, Southampton, New York, by a great-granddaughter, Mrs. Margaret Berry Garguilio, granddaughter of Margaret Ayer Cobb. A study for the painting by Johnson was passed down in the family until it was sold in 1977 to the Fort Wayne Museum of Art, Indiana, in 1986.

93. Today, only a few of Dearborn Street's single-family town houses remain.

94. Charles Collins, "The Fantastic Life of Harriet Hubbard Ayer," *Chicago Daily Tribune*, September 29, 1957, 92. Ayer and Taves is the source for Collins's description of 362 Dearborn, near Maple. This grand house, although perhaps instigated by John, was certainly completed well after his death in 1877.

95. "Troubles in Her Life," *Boston Globe*, December 19, 1886, 4; "Mrs. Ayer Sent to An Asylum," *New York Herald*, February 28, 1893, 3.

96. "Mrs. Ayer in an Asylum," *New York Times*, February 28, 1893, 8.

97. Ayer and Taves, *Three Lives*, 83.

98. Ibid., 82.

99. Kirkland, *Chicago's Yesterdays*, 262.

100. "Announcement," *Chicago Daily Tribune*, February 1, 1880, 12.

101. Kirkland, *Chicago's Yesterdays*, 262–63.

102. *The Widow* (New York: DeWitt Publishing House, 1877) duly protected Harriet's version by copyright. Harriet also wrote directions for costumes, settings, actors and directors.

103. I am grateful to Dr. Wayne Wood, a Jacksonville historian, for a picture of the edifice and information about the Riverside house. *New York Times*, March 11, 1893, 8, mentioned the mortgage and the value of $8–10,000. Alfred Bishop Mason, "Committee of Person and Estate of Harriet Hubbard Ayer, a Lunatic," sold Lot 4, Block 5, for $8,000 to Telfair Stockton, a Jacksonville businessman. Another article on September 12, 1888, states that the Knights Templar may have used the villa for a fundraiser.

104. "Wealth That Took Wings," *Brooklyn Eagle*, October 10, 1891, 2.

105. "Sunday Morning News," *Chicago Daily Tribune*, December 20, 1886, alleged that Harriet had $150,000 and that Herbert left her free of debt.

CHAPTER 5

106. "A Wrecked Society Queen," *Atlanta Constitution*, March 24, 1893, 2.

107. Appignanesi, *Mad, Bad and Sad*, 106–07.

108. Harriet's ownership of the house is not recorded in the police census of 1880 or 1890 since she lived there between those dates. See Book 193 for police record of 1890. The family of Henry Miller lived in the house and may have replaced Harriet. Number 122 West Thirteenth Street was listed as a private house. (Block 608, tax lot # 29).

109. "Sunday Morning News," *Chicago Daily Tribune*, December 20, 1885, 7.

110. "Herbert Ayer Sanguine," *Chicago Daily Tribune*, December 19, 1886, 9.

111. Built in 1846; rebuilt after a fire in 1855.

112. Ayer and Taves, *Three Lives*, 108–09.

113. Ibid., 113.

114. Ibid., 114.

115. Ibid., 115.

116. "Obituary: John V. Ayer," *Chicago Daily Tribune*, May 1, 1877, 8.

117. "The Old and Heavy House of John V. Ayers' Sons in Straightened Shape, The Cause Declared to Be Tariff-Tinkering and General Stagnation in Trade," *Chicago Daily Tribune*, June 29, 1879, 3; "Contempt," January 31, 1879, 7.

118. Kevin Baker, "Blood on the Street," *New York Times Book Review*, February 22, 2009, 12.

119. "Iron and Steel," *Chicago Times*, February 18, 1883, 7.

120. "Herbert Ayer Sanguine," *Chicago Daily Tribune*, December 19, 1886, 8.

121. Ayer and Taves, *Three Lives*, 118. See also Divorce Papers, *Ayer v. Ayer*, Clerk of the Circuit Court of Cook County, Illinois.

122. "The Rev. Clinton Locke," *New York Times*, February 24, 1904, 7.

123. Ayer and Taves, *Three Lives*, 118.

CHAPTER 6

124. "Successful Women," *New York Times*, September 5, 1886, 7.

125. "New York," *Chicago Daily Tribune*, October 22, 1883, 2.

126. *New York Graphic*, ca. 1888.

127. "A Former Chicago Lady of Fashion Clerking in Sypher & Co. Store," *Chicago Daily Tribune*, October 22, 1883, 2.

128. For more about Sypher & Co., see J.F. Sypher, "Sypher & Co., A Pioneer Antique Dealer in New York," *Furniture History* 28 (1992): 168–79. For an image of their advertisement, see Doreen Burke, *In Pursuit of Beauty: Americans and the Aesthetic Movement* (New York: Random House Inc., 1986), 171ff.

129. "A Former Chicago Lady," 2.

130. Ayer and Taves, *Three Lives*, 120.

131. Ibid., 135.

132. "Mrs. M.E.W. Sherwood, Writes a Homily on the Subject of Honest Labor," *Chicago Daily Tribune*, February 10, 1889, 5.

133. "Mrs. James Potter, A Practical Business Woman Expresses an Opinion," *New York Times*, December 4, 1887, 14.

134. "A Former Chicago Lady."

135. "Sypher & Co.," *Chicago Daily Times*, April 4, 1884, 13.

136. "Mrs. Ayer in an Asylum," *New York Times*, February 28, 1893, 1.

137. Listed in the Chicago Directory under her name and Sypher's

138. Ayer and Taves, *Three Lives*, 134.

139. Ibid., 125.

140. Ibid.

CHAPTER 7

141. May 16, 1877 passport to European countries; Ayer and Taves, *Three Lives*, 125, described him as having prematurely silver hair.

142. "Trouble About the *Radha*," *New York Times*, December 11, 1886, 8.

143. Radha was the Indian god Krishna's supreme love.

144. According to his 1886 passport.

145. "The Courts," *Chicago Daily Tribune*, September 21, 1881, 8.

146. Dun & Co. records, New York City, vol. 367, February 7, 1879, Baker Library, Harvard University Business School, p. 1,849.

147. Ibid., vol. 424, May 1886, p. 819.

148. "The Title to a Mine," *New York Tribune*, February 20, 1887, 5.

149. "Howard's Gossip, Interesting Facts about the Rise and the Fall of the Phoenix Mine," *Boston Globe*, March 1, 1887, 4.

150. "J.M. Seymour's Career," *Chicago Daily Times*, May 23, 1889, 3.
151. Suit brought by George A. Treadwell of Brooklyn. See "Phoenix Mine Litigation," *New York Times*, September 6, 1889, 5.
152. "The Phoenix Mine," *New York Tribune*, October 4, 1887, 8.
153. Dun & Co. records, vol. 424, March 1889, p. 819.
154. "Phoenix Mine Litigation," *New York Times*, September 6, 1889, 5.
155. Dun & Co. records, vol. 424, February 20, 1883, p. 19.
156. Susan Yohn, "Men Who Wouldn't Cheat Each Other…Seem to Take Delight in Cheating Women: Court Challenges Faced by U.S. Businesswomen in the Nineteenth Century," Paper presented at the Fourteenth International Economic History Congress, Helsinki, Finland, August 21, 2006.
157. "Eno's Stock Transactions Recalled," *New York Tribune*, July 28, 1894, 5.
158. "That Yacht Radha," *New York Times*, December 18, 1886.
159. Ayer and Taves, *Three Lives*, 128.
160. Ibid., 128–29.
161. Ibid., 131.
162. Ibid., 133.
163. Ibid., 136.
164. "A Law Suit About the *Radha*," *New York Times*, September 25, 1885, 8; "Mr. Lorillard to Pay," *New York Times*, December 3, 1886, 8; "Was the *Radha* Seaworthy," *New York Times*, October 12, 1886, 8; "Defects in the *Radha*," *New York Times*, December 10, 1886, 10; "Trouble about the *Radha*," *New York Times*, December 11, 1886, 8; "That Yacht *Radha*," *New York Times*, December 18, 1886, 5; "All Testimony In," *New York Times*, December 21, 1886, 3; "End of the *Radha* Suit," *New York Times*, December 22, 1886, 3.
165. Ayer and Taves, *Three Lives*, 136.

CHAPTER 8

166. The Blanche W. Howard Papers and the Maine Women Writers Collection reveal Blanche's trip to Maine in 1885.
167. Biography of Blanche Willis Howard (Madame Von Teuffel), "Authors at Home," *New York Times*, July 16, 1898; and others.
168. In 1871, the autonomous kingdom of Wurttemberg joined the German Empire created by Otto von Bismarck, prime minister of Prussia.
169. "Authors at Home."
170. Ayer and Taves, *Three Lives*, 139.
171. Ibid., 154.
172. Hattie Seymour obituary: "Mrs. A. L. Seymour Musical Therapist," *New York Times*, July 31, 1944, 4.

173. After Lewis Seymour died, Hattie went to work like her mother in order to support her children. In the early twentieth century, she taught music and later founded the Seymour School of Musical Reeducation.

174. Ayer and Taves, *Three Lives*, 144.

175. Ibid., 147.

176. Letter in Blanche W. Howard Papers.

177. Ayer and Taves, *Three Lives*, 155.

CHAPTER 9

178. Divorce Papers, Clerk of the District Court of Cook County, Superior Court, Bureau of Vital Statistics, Chicago, IL.

179. "Trouble of Her Life," *Boston Daily Globe*, December 19, 1886, 4.

180. "Restrain Mrs. Ayer," *Chicago Daily Tribune*, February 28, 1893, 3.

181. Divorce Papers, Superior Court, Bureau of Vital Statistics, Chicago, IL.

182. Ibid.

183. "Successful Women," *New York Times*, September 5, 1886, 7, for example.

184. Decree for Divorce, Superior Court, Bureau of Vital Statistics, Chicago, IL.

185. Ayer and Taves, *Three Lives*, 167–68.

CHAPTER 10

186. Ayer and Taves, *Three Lives*, 73, 149. None of the Paris directories that I examined listed Monsieur Mirault, the chemist. See *Les Bottin* 1880s and 1890s at the Archives de Paris, France.

187. "Rivaling Mme. Récamier," *Chicago Daily Tribune*, March 20, 1887, 16.

188. "Harriet Hubbard Ayer," *New York Times*, May 29, 1887, 13.

189. Ayer and Taves, *Three Lives*, 151.

190. Peiss, *Hope in a Jar*, olt and Company 20.

191. Oleson, *Secret Nostrums*.

192. The telephone had been invented ten years earlier, and by 1886, phones were found in business offices and the homes of the well-to-do.

193. Ayer and Taves, *Three Lives*, 157.

194. 1886 advertisement found on the web, collection of the author.

195. U.S. Government Works, Récamier MFG.

196. Peiss, *Hope in a Jar*, 77.

197. "Mrs. Ayer in An Asylum," *New York Times*, February 28, 1893.

198. "Successful Women," *New York Times*, September 5, 1886, 7.

199. "Mrs. James Brown Potter," *New York Times*, December 11, 1887, 5, col. 3, reprint in *Chicago Daily Tribune*, December 11, 1887.

200. "Rivaling Mme. Récamier," *Chicago Daily Tribune*, March 29, 1887, 16.

201. Undated, unidentified article in the miscellaneous file of the Blanche Howard Collection at Bowdoin College Library.

202. "Rivaling Mme. Récamier," 16.

203. Altman's, founded in 1864, was located on Sixth Avenue between West Eighteenth and Nineteenth Streets in a grand cast-iron emporium. "Mrs. James Potter Brown," *Chicago Daily Times*, December 11, 1887, 14.

204. "Rivaling Mme. Récamier," 16

205. "Society Women Who Are Going to Europe This Season," *Chicago Daily Tribune*, April 10, 1887, 13.

206. "Harriet Hubbard Ayer," *Brooklyn Eagle*, March 22, 1887, 8.

207. "Harriet Hubbard Ayer," *Brooklyn Eagle*, May 25, 1887, 5.

208. "A Successful Woman," *Chicago Daily Tribune*, June 3, 1887, 3, reprint from the *New York World*. *Chemist and Druggist*, August 17, 1889, 245, also mentions Frenzel and the ingredients in Récamier products, stating how profitable her products were and how the cocaine in Vita Nuova was "producing a temporary exhilaration."

209. Oleson, *Secret Nostrums.*

210. "What Does It Mean?" *New York Times*, July 3, 1887, 11. See also "Society Women," *Chicago Daily Tribune*, April 10, 1887, 13, advertorial; "Interesting Format," January 27, 1889, 2 (questioning her products).

211. "Mrs. James Brown Potter," *New York Times*, December 12, 1887, 14.

212. "Halt," *New York Times*, June 12, 1887, 13.

213. "Twenty Dollars Is the Usual Fee," *Boston Globe*, November 6, 1887, 18.

214. "Theodore Houston's Death," *New York Times*, January 15, 1888, 5.

215. "Practical Charity," *Chicago Daily Tribune*, April 7, 1889, 31.

216. "Business Notices," *Brooklyn Eagle*, May 29, 1887, 8.

217. "American Exhibition" *London Times*, May 6, 1887, 5.

218. "Buffalo Bill," *New York Times*, December 18, 1887.

219. "The American Exhibition," *London Times*, November 1, 1887, 9.

220. Not listed in *Les Bottins*, 1880s and 1890s. Not all companies or people were listed, and there were no listings for Ayer or Récamier even in the *Bottins* of "étrangers" and "la tout Paris" or in the museum archives of Musée et Bibliothèque des Arts Décoratifs, Musée de la Publicité, Bibliothèque Forney, Bibliothèque Historique de la Ville de Paris and Bibliothèque National de France digital services (SINBAD).

221. See, for example, the following articles and ads in the *Winnipeg Free Press*, November 26, 1903 (about her death); March 20, 1890 (about her coining money); December 9, 1890, and September 26, 1890 (about her endorsers); December 11, 1890 (about her success and her sumptuous quarters), as well as other ads.

222. Numerous ads included the portrait of Madame Récamier by Francois-Pascal Gerard (1770–1837), collection Musée Carnavalet, Paris.

223. *Chicago Tribune*, December 16, 1888; *Chicago Daily Tribune*, October 22, 1883, 2. Langtry became an American citizen in 1887 and bought property in California. While Langtry was using Harriet's house, Harriet rented space in the elegant Colonnade Row. Built in 1833, it was nine houses combined into one by a Greek Revival façade of graceful fluted columns and Corinthian capitals. This cul-de-sac on the two-block-long Lafayette Place provided privacy for the wealthy. See Christopher Gray, "The Mystery of the Lost City," *New York Times*, August 8, 2010.

224. "The Four Cleopatras," *New York Times*, March 22, 1891.

225. Ibid.

226. "Adelina Patti Nicolini," *Chicago Daily Tribune*, December 16, 1888, 15.

227. "Business Notices, Harriet Hubbard Ayer," *New York Times*, May 29, 1887.

228. Advertisement, *New York Times*, April 12, 1891.

229. "Miss Clara Louise Kellogg," *Brooklyn Eagle*, July 17, 1887, 16.

230. "The Largest Sign in the World," *Harper's Weekly*, May 4, 1888, 355. *Harper's Weekly* republished an advertorial from the *New York Herald* of February 23, 1889, and the *Philadelphia Times* repeated some of the same stories and letters.

231. "More Household Idols Shattered," *Chicago Daily Tribune*, August 5, 1888, 8.

232. "Interesting Information," *Chicago Daily Tribune*, January 27, 1889, 2.

233. "Mrs. Ayer and her Foes," *Chemist and Druggist*, August 17, 1889, 245.

234. *Harriet Hubbard Ayer's Book*, 80.

235. Clark, *Elegant Eighties*, 88.

236. "Mrs. M.E.W. Sherwood," *Chicago Daily Tribune*, February 10, 1889, 5.

237. "The Talk of New York," *Washington Post*, August 11, 1889, 16.

238. For sale of company figures see, *Récamier Manufacturing Co., Inc., v. Harriet Hubbard Ayer, Inc.*, District Court, S.D. New York, 59 F. 2d 803; U.S. Dist. LEXIS 1293 (April, 13, 1932). I am grateful to Professor Melanie Gustafson, University of Vermont, for providing a copy for me.

CHAPTER II

239. Ayer and Taves, *Three Lives*, 170–72.

240. Letter from Blanche to her niece Marion Stuart Smith, June 2, 1895, referring to the actor John McCullough, who was one of Harriet's frequent visitors in Chicago, University of New England Women Writers Collection.

241. Hubbard Cobb's unpublished manuscript, collection of Deke Simon.
242. "Married," *New York Times*, November 13, 1888.
243. Ayer and Taves, *Three Lives*, 185; "Crazed By Drugs, Left at Death's Door," *New York Herald*, May 21, 1889, 3.
244. "Ayers Domestic Woes," *Washington Post*, July 14, 1889, 1.
245. "Crazed By Drugs, Left at Death's Door," *New York Herald*, May 21, 1889, 3.

CHAPTER 12

246. "Crazed By Drugs, Left at Death's Door," 3. The reference to two venal doctors was because of the law calling for two physicians to declare someone insane.
247. "Ayers Domestic Woes," *Washington Post*, July 14, 1889, 1.
248. Newspaper articles during 1889 mentioned previously and legal brief.
249. A legal brief explained the situation:

> *In reply to the motion to discontinue the action the affidavit of Mrs. Ayer, the president of the company, who instituted this action in the name and on behalf of the company, is read, in which she shows that of the 1000 shares of the stock of the company she owns 968, of which 498 are pledged to the defendant James W. [sic] Seymour to secure a debt which she is informed and believes had been paid; that she had begun an action to recover that stock; that the trustees A. Lewis Seymour and Albert Watson, own each one share of stock; that no meeting of the board of trustees has been held for over one year; no annual meeting of the stockholders has been held since the formation of the company in 1887.*

250. I am grateful to Franklin Feldman, Esq., for helping me interpret the legal documents from Harriet's various lawsuits. "Mrs. Ayer Gains Control," *The Sun*, May 28, 1889:

> *The Judge says the question presented for decision is whether the President of a corporation, being a trustee, may maintain an action in the name of the corporation without the authority of the Board of Trustees and against the express direction of the Board: Ordinarily he may not. But this rule has manifestly no application where a majority of the directors or trustees are engaged in the wrongful division of the corporate funds or other injury to its business…Motion to discontinue the action and dismiss the complaint denied. Motion to continue the injunction granted.*

251. "Mrs. Ayer Gains Control."

252. "Mrs. Ayer's Queer Story," *New York Times*, May 21, 1889, 8.

253. Dates come from printed opinions of Judge J.F. Daly, Court Papers New York (CPNY), New York Supplement, vol. 5, p. 655.

254. "J.M. Seymour's Career," *Chicago Daily Tribune*, March 23, 1889, 3.

255. Opinion of Judge Daly in CPNY, New York Supplement, vol. 5, p. 656.

256. "Three Awful Charges," *Trenton Times*, May 21, 1889.

257. "Ayer's Domestic Woes," *Washington Post*, July 14, 1889, 1.

258. Ibid.

259. The story was also carried in a short paragraph in the Paris edition of the *New York Herald*. "Crazed by Drugs," *New York Herald*, May 21, 1889, 3.

260. "Stuttgart's Scandal," *New York Herald*, Paris, June 4, 1889.

261. "Mrs. Ayer's Strong Talk," *Chicago Daily Tribune*, May 22, 1889, 5.

262. This could have been related to her preeclampsia during pregnancy and the ultimate diagnosis at her death: pneumonia and nephritis. See "Stuttgart's Scandal."

263. "Mrs. Ayer Gains Control. Similar to "Hot Shot for Seymour," *New York Herald*, May 28, 1889.

264. Court records, 31 Chambers Street, "In the Matter of Election of Trustees of the Récamier Manufacturing Company," June 5, 1889.

265. "Mrs. Ayer Wins," *New York Times*, June 5, 1889, 8; "The Ayer-Seymour Case Settled," *New York Tribune*. Both June 5, 1889.

266. "Mrs. Ayer Grateful," *New York Times*, June 9, 1889, 5.

267. "James Seymour's Case," *Chicago Tribune*, March 23, 1889, 3.

268. "Phoenix Mine Litigation," *New York Times*, September 6, 1889, 5.

269. "J.M. Seymour's Career," *Chicago Daily Tribune*, May 23, 1889, 3.

270. "[E]ntrenched in the Office," *New York Tribune*, May 30, 1889, 3.

271. Ibid.; *New York Tribune*, May 30, 1889, 3.

272. On July 2, 1889, the *New York Times*, *New York Herald* and *Chicago Daily Tribune* published articles "Suit Against Harriet Hubbard Ayer," "Mrs. Ayer's Romances Rudely Shattered" and "Spoiling the Romance," respectively.

273. "Spoiling the Romance," *Chicago Tribune*, July 2, 1889, 1; "Suit Against Harriet Hubbard Ayer," *New York Times*, July 2, 1889. Hattie's use of Récamier products has never been mentioned in any ads or articles I have found.

274. "In the Matter of Application of Lutie Lawton Frenzel for a Peremptory Mandamus against the Récamier Manufacturing Company and Harriet Hubbard Ayer, president, etc.," New York Supreme Court.

275. "Mrs. Ayer's Romances Rudely Shattered," *New York Herald*, July 2, 1889.

276. "City and Suburban News," *New York Times*, June 7, 1889, 3.

277. "Mrs. Ayer Declares War," *Chicago Daily Tribune*, July 21, 1889.

278. "Mr. Ayer Gets His Daughter," *New York Times*, November 15, 1889.

279. Letter, June 2, 1895, from Blanche Howard to her niece Marion Smith insinuating that Harriet had an affair with Grubb, Bowdoin College Library.

280. Court papers, Chicago Bureau of Vital Statistics.

281. "Mrs. Ayer Wins her Daughter," *New York Times*, November 27, 1889, 3.

282. Letter in Blanche W. Howard Papers.

283. CPNY, New York Supplement, vol. 5, p. 657.

284. "The Ayer Case Settled," *New York Tribune*, June 5, 1889, 3.

285. "How Women May Succeed," *Harper's Weekly*, March 4, 1889, 355.

286. "Mrs. Ayer's Effects Go Cheap," *New York Times*, June 6, 1889, stated that the Chase portrait was sold for fifteen dollars, but Harriet had it in her estate when she died, so the article was mistaken, or else she bought it back sometime later.

287. "Mrs. Ayer in an Asylum," *New York Times*, February 28, 1893, 8.

288. "Mrs. Harriet Hubbard Ayer's Jewels," *Los Angeles Times*, April 13, 1890, 10; Cardinal Mazarin, an Italian cardinal who rose to be chief minister of France from 1842 to 1861, had a great fondness for jewels.

289. Ibid.; "The Ayer Seymour Case Settled," June 5, 1889, 3; "Mrs. Ayer's Effects Go Cheap." One said that the Eastman Johnson painting was sold and the other that the Chase painting went for fifteen dollars. Since both were bequeathed to her daughters when she died, Harriet either bought them back or they did not sell. Even the *Washington Post*, June 6, 1889, carried a notice about the sale of Harriet's possessions at auction.

290. "On the Voyage to Europe," *New York Times*, June 4, 1891, 8; "Passengers on the *Ocean*," July 9, 1891, 8.

291. Letter, May 2, 1890, from Blanche to Hattie, Bowdoin College Library.

292. Two undated letters from Blanche to Marion, University of New England Library.

293. The baroness was Blanche-Augustine-Angele Soyer, a French author known for her books on manners who used a pseudonym with an assumed title. The book was published in French as *Le Cabinet de Toilette* in 1891.

294. Undated article about Harriet from the graphic collection of the Harvard Fine Art Library. See also Staffe, *My Lady's Dressing Room*.

295. New York City Municipal Archives, Death Certificate, Juliette Hubbard. St. Rosedale Cemetery has no record of her being buried there.

CHAPTER 13

296. Dr. Morton was a distinguished member of the medical profession who graduated from Harvard in 1867 and from medical school in 1872. With his colleague Dr. Graeme Hammond, between 1879 and 1880,

he published a short-lived journal called *Neurological Contributions*. Diane E. Richardson, special collections librarian, Oskar Diethelm Library, Department of Psychiatry, Weill Cornell Medical College, graciously supplied this information.

297. Dr. Morton apprenticed with Hammond's distinguished father, Dr. William A. Hammond, at the Clinic for Diseases of the Mind and Nervous System, New York University.

298. "Mrs. Ayer Sent to an Asylum," *New York Herald*, February 28, 1893, 6.

299. "Mrs. Ayer in an Asylum," *New York Times*, February 28, 1893, 8.

300. "Restrain Mrs. Ayer," *Chicago Daily Tribune*, February 28, 1893, 3.

301. "Mrs. Ayer in an Asylum."

302. Ibid.

303. Miller, *Central Park*, 125.

304. Morgan, "Bronxville's Insane Asylum," 22. I am grateful to Eloise Morgan, village historian, for her willingness to share information about Bronxville, Vernon House and Dr. Granger, which I have incorporated in these several paragraphs.

305. "Mrs. Ayer in an Asylum."

306. "Mrs. Ayer, Her Divorced Husband Tells Why He Had Her Placed in an Asylum," *New York Times*, April 3, 1893, 6.

307. Recently, some psychiatrists have conjectured that she suffered from hypomania, a mild form of bipolar disease, given her dynamic energy in business and advertising.

308. E.L. Johnson, "Mania and Dysregulation in Goal Pursuit: A Review," *Clinical Psychology Review* 25, no. 2: 241–62. Dysregulation is an impairment of the physiological regulatory mechanism.

309. Lunacy certificate, signed February 8, 1893.

310. Ibid.

311. The words "insane" and "lunatic" were interchangeable at this time.

312. Lena apparently married at some point and was listed in the New York City directory under the name Tooms as a seamstress.

313. "Found Mrs. Ayer Insane," *New York Times*, March 11, 1893, 8.

314. Deposition from lunacy trial.

315. William Granger, *How to Care for the Insane: A Manual for the Insane Asylum Attendants* (New York: G.P. Putnam Sons, 1887), 38–39.

316. Ibid., 94–95.

317. Ayer and Taves, *Three Lives*, 240–41.

318. Ibid., 242.

319. Inventory of Harriet's property by Alfred Bishop Mason, court-appointed person in charge of appraising and selling her estate to pay for her incarceration.

320. Ayer and Taves, *Three Lives*, 240.

321. Ibid., 242.

322. "To Care for Mrs. Ayer's Estate," *New York Times*, May 11, 1893, 9.

323. "The Case of Mrs. Ayer," *New York Times*, March 29, 1893, 5.

324. "Declared Sane," *Boston Globe*, August 12, 1894, 6.

325. "Over Mrs. Ayer's Property," *New York Times*, March 26, 1893, 10.

326. According to Dr. Wayne Wood, in October 1893, Lots 4 and 5 in Riverside were sold to Telfair Stockton for $8,000 by Alfred Bishop Mason. Stockton completed the house and took possession in December 1893.

327. Letter from Owen E. Abraham, Notary Public, New York, June 27, 1893.

328. Letter. May 5, 1893; "Found Mrs. Ayer Insane," *Chicago Tribune*," March 11, 1893, 8.

CHAPTER 14

329. "Harriet Hubbard Ayer's Mission," *Chicago Daily Tribune*, January 5, 1895, 3.

330. Ibid.

331. "Declared Sane."

332. "Harriet Hubbard Ayer Sane Again," *New York Times*, August 12, 1894, 17:6. Dr. Hulse worked with Dr. Smith and took care of Harriet when she spent July 1891 in Islip, Long Island.

333. The Lockwoods were living in Elberon at this time. "Lays Her Fate to an Absurd Blunder," *Chicago Daily Times*, September 9, 1894, 3. John Lockwood probably died or retired sometime around 1903, for he is no longer listed in the New York city directory.

334. "Harriet Hubbard Ayer's Mission."

335. Wetherill left an estate valued at $50,000 to care for their daughter and two sons. May lived until November 4, 1928, and both she and Alexander are buried at Arlington National Cemetery, along with their son, Colonel Alexander Macomb Wetherill Jr. (1878–1940). One of their daughters, May Hubbard Wetherill, married Dr. Benjamin F. Van Meter of Lexington, Kentucky.

336. *Harriet Hubbard Ayer's Book*, 46.

337. Ibid., 456.

338. Ibid., 46.

339. "Life in Insane Asylums," *Chicago Daily Tribune*, April 16, 1896, 6.

340. There were several versions of her incarceration in the newspapers. See "To Aid the Insane," *Sunday Daily Inter Ocean*, April 12, 1896, 13.

341. "She Starts a Crusade," *Chicago Daily Tribune*, April 10, 1896, 10; "Life in Insane Asylums," 6.

NOTES TO PAGES 147–158

342. Ibid.

343. Ibid.

344. "The Gate to a Madhouse" and "Insanity and Quarantine" *New York Times*, April 7, 1892; November 18, 1892.

345. Gallery of History, document for sale on the Internet, now in collection of Katina Jones, a very distant cousin of Harriet.

346. "Receiver for the Récamier Company" and "Récamier CO. Fails," *New York Times*, February 6, 1896, 12.

347. Westlaw Legal Research service, Claim to original government works, 59 F.2d 802, *804 & 805, 6.

CHAPTER 15

348. Post was a student of Richard Morris Hunt (who had designed the Tenth Street Studio Building, where Harriet sat for her portraits by William Merritt Chase). Although Hunt was on the selection committee to choose the architect, Post boldly solicited Pulitzer's support and thereby won the competition.

349. "Cure for Wrinkles in the Neck," *Chicago Daily Tribune*, May 3, 1896, 14, is an example.

350. The rival *New York Evening Journal*, published by William Randolph Hearst, wooed Brisbane away less than a year later.

351. Pulitzer also donated money to Columbia University to establish the first school of journalism in the world.

352. Bly married in 1894 and within a few years retired from journalism and went into business.

353. Henry Ward Beecher had a proven reputation as a philanderer. See Goldsmith, *Other Powers*, re: Victoria Woodhull.

354. "Kate Swan Scales the Harlem River Bridge," *New York World*, April 2, 1896, 29. I could find no information about Kate Swan.

355. *New York World*, October 24, 1997, headline axiom.

356. Agnes Hooper Gottlieb, "Networking in the Nineteenth Century: Founding of the Women's Press Club of New York City," *Journalism History* 21, no. 4: 156. In addition, I have searched the original minutes of the club, Rare Book Room of Butler Library, Columbia University; Harriet is not mentioned. Even after she died, there was no acknowledgement of her writing or of any other woman journalist at the *World*.

357. "Women's Beauty and Health," *New York World*, December 6, 1896.

358. "Mrs. Harriet Hubbard Ayer, the Beauty Expert Makes a Study of Yvette Gilbert," *New York World*, December 13, 1896.

359. "Mrs. Grover Cleveland Analyzed," *New York World*, December 20, 1896.

360. "The Political Woman, The Strangest Product of '96," *New York World*, December 27, 1896. See also Goldsmith, *Other Powers*.

361. Elizabeth Cady Stanton, *Eighty Years and More: Reminiscences* 1815–1897 (Boston: Northeastern University Press, 1898), 148.

362. *Harriet Hubbard Ayer's Book*, 49.

363. Ibid., 36.

364. Ibid., 49.

CHAPTER 16

365. "Mrs. Ayer on Aids to Beauty, Suggestions About Face Blemishes and the Care and Growth of the Hair," *New York World*, January 17, 1897, 20.

366. Various articles in the *New York World*, January–June 1897.

367. "Daughters of the Cross," *New York World*, June 13, 1897, 34.

368. *Harriet Hubbard Ayer's Book*, 496; Sunday Magazine, *New York World*, July 7–August 13, 1897.

369. "It Is Right and It Is Wrong," *New York World*, October 24, 1897.

370. "The Proper Way to Care for Eyes," *New York World*, October 16, 1897.

371. Ibid.; "Suggestions for Personal Improvement," *New York World*, October 14, 1897, 34.

372. "How to Read your Sweetheart's Character," *New York World*, December 12, 1897, 39.

373. "The Proper Thing to Do," *New York World*, January 9, 1898, 44.

374. This story became Appendix A in *Harriet Hubbard Ayer's Book*.

375. *Harriet Hubbard Ayer's Book*, 457.

376. Electric baths connected the patient to a negative and positive electrode in water and were a very popular remedy. Oxygen was used in this case, possibly to increase blood supply.

377. " Maggie Was Not Married," *New York Herald*, March 17, 1887; "Sergt. Crowly's Crime," *Boston Globe*, March 17, 1887, 1.

378. "The Etiquette of Lent, How to Conduct Yourself During the Solemn Season," *New York World*, March 6, 1898, 6.

379. On November 13, her name was misspelled as Mrs. Harriet Hubbard Ayres.

380. "In What Country Do Woman Have the Best Time?" June 30, 1901, 7; "The Child's Toilet," October 30, 1901, 11; "How to Make Your own Cosmetics," April 20, 1902, 11; "Parisian Institute of Beauty," July 13, 1902, 11; "Recipe for Vegetarians," November 7, 1902, 11, all in *New York World*; and then several in 1903 with Asian influences on Buddha, yoga and Hindu concepts most by the Hindu savant Yogi Ramacharaka, May 24, September 20 and October 11, 1903.

381. "In What Country?" 7.

382. *New York Times*, November 8, 1913. Margaret's middle name was Rathbone. I am conjecturing that perhaps it was a pen name.
383. *New York World* Papers, Box 1, 89-A962, Harriet to Joseph Pulitzer, March 22, 1902, Butler Library, Columbia University.

384. "The Countess Who Thinks She Cured King Edward VII by Absent Treatment," *New York World*, August 10, 1902.
385. "The American Woman Who Has Been Imprisoned in England for Thirteen Years Still Looks Forward Hopefully to Her Release But Declares that King Edward Is Powerless to Help Her," *New York World*, October 17, 1902, 3.
386. "Harriet Hubbard Ayer's Mission," *Chicago Daily Tribune*, January 5, 1895, 3.
387. "The American Woman," 3.
388. Letter, July 7, 1902. She sailed on the *Pennsylvania*, the Hamburg & American Line.
389. "Their Rainy Day Garb," *Chicago Daily Tribune*, December 12, 1896.
390. "Rainy Day Club Election," *New York Times*, January 7, 1897, 16.
391. "The Shoe That Makes a Pretty Foot—Yet Is Neither Unhealthful nor Common Sense," *San Francisco Chronicle*, October 1, 1903, 2.
392. "Their Rainy Day Garb."
393. "What Not to Wear for Walking," *New York World*, October 24, 1897.
394. "Dr. Schrady's Views," *New York World*, March 20, 1898, 31. This was accompanied by "The Modiste's Opinion," "Artist Blashfield's Views" and "Ella Wheeler Talks." Blashfield liked the new slimmer dresses that accentuated the human figure, while other artists denounced the new form.
395. "The Sunday *World*'s School of Manners: Good Form for the Street, How Men and Women Should Dress for the Thoroughfares," *New York World*, January 19, 1902.

CHAPTER 17

396. *Harriet Hubbard Ayer's Book*, dedication.
397. Ibid., preface.
398. Ibid., 40.
399. Ibid., 46
400. Ibid., 48–49
401. Ibid., 56
402. Ibid., 63
403. Ibid., 68
404. Ibid., 72

405. Ibid., 76
406. Ibid., 79–84
407. Ibid., 85
408. Ibid., 125
409. Ibid., 189
410. Ibid., 266
411. Ibid., 275–276
412. Ibid., 320
413. Ibid., 325
414. Ibid., 326
415. Ibid., 374–45
416. Ibid., 428
417. Ibid., 435
418. Ibid., 437
419. Ibid., 446
420. Ibid., 471
421. Nancy Etcoff, *Survival of the Prettiest: The Science of Beauty* (London: Abacus Books, 2000).
422. Staffe (pseudo.), *Lady's Dressing Room*, preface.

CHAPTER 18

423. *American Women*, revision of *Women of the Century*, 1893, notes that she had chronic nephritis and died after an illness of four days.
424. "Mrs. H.H. Ayer Dies From Pneumonia," *New York World*, November 26, 1903, 4.
425. Death certificate #33455 filed with the City of New York Department of Health. Dr. Cyrus Edson of 56 West Fiftieth Street signed the death certificate.
426. Terhune is best remembered for his novels about dogs; nevertheless, he worked at the *Evening World* from 1894 to 1914. *To the Best of My Memory* (New York: Harper & Brothers, 1930).
427. Ayer and Taves, *Three Lives*, 284.
428. "Mrs. Harriet Hubbard Ayer Dead," *New York World*, November 26, 1903, 4.

EPILOGUE

429. Ayer and Taves, *Three Lives*, 262–63.
430. Letters at Bowdoin College; Ayer and Taves, *Three Lives*, 266.
431. Chicago directory lists him there in 1892.

432. Ayer and Taves, *Three Lives*, 267.

433. Ibid., 270.

434. Kirkland, *Chicago Yesterdays*, 264.

435. "Herbert C. Ayer Dies," *Chicago Daily Tribune*, January 13, 1899, 1.

436. Ibid.; "Herbert C. Ayer Dead," *New York Times*, January 14, 1899; Graceland Cemetery records; telephone call to Rosedale, July 2009.

437. Ayer and Taves, *Three Lives*, 272–73.

438. Ibid., 272.

439. Stated in article citing Margaret's marriage to Cobb. There was no listing for M.R. Kent in the New York directories, census or passports.

440. Dr. Faisst, an organist and composer, founded the school in 1857.

441. "Miss Margaret Ayer Here to Begin Musical Career," *New York World*, August 7, 1902, 12.

442. "Not You Miss Barton," *New York Times*, August 7, 1902; "London Theatres' Gossip," *Boston Daily Globe*, August 3, 1902, 20; *New York World*, August 7, 1902, 12.

443. Melanie Gustfson, "Beautiful Faces, Strong Bodies," Paper delivered at the Hagley Museum and Library, February 2010.

444. "Mrs. Frank Cobb, Widow of Editor," *New York Times*, February 4, 1965, 31.

445. He was arraigned and waived examination. Bail was fixed at $5,000. The questions he refused to answer had to do with a branch of his firm in Washington and the possible sale or purchase of American Sugar Refining Company stock by several senators. Ultimately, he made a statement and then withdrew it. "Broker Allen L. Seymour Arrested," *New York Times*, October 19, 1894.

446. "Seymour Brothers Fail," *New York Times*, September 16, 1897.

447. No obituary found. In an article, "Orange's Great Society Event," *New York Times*, February 16, 1896, Mrs. Lewis Seymour and Mrs. James M. Seymour were listed as patronesses, but only Lewis and Hattie were mentioned as attending the event.

448. "Mrs. A.L. Seymour Musical Therapist," *New York Times*, July 3, 1944, 4. She is listed in the New York city directory as a teacher in 1909.

449. Harriet Ayer Seymour, *What Music Can Do for You: A Guide for the Uninitiated* (New York: Harper & Brothers, 1920), preface.

450. Hattie died on July 30, 1944, at the Hotel Volnay, 23 East Seventy-fourth Street, at the age of sixty-eight, leaving two daughters, Mrs. Jerome Brush and Mrs. Valentine Macy. See "Mrs. A.L. Seymour, Musical Therapist," *New York Times*, July 31, 1944, 4. According to the New Jersey Soundex record in 1900, there were four children: Lewisa (b. 1888), Allen L. Jr. (b. 1891), Caroline (b. 1897) and Harriet S. (b. 1899); the *New York Times* lists only two, therefore one must assume that by 1944 the other two had died.

451. *Récamier Manufacturing Co., Inc., v. Harriet Hubbard Ayer, Inc.*, District Court, S.D. New York, 59 F. 2d 803; U.S. Dist. LEXIS 1293 (April, 13, 1932)

452. "Mrs. Dodge Is Decorated," *New York Times*, July 21, 1929. She was president of the Harriet Hubbard Ayer Society and, "for great services in the cause of Franco-American amity,' was awarded the Cross of the Chevalier of the Legion of Honor on July 20, 1929, in Paris.

Selected Bibliography

Primary Sources

Certificate of Incorporation. April, 1887, Albany, New York.

Chicago City Directories

Clerk of the District Court of Cook County, Superior Court, Bureau of Vital Statistics, Chicago, IL. [*Ayer v. Ayer* divorce documents; John V. and Elida Ayer wills; *Ayer v. Ayer* custody suit.]

Hamilton, Henry. Manuscripts. Chicago Historical Museum Library, Chicago, IL.

Howard, Blanche W. Papers. George J. Mitchell Department of Special Collections and Archives, Bowdoin College Library, Brunswick, ME.

————. Maine Women Writers Collection. Abplanalp Library, University of New England, Portland, ME.

Les Bottins, 1880s and '90s. Archives de Paris, France.

New York, City and County of, Supreme Court. [*Ayer v. Seymour*, May 27, 1889; *Frenzel v. Ayer*, May and August 1889; Lunacy Certificate. "In the Matter of Harriet Hubbard Ayer, a Lunatic," 1893.]

New York City Directories

New York Municipal Archives. [Buildings Department; Death Certificate; Department of Health.]

New York World Papers, Box 1, 89-A962. Butler Library, Columbia University, New York.

R.G. Dun & Co. Credit Report Volumes. Baker Library Historical Collections, Harvard Business School, Boston, MA.

U.S. Government Works. *Récamier MFG. Co., Inc. v. Harriet Hubbard Ayer, Inc.* 59 F. 2nd 802. District Court, S.D. New York, April 13, 1932.

NEWSPAPERS

Atlanta Constitution
Boston Daily Globe
Brooklyn Daily Eagle
Chicago Daily Times
Chicago Tribune
London Times
Los Angeles Times
New York Herald
New York Herald [Paris edition]
[New York] *Sun*
New York Times
New York Tribune
New York World
Philadelphia Times
San Francisco Chronicle
Trenton Times
Washington Post
Winnipeg Free Press [Canada]

AYER BIOGRAPHIES

Ayer, Margaret Hubbard, and Isabella Taves. *The Three Lives of Harriet Hubbard Ayer*. Philadelphia: J.B. Lippincott Company, 1957.

Bird, Carolyn. *Enterprising Women*. New York: W.W. Norton & Company, 1976.

"Harriet Hubbard Ayer." *Harper's Bazaar* July 7, 1888.

Perry, Marilyn E. "Ayer, Harriet Hubbard." *American National Biography* (1999).

Weisberger, Bernard E. "Ayer, Harriet Hubbard." in *Notable American Women 1607–1950*. James, Edward T., Janet Wilson James and Paul S. Boyer, eds. Cambridge, MA: The Belknap Press of Harvard University, 1971.

White, James T., ed. "Ayer, Harriet Hubbard." *National Encyclopedia of American Biography*. Vol. 43. Clifton, NJ: J.T. White, 1979.

Yard, Amy. "An American Society Matron, Cosmetic Entrepreneur and Journalist." Women's History Series, 2002.

BOOKS WRITTEN OR TRANSLATED BY AYER

Harriet Hubbard Ayer's Book. Springfield, MA: King Richardson Company, 1899. Reprint, Arno Press, 1974.

Meilhac, Henry, and Ludovic Halevy. *The Widow: A Comedy in Three Acts.* Translated and annotated by Harriet Hubbard Ayer. New York: DeWitt Publishing House, 1877.

Staffe, Baroness (pseud.). *My Lady's Dressing Room.* Adapted and translated from the French, with an introduction and annotations by Harriet Hubbard Ayer. New York: Cassell & Company, 1892.

BOOKS AND ARTICLES

Andreas, Alfred Theodore. *History of Chicago.* Vol. 3. New York: A.T. Andreas Publisher, Arno Press, 1975.

Appignanesi, Lisa. *Mad, Bad and Sad, Women and the Mind Doctors.* New York: W.W. Norton & Company, 2008.

Banner, Lois W. *American Beauty.* New York: Alfred Knopf, 1983.

Bird, Carolyn. *Enterprising Women.* New York: W.W. Norton & Co., 1976.

Blaugrund, Annette. *The Tenth Street Studio Building: Artists and Entrepreneurs, from the Hudson River School to the American Impressionists.* Southampton, NY: Parrish Art Museum, 1996.

Clark, Herma. *The Elegant Eighties.* Chicago: A.C. McClurg & Company, 1941.

Goldsmith, Barbara. *Other Powers.* New York: Harper Perennial, 1999.

Kirkland, Caroline. *Chicago Yesterdays: A Sheaf of Reminiscences.* Chicago: Daughaday and Company, 1919.

Laurence, Anne, Josephine Maltbym and Janette Rutterford. *Women and Their Money, 1700–1950.* London: Routledge, Taylor & Francis Group, 2008.

Ledbetter, Suzann. *Shady Ladies: Nineteen Surprising and Rebellious American Women.* New York: 2006.

Miller, Sara Cedar. *Central Park: An American Masterpiece.* New York: Harry N. Abrams, Inc., 2003.

Morgan, Eloise L. "Bronxville's Insane Asylum." *Bronxville Journal* 1 (2001–02).

Oleson, Charles W., MD. *Secret Nostrums and Systems of Medicine: A Book of Formulas.* Chicago: Oleson & Co. Publishers, 1889.

Peiss, Kathy. *Hope in a Jar: The Making of America's Beauty Culture.* New York: An Owl Book, Henry Holt and Company, 1998.

Sandweiss, Martha A. *Passing Strange*. New York: Penguin Press, 2009.

Terhune, Albert Payson. *To the Best of My Memory*. New York: Harper & Bros. Publishers, 1930.

Van Renssaelaer, Mariana. "William Merritt Chase." *American Art Review* 2, no. 1 (1881).

About the Author

Annette Blaugrund, an art historian, former curator and museum director, has written a number of award-winning books about American art and artists. She has worked as director of the National Academy Museum and School of Fine Arts (1997–2007); as the Andrew W. Mellon senior curator of paintings, drawings and sculpture at the New York Historical Society (1989–1995); and as a curator at the Brooklyn Museum (1980–1985) and has held positions at several other institutions. Dr. Blaugrund has written six books about American art and contributed seven chapters and twenty-nine articles to other books and journals. For her accomplishments she received a Lifetime Achievement Award from the National Academy in 2008 and was named a chevalier in the Order of Arts and Letters by the French government in 1992, among other honors. She currently sits on several philanthropic boards, juries art competitions and writes essays for magazines and catalogues. She holds a PhD in art history from Columbia University (1987), where for six years (1996–2001) she taught American art and culture and currently sits on the advisory council of the Department of Art History and Archaeology. She has lectured on subjects from her books at museums around the world and has appeared on television and radio programs. A member of Women Writing Women's Lives, a group of sixty published biographers, she has spent the last three years researching and writing the biography of Harriet Hubbard Ayer.

Visit us at
www.historypress.net